*A Preface to Sartre*

*Emile Durkheim: Sociologist and Philosopher*
*History and Criticism*
Madame Bovary *on Trial*
*Rethinking Intellectual History: Texts, Contexts, Language*

*Modern European Intellectual History: Reappraisals*
*and New Perspectives*

# A Preface to Sartre

Dominick LaCapra

*Cornell University Press*

First published 1978 by Cornell University Press.
First printing, Cornell Paperbacks, 1987.


Printed in the United States of America

The paper in this book is acid-free and meets the guidelines for permanence and durability of the Committee on Production Guidelines for Book Longevity of the Council on Library Resources.


Library of Congress Cataloging in Publication Data
(For library cataloging purposes only)

LaCapra, Dominick, 1939–
  A preface to Sartre.

  Includes bibliographical references and index.
  1.  Sartre, Jean-Paul, 1905–       I.   Title.
B2430.S34L24        848'.9'1409        78-58022
ISBN 0-8014-1175-0 (cloth)
ISBN 0-8014-9448-6 (pbk.)

Reading must always aim at a certain relationship, unperceived by the writer, between what he commands and what he does not command of the schemata of the language that he uses. This relationship is not a certain quantitative distribution of shadow and light, of weakness and force, but a signifying structure that critical reading must *produce*.... [Without] all the instruments of traditional criticism, ... critical production would risk developing in any direction and authorize itself to say almost anything. But this indispensable guardrail [*garde-fou*] has always only *protected*, never *opened*, a reading.

Jacques Derrida, *Of Grammatology*

But if nobody can escape this necessity [of employing traditional concepts], and if no one is therefore responsible for giving in to it, however little, this does not mean that all the ways of giving in to it are of equal pertinence. The quality and the fecundity of a discourse are perhaps measured by the critical rigor with which this relationship to the history of metaphysics and to inherited concepts is thought.

Jacques Derrida, "Structure, Sign and<br>Play in the Discourse of the Human Sciences"

The trust in life is gone: life itself has become a *problem*. Yet one should not jump to the conclusion that this necessarily makes one gloomy. Even love of life is still possible, only one loves differently. It is the love for a woman that causes doubts in us.

The attraction of everything problematic, the delight in an *x*, however, is so great in such more spiritual, more spiritualized men that this delight flares up again and again like a bright blaze over all the distress of what is problematic, over all the danger of uncertainty, and even over the jealousy of the lover. We know a new happiness.

Nietzsche, Preface for the Second Edition, *The Gay Science*

# Contents

# Preface

Kierkegaard wrote a book made up entirely of prefaces. For him, all thinking was a preface. I look upon what follows as a critical preface to Sartre. I also see it as a contribution to the rather ill-defined but challenging field of intellectual history. The two perspectives are one. I envision intellectual history as a critical, informed, and stimulating conversation with the past through the medium of the texts of major thinkers. Who in our recent past is a more fascinating interlocutor than Sartre?

Indeed, Sartre has often been seen as the leading Western intellectual of this century—an "ideal-typical" figure. Whether in admiration or in admonition, many have perceived Sartre's life as the existential embodiment of his ideas. He has written influential works in an often bewildering variety of areas: philosophy, literature, biography, autobiography, and the theory of history. I discuss Sartre's contribution in all of these areas, taking as a leitmotif the critical investigation of Sartre's conception of a dialectical "totalization" of knowledge.

The objectives of this book are multiple. I attempt to make a contribution to the scholarship on Sartre by providing a "deconstructive" reading of certain of his most well-known and influential writings—a reading that has implications for the interpretation of Sartre's work as a whole. I focus on centers of self-contestation in Sartre's texts and raise the more general questions of his relation to tradition and of the theoretical foundations for his radical politics.

Relying on a discriminating use of recent tendencies in French thought (notably, in the writings of Jacques Derrida), I try to

bring about an active confrontation between Sartre and his critics in terms that go beyond the often sterile opposition between
existentialism and structuralism. I also engage in a polemic with
prevalent approaches to intellectual history and defend by argument and example the idea that critical strategies developed
in recent philosophy and literary criticism are relevant to historical interpretation. In these senses, theoretical and methodological questions that go beyond a reading of Sartre are very much at
issue in this book.

A major task of intellectual history is to help make the works
of seminal thinkers more accessible as forces in social life—to
socialize these works without vulgarizing them. This task is
paradoxical, but I believe that the paradox here is a fruitful one.
The intellectual historian should do more than provide the occasion for a cultural sun tan. In fact, he should try to do something
entirely different: mediate between specialized and general
knowledge and contribute to the rethinking of significant problems. At times the pages that follow—especially the introductory ones—may not adequately negotiate the problem of addressing both the specialist and the generally educated person.
These introductory pages dealing with the methodological argument were difficult to write, and they are difficult to read,
perhaps especially for the reader I would most like to reach: the
one who is genuinely interested in the issues discussed but who
thus far has not had the occasion to become thoroughly familiar
with all the texts I treat. This book will be successful to the extent
that it helps to induce this reader to critically confront the texts
and the issues themselves. The methodological argument, with
its asperities, is nonetheless necessary, I believe, given the
controversy among professional historians concerning the nature of intellectual history. I also ask the indulgence of the literary critic for whom some of what I say may seem self-evident. I
would further note that an Introduction should be read as it is
written, both at the beginning and at the end of the principal
text.

Sartre is a difficult writer. Derrida, whom many see as Sartre's
successor as the most important philosopher in France, is even
more inaccessible: on first reading he *must* appear incomprehen-

sible or simply perverse. Recent French thought has bade a bittersweet adieu to the older Cartesian virtue of a plain style that, in its classical purity, seemed to express immediately intelligible, clear and distinct ideas. But there are no gains without losses. The problems addressed in recent French thought are terribly important ones. Style itself—style in the largest and most ambitious sense of the word—is among these problems. The diverse and divergent styles of recent French writers share certain elements that aid in explaining their difficulty: these styles are contestatory and have political overtones. At their best, they force us to look at things anew and may even rekindle a carnival spirit. At their worst, they allow difficulty to settle into obscurity, indeed into obscurantism. A contestatory style must, at least on first acquaintance, appear difficult; it need not push the testing of accepted virtues to self-defeating extremes. On the contrary, it should attempt to create the regenerative interplay between structure and openness that its proponents often find lacking in the dominant culture. In this venture, success is in no sense assured; but the effort counts. I have tried to convey something of the invigorating debate currently going on in France and to contribute a little to it.

I am grateful to Steven L. Kaplan for reading this work and, more generally, for his ability to demonstrate, time and again, that colleagues with significantly different approaches to history can engage in mutually beneficial exchange. Most especially, I thank Jane Pedersen, whose criticisms and suggestions helped inestimably in giving the book whatever value it may have. Finally, I thank the National Endowment for the Humanities for a fellowship that enabled me to write this study.

DOMINICK LaCAPRA

*Ithaca, New York*

# Abbreviations for Sartre's Works

B     *Baudelaire.* Précédé d'une note de Michel Leiris. Paris: Editions Gallimard (Collection Idées), 1963 [first pub. 1947]. Translated as *Baudelaire* by Martin Turnell. Norfolk, Conn.: James Laughlin, 1950.

*Critique*     *Critique de la raison dialectique* (Précédé de *Question de méthode*). Paris: Editions Gallimard, 1960.

Translated as *Critique of Dialectical Reason, Theory of Practical Ensembles* by Alan Sheridan-Smith (edited by Jonathan Rée). London and Atlantic Highlands, N.J.: Humanities Press, 1976.

*EN*     *L'Etre et le néant, essai de phénoménologie ontologique.* Paris: Editions Gallimard (Bibliothèque des Idées), 1943.

Translated as *Being and Nothingness* by Hazel E. Barnes. New York: Washington Square Press, 1953.

*G*     *Saint Genet, comédien et martyr.* Paris: Editions Gallimard, 1952.

Translated as *Saint Genet, Actor and Martyr* by Bernard Frechtman. New York: Braziller, 1963.

*L'Idiot*     *L'Idiot de la famille. Gustave Flaubert de 1821 à 1857.* Paris: Editions Gallimard (Bibliothèque de Philosophie), vols. 1 & 2, 1971, vol. 3, 1972.

*L'Imaginaire*     *L'Imaginaire, psychologie phénoménologique de l'imagination.* Paris: Editions Gallimard, 1940.

Translated as *The Psychology of the Imagination* by Bernard Frechtman. New York: Washington Square Press, 1966.

*M*     *Les Mots.* Paris: Editions Gallimard, 1964.

Translated as *The Words* by Bernard Frechtman. New York: Braziller, 1964.

*N*     *La Nausée.* Paris: Editions Gallimard, 1938.

Translated as *Nausea* by Lloyd Alexander. New York: New Directions, 1949.

Also translated as *The Diary of Antoine Roquentin.* London: John Lehmann, 1949.

13

Plea        "Plaidoyer pour les intellectuels." *Situations VIII*. Paris: Editions Gallimard, 1972. Pp. 373–455.
            Translated as "A Plea for Intellectuals" by John Mathews in *Between Existentialism and Marxism*. New York: Pantheon Books, 1974. Pp. 227–285.

QL          *Qu'est-ce que la littérature? Situations II*. Paris: Editions Gallimard, 1948. Pp. 55–330.
            Translated as *What Is Literature?* by Bernard Frechtman. New York: Philosophical Library, 1949.

S. I–S. X   *Situations I–X*. Paris: Editions Gallimard, 1947–1976.
            Selected essays from *Situations I* and *III* are translated as *Literary Essays* by Annette Michelson. New York: Philosophical Library, 1957.
            *Situations IV* is translated as *Situations* by Benita Eisler. New York: Braziller, 1965.
            *Situations VIII* and *IX* are translated as *Between Existentialism and Marxism* by John Mathews. New York: Pantheon Books, 1974.
            *Situations X* is translated as *Life/Situations: Essays Written and Spoken by Jean-Paul Sartre* by Paul Auster and Lydia Davis. New York: Pantheon Books, 1977.

Search      *Search for a Method*. Translation of *Question de méthode* by Hazel E. Barnes. New York: Knopf, 1963.

TE          *La Transcendance de l'ego: esquisse d'une description phénoménologique*. Introduction, notes, and appendixes by Sylvie Le Bon. Paris: Librairie J. Vrin, 1966 [first pub. 1936].
            Translated as *The Transcendence of the Ego* by Forrest Williams and Robert Kirkpatrick. New York: Noonday, 1957.

Except in the case of *Search for a Method*, page references are to the French edition, and translations are my own. For an exhaustive bibliography of Sartre's works to 1970, see Michel Contat and Michel Rybalka, *Les Ecrits de Sartre: chronologie, bibliographie commentée* (Paris: Editions Gallimard, 1970). For an extensive bibliography of works on Sartre, see Robert Wilcocks, *Jean-Paul Sartre: A Bibliography of International Criticism* (Edmonton, Canada: University of Alberta Press, 1975).

*A Preface to Sartre*

# Introduction

Introduction. Obscene word.

Flaubert, *Dictionary of Received Ideas*

M. CONTAT: In other words, to contest you, one must reject you *en bloc?*
SARTRE: I believe that this is necessary and besides that's the way it is with most philosophers. . . .
M. CONTAT: And if it were a question [of self-criticism], what would you say?
SARTRE: In general it would always be a question of not having gone to the end of my radicalism. I naturally committed in my life a vast number of mistakes, but the bottom line [*le fond de l'affaire*] is that each time I made a mistake, it is because I was not radical enough.

*Situations X*, Interview of 1975

It is not hard to see how the history of ideas differs from political, social, or institutional history. It focuses on men's ideas, on the "inner world of thought," whereas they dwell largely in "the external world of action."

Franklin L. Baumer, *Modern European Thought*

Intellectual history has often followed one of three models in investigating "ideas," or "consciousness." These are, broadly speaking, the "internal" history of ideas, referring to formal structures and purely intellectual traditions; the "external" social or cultural history of ideas; and an attempt to reconcile these two approaches in accordance with some notion of "dialectical" synthesis. Other critics are increasingly contesting these models, and through my analysis of the works of Jean-Paul Sartre, I further examine the claim that these are inclusive and exhaustive definitions of the field. By aligning intellectual history with a critical history and theory of texts, I hope to further a shift in our perspective on the way one "does" intellectual history.

More specifically, I would like to provide an active interpretation of texts through which particular readings may be related to a general critical perspective in an open and self-critical process of mutual refinement and testing. Sustained attention will be paid to the way in which a text is made and to the way in which, through its own procedures, it internalizes or represses certain contexts. I take a critical approach to the inside/outside dichotomy and its application to the relation between a text and its contexts. The text is never without context. And the context is itself a text of sorts. The interesting question is that of the precise way in which the text relates to its various contexts and vice versa. At least in the modern period, the writings of important figures such as Sartre tend to have a markedly critical or contestatory relation to the dominant sociocultural context and, in however divided or inadequate a way, demand a significantly different society and culture. For their writings are often the scene of broken dialogues that, in their most forceful moments, point to the need for fuller dialogue in modern life.

I attempt to indicate certain ways in which a rethinking of the dialectical model may be necessary. But I especially resist one popular approach to intellectual history—what may be termed a relatively weak synthesis of internal and external methods. In this approach, a synoptic content analysis of essential "ideas," forms of "consciousness," or "world views" is combined in the same narrative with references to events or developments in the life of the individual and society. This approach tacks between "ideas" and "events" in a seemingly unified story modeled uncritically upon the most traditional kind of narrative history. It gives rise at worst to a quasi-journalistic and relatively superficial type of intellectual history. And, even at its best, the traditional narrative of "men and ideas" threatens to domesticate or neutralize potentially disconcerting texts. Whatever is uncanny or even revolutionary in "textual praxis" is leveled off in a highly readable but diverting mode of introducing readers to the text. Indeed, domestication is at least one possible function of the familiar demand that texts be placed squarely in their own times or that social history, geared to the investigation of the dominant culture, provide the models of explanation for the reading of texts. What escapes in this way of doing intellectual history is the complex work (or play) of the text and whatever it may disclose, including at times elements critical of one's own assumptions about the nature of interpretation and of history.

The relatively close reading of texts attempted here does not identify intellectual history with traditional *explication de texte*. Nor does it advocate a formalism fixated on the presumably pure internal structure and workings of texts. Although the following pages do center intellectual history on texts, they simultaneously "define" the text in a way that is critical of a conception of the text in terms of formal purity. A writer may strive for purity in his writings, as does Sartre himself on one important level of his thought. But this desire is contested and displaced by heterogeneous and disseminating tendencies in the text itself. A text has no pure and virginal "inside" that may find sanctuary in formalistic interpretation. Its "inside" is "always already" contaminated by an outside—the outside of internal self-questioning, other texts, and the text of life. Nor does the putative intention of the writer unproblematically govern what the text does, especially when the intention is a retrospective one provided by a self-reading or self-commentary. At best, one may set up a relationship between the more or less plausible account of intentions (or what the writer meant to say) and what the text may plausibly be argued to do or to disclose—and this relationship may be one or another form of difference (such as tension, contradiction, supplementarity, lack of communication).

Historians are, I think, always confronted with the problem of how to approach or "use" texts. For all historians, the text is the "given." Reality is an inference—often a shaky one, always a problematic one. It is becoming more difficult, even for practitioners of the craft resistant to theory, to confide in an epistemology of documentary realism that presents the text as a simple transparency representing reality and requiring, not interpretation, but merely a "literal" reading. Even more important is the growing realization that a cognitively responsible and self-critical historiography cannot rest content with approaches to problems that resist complex models of interpretation. One can neither simply believe nor structure a study such that the revelation of some piece of biographical or other "contextual" information marks the "bottom line" where all questions come to an end. The relationship between text and context does not admit of oversimplified, reductionist solutions.

I would draw a distinction (but not mark a dichotomy) between treating an artifact as a document and treating it as a text. To approach the artifacts of intellectual history as documents making "literal" statements about the times or the life of the author is to engage in an enterprise of limited and dubious value. At worst, one makes the artifacts redundant. At best, one reduces them to a merely suggestive status or to the position of second-class citizens in the world of historical scholarship. When these artifacts are conceived as sources for facts and hypotheses about the author's life or as tableaux providing a "concrete" sense of how life is lived in a given period, whatever one derives from them must be checked against more "objective" documents to corroborate one's conclusions. If one's conclusions cannot be checked against other documentary sources, the putative facts or "insights" are not naturalized; they must remain "merely suggestive" aliens in the historical mind. The overall danger of a predominantly documentary approach is that it reduces artifacts to objects adapted to a narrowly positivistic perspective on history. From this perspective, literature and philosophy tend to lose their point. And the problem of the text is avoided. Whatever is valuable in the documentary approach itself may become more valuable if questions are posed in a different way.

One might suggest that texts available to the historian fall on a spectrum ranging from relative poverty to relative richness. Tax rolls, marriage contracts, bureaucratic reports, diplomatic correspondence, and even the memoirs of businessmen or other "men of action" tend to be relatively poor texts. The writings of someone like Sartre are relatively rich, although controversial, texts. The crucial problem is how to read them. There is at least something dubious in the attempt to center a reading of rich texts on models of reality inferred—at times on the basis of unexamined assumptions (for example, about "total history") —from a narrowly documentary reading of relatively poor texts. Reversing the procedure may have some value, using the reading of relatively rich texts to render more intricate and perhaps more "realistic" our inferential reconstructions of past "reality." To the extent that it is feasible (given the nature of certain documentary sources), this reversal of perspectives might provide an initial basis for a more fruitful exchange between intellectual historians and those engaged in the extremely important projects of writing social history and individual biography.

The "reading," or interpretation, of an individual's life or a society's "structure" is often as intricate a problem as the reading and interpretation of the most complicated written text. This study focuses on Sartre's written texts and poses the problem of context largely in terms of its relevance for the reading of these texts. But it attempts to do so in a way that suggests the complementarity and supplementarity of perspectives on written texts and on the "text" of life. One of Sartre's most fascinating "texts" is his life. Facets of it appear in the pages that follow with reference to specific problems of interpretation. I do not undertake a full-scale investigation of the interaction between the text of writing and the text of life, although such an investigation may be seen as the horizon of the form of inquiry I attempt. An aspect of research into the life must be the realization of the need for a convincing understanding of the written texts in all their subtlety; otherwise, one may end up illustrating only one's own desire for "totalizing" explanations. In addition, the relationship between written text and life must explicitly be seen as a problem. I attempt to cast doubt upon the belief that an idea of "identity" or comprehensive unity may be taken as the guide to interpreting this relationship. At least in the case of major figures, there is, I think, always a tense interplay between unifying and disseminating movements, involving more or less self-conscious forms of "non-identity," self-contestation, and dissonance. The text is the scene of this interplay. In his writing, a person may place his life in question (or vice versa). Indeed, the turn to the life never simplifies issues for the interpreter: it supplements the written texts with a "lived" text that is itself reconstructed from other texts. If the putative "lived" text is as difficult to decipher as the most intricate written text, one further complicates the problem of eliciting some overall structure or pattern of development.

Sartre is an especially challenging object of study for the approach to intellectual history exemplified by this critical preface, for he has himself attempted to develop a totalizing, dialectical model of intelligibility in the investigation of thought, society, and individual life.[1] In so doing, he has explicitly rejected a theory of the text on the lines suggested above. In an interview, Sartre declared: "I am completely opposed to the idea of the text. . . . For example, I have just read [Mikhail] Bakhtin on Dostoevsky and I do not see what the new formalism—semiotics—adds to the old one. On the whole, what I reproach these studies for is that they lead to nothing: they do not encircle [elles n'enserrent pas] their object; they are forms of knowledge that dissipate themselves" (S. X, pp. 106, 109–10). The approach to Sartre's own texts here is inspired, in a relatively reserved and limited way, by the notion of "deconstructive" reading elaborated by Jacques Derrida (who is himself—but for very different reasons—critical of semiotics). And the question addressed to Sartre here is whether the attitude toward the text expressed in this quotation indicates that he is not being radical enough: for the very notion of understanding in the passage is one geared to the mastery, if not the domination, of the object. And the larger question raised by it is whether a logic of domination—which Sartre criticizes in others—is central to the forms of analytic rationality that Sartre both employs and contests as well as to the totalizing dialectic he more and more explicitly espouses. What escapes theoretical recognition by Sartre is what escapes the grasp of his analytic oppositions and dialectical project. What also threatens to escape him is the possibility that his own thought is reappropriated by the very traditions or institutions he explicitly rejects.

Consciousness itself may be seen on the analogy of the text. And the situation with which consciousness begins, or the larger text in which it is "always already" inscribed, is tradition. Sartre's ultraphenomenological view of consciousness as an empty spontaneity inhibits him from explicitly posing as a problem the relation of consciousness and of his own discourse about it to tradition and institutions in the largest sense. Sartre centers philosophy on man, and he centers man on consciousness, freedom, and a certain conception of praxis. On the inert foundation of the brute existent (in-itself, thing, matter), man in his consciousness and freedom defines the meaning of the situation through his intentional projects. However empty and internally problematic consciousness (or freedom) may be for Sartre, it is presented in perhaps the dominant tendency of his thought as pure and homogeneous within itself, split off from the "other" with which it seeks an impossible reconciliation, and devoid of any internal alterity that might impair its translucent spontaneity. The "other" is at first outside and has no meaning. But, given the necessity that freedom be situated in a contingent situation, freedom must "fall" into the world through bad faith or alienation and confront the problem of counterfinality. This notion of an internally pure intentional consciousness as the basis of free praxis that generates meaning and value is repeated in different guises throughout Sartre's thought, for example, in his later Marxist phase as the supposedly "translucent praxis of the organic individual."

Sartre's notion of consciousness as an empty spontaneity is plausible to the extent that the text of tradition has, or is made to have, blanks and discontinuities in its discourse. This is always the case, even with the most "solid" traditions. ("Tradition," as used in this study, may be defined on the analogy of the text as a problematic unitary concept designating a series of displacements over time that raise the question of the relationship between continuity and discontinuity.) But the problem of tradition has perhaps become especially forceful in what we term the "modern period." It has been most explicitly formulated in the notion of the death of God or absence of center. Sartre's interpretation of consciousness becomes increasingly plausible to the extent that the absence of center becomes generalized as a problem and to the extent that the text of tradition is erased, leaving relatively empty or exhausted forms and more or less random contents. Sartre, I think, assumes this condition of tradition as the cultural context for his thought. But the fact that this assumption remains implicit or is repressed by the phenomenological belief that he is going "to the things themselves" makes Sartre's writing the scene of relatively blind internal contestation. Sartre writes a hidden history of the exhaustion of traditional forms whose ghostlike presence threatens to repossess his own thought. In this respect, his thought is perhaps symptomatic of all modern thought. But his failure to make the "centering" and "decentering" interplay of tradition and critique an explicit theme of reflection blinds him to the form of the history he is writing and impairs his ability to situate the tensions of his own thought in a self-critical manner. Sartre does not systematically explore the possibility that the only "original," "spontaneous," or "naive" experience to resist mystification is one that is *derived* from a disciplined and self-conscious critique of traditions in the effort to eliminate what is abusive and to revitalize or transform what is valid in them.

A sign of Sartre's difficulties is the status in his thought of language and of institutions in general. Certain of his views on these matters will be discussed at some length in the course of this study, but a few constants in his approach to language may be noted in an introductory manner. Although he has written a great deal about language, Sartre in his principal works never focuses directly and in a sustained way on the problem of language as a topic of philosophical reflection. His discussion of language is always attendant upon the investigation of some other problem, and it often has a marginal or even ancillary status. Nor does Sartre see language as a microcosm of the question of the nature and the role of institutions in society. His largely instrumentalist perspective on the problem of language is of a piece with his approach to tradition and the text. A critical focus on language would necessarily raise questions about the terms on which Sartre would like to center thought and life. "Consciousness" and "man" would, for example, be situated as terms in a more general field that cannot be oriented around them in an uncontested or absolute fashion. A more open reckoning with the critique of language in its more modern forms would not only create difficulties for Sartre's attempt to organize all problems—for example, that of meaning or signification— around a term or opposition taken as absolute master of the field and ultimate origin of all perspectives. It would also constrain Sartre to engage in self-critical reflection about his own use of language in the effort to master problems. What is almost invariably left in the dark or repressed by Sartre is the intercourse between structure and play in his own use of language. Sartre has always insisted that philosophical language is based on the univocal usage of terms. In a recent interview, he has asserted that philosophy differs from science in that the usage of a term may vary from place to place in a philosophical text, and that the overall "communication" of philosophy may not be univocal. But he still insists on a clear divide between literature and philosophy, for in philosophy each usage of a term in the same place must be univocal and "each sentence must have only one meaning" (S. X, pp. 137–38). This view would seem to condemn philosophy to blind and unthematized inconsistency, or even to self-contradiction, in the sustained use of language in discourse. Sartre's intention is apparently to keep philosophy, as a primary voice, pure of the dangers of ambiguity, multivalent meaning, and figurative usage, which more recently he has been willing to admit in the literary use of prose. The price paid for this intention is equivocation and a relatively unexamined internal self-contestation in his writings. He defines himself into a position where he is unable to elucidate—and perhaps exercise some measure of critical control over—the interplay between the totalizing and unifying desire of philosophy "proper" (or "proper" philosophy) and disseminating tendencies related to the role of self-questioning, ambivalence, and the use of metaphor. His philosophy does not—and perhaps cannot—conform to his own criterion of proper usage. And his belief in this criterion prevents him from exploring more fully both the disabling and the enabling aspects of the interaction among various uses of language in a given text. It is even conceivable that a certain approach to language—precisely the one Sartre explicitly resists—might provide an intimation and even a regional "exemplification" of the possibility Sartre cannot imagine: a way in which institutions might be structured and yet allow if not encourage contestation, freedom, and play.

Sartre's best-known critics in France over the years—Derrida, Foucault, Lévi-Strauss, Merleau-Ponty to a certain extent, and perhaps even Camus—have attempted in various ways to develop such an approach. This group is of course heterogeneous enough even if one excludes Merleau-Ponty and Camus. But one may perhaps hazard some tentative generalizations explicitly oriented to the argument developed here. An initial way of broaching the problem is to relate Sartre and certain of his critics to a common set of philosophical antecedents or reference points—Hegel, Husserl, Marx, Freud, Nietzsche, and Heidegger.[2]

Sartre's own relation to Hegel and Husserl is relatively clear. To schematize drastically, one might say that Sartre follows Hegel until the final idealistic *Aufhebung*, which brings absolute knowledge and the ultimate reconciliation of opposites, although he accepts even this as an impossible desire that ontologically characterizes man. He believes that Marx critically transformed or dialectically overcame Hegel's dialectic by rejecting *Geist* and making concrete men the subjects and agents of history. Sartre's critique of Husserl's notions of a transcendental ego and the phenomenological reduction—a critique not free of problematic elements—is attended by an even more basic retention of the intentionality of consciousness, a notion that has always remained essential to Sartre's understanding of man as "freedom in a situation." Sartre's relation to Marx and Freud is more difficult to characterize, even on the level of scandalously oversimplified categorizations. He rejects the positivistic and deterministic interpretations of Marxism in Engels and later theorists, even though he is aware of the ways in which Marx, especially in his later works, may have invited them. Yet his own existential Marxism—which centers history and its dialectical explication upon the role of free, conscious agents—itself depends upon a Hegelian and humanistic reading of Marx. He resists the elements in Marx that have been elaborated by his own critics in France. These elements decenter man in the historical process, allow for the distinction between alterity and alienation, introduce repetition into history, interpret freedom not as pure and total but as "always already" situated, and construe the situation as more than the resultant of free projects and counterfinalities. In other words, they place in question the philosophical foundation that Sartre tried to lay for Marxism in the *Critique of Dialectical Reason*.

Sartre has always rejected Freud's notion of the unconscious as either deterministic cause or interpretive myth. In his later works, Sartre makes freer use of Freudian language as he attempts a dialectical reconciliation of existential psychoanalysis and Marxism. Nevertheless, he always explicitly resists the most interesting sense of Freud's notion of the unconscious as it has been interpreted by theorists like Derrida and, to a certain extent, Lacan. In this sense, the unconscious introduces alterity into the self in a manner that undermines the belief in an inviolate or pure sanctuary of total freedom or consciousness. The unconscious is not another "text" present beneath the text of consciousness and potentially open to unmasking and full reappropriation by the ego or consciousness in quest of identity. "It" is radically "other," yet not simply separate from the consciousness that it decenters and whose appropriative grasp it resists and continually defers. It is the different and the differing play

within the "same" text as consciousness—the play of ambivalence, which a philosophical consciousness, devoted to univocal
meaning and self-possession, would repress. In this sense, the
unconscious (or whatever term may be substituted for it) provides the theoretical basis for the interminability of analysis and
the openness of any system of interpretation. Sartre's refusal to
admit the unconscious or some analogue of it in his own
thought is one reason why his explicit affirmation of an open
dialectical system is theoretically unfounded and depends for its
acceptance upon ontological fiat.

Sartre's relation to Heidegger and Nietzsche is perhaps even
more problematic than his relation to Marx and Freud. Especially in his early work, Sartre borrows certain terms and themes
from Heidegger—being-in-the-world, temporality, the conditions of historicity, among others. (Comments in the *Critique*
suggest that Sartre has not given a careful reading to Heidegger's later works.) In *Being and Nothingness,* as we shall see,
Sartre translates *Dasein* as "human reality" and proceeds to
center human reality on consciousness. Despite his admission
that the humanistic interpretation of *Dasein* was in certain ways
plausible within the context of *Being and Time,* Heidegger has
attempted to show why this interpretation is misleading. Sartre
has made only scattered references to Nietzsche and has never
undertaken an extended discussion of his understanding of
Nietzsche's work. Nor has he indicated an awareness of the way
in which Nietzsche's critique of traditional assumptions and his
affirmation of play, laughter, and destructive-regenerative ambivalence may be seen to place in question the dominant motifs
of Sartre's own conception of philosophy. In general, I think
that Sartre's use and abuse of Heidegger and Nietzsche display
in extreme form something present in virtually all of his
readings, notably including those in his existential biographies:
his readings tend to be selective, one-way appropriations that
do not recognize the other as having a voice, especially in respects that might generate radical doubts about his own
framework of interpretation.

Sartre's critics in France are in no sense invariably right and
Sartre is not invariably wrong. His criticisms of a certain kind of
structuralism, for example, are pointed in so far as he argues

that one must account for history and human agency other than in terms of synchronic structures, epistemological breaks, and the reduction of the human being to a purely passive cipher of impersonal processes. But these criticisms do not confront the views of his opponents on repetition, alterity, play, supplementarity, decentering and regeneration of the center as a function or a fiction. On one level, Sartre's critics explicitly attempt to develop "pointless" approaches to the text (and to history) that radically contest teleological and totalizing interpretations. But there is a point to this pointlessness. It is to rehabilitate notions like that of repetition as the displacement of the "same" in the "other"—notions that are de-emphasized in the dominant philosophical tradition and in Sartre, but that are necessary to explicate more submerged elements of both that tradition and Sartre's thought. An attempt is made to give these notions *droit de cité* in a forceful manner that questions the analytic and dialectical commitment to mastery and domestication of the object. And the "point" of the critique of humanism is not to defend inhumanity. Nor is it—at least in its more cogent forms—made to deny a highly significant role for man as subject and agent. It is rather to see man not as absolute master of the situation but as a decentered subject fully at play and at stake in the world. The views of his critics suggest why Sartre is condemned, at least in his explicit theoretical ideas, to remain a master analyst of alienation largely "from the inside": for his resistance to any basic challenge to the assertion of a paradoxical pure freedom helps to explain why he cannot provide any perspective on alienation— the primary alienation in terms of a split of freedom (and purpose) from things (and causes), which prefaces a kind of fall of freedom into things that generates counterfinality. Sartre never fully recognizes the ambiguity of—or overlap between— freedom or consciousness and the world, their "intertextuality." Thus he cannot see that a basic problem in the dominant metaphysical tradition is the avoidance or repression of that recognition. And he never attempts to "think through the ontological difference" that gives rise to conceptual dichotomies, double binds, and "originary" alienation. Hence he does not explore the ways in which the thought of those he criticizes may be seen in the light of such an attempt. Sartre's thought begins with a largely "unproblematicized" ontological difference (for-itself/in-itself, consciousness/thing, praxis/practico-inert, and others) and intellectually institutionalizes it in various repetitive formulations from *Being and Nothingness* to the *Critique*. Thus, despite internal self-contestation of a largely unthematized sort, there is in one sense no way for him to think in terms other than those of alienation. He denies himself the necessary "space."

Sartre's French critics have taken a rather different approach both to the question of specific philosophical antecedents and to the more general problem of the relation of one's own discourse to the tradition of Western metaphysics. Derrida especially has provided penetrating analyses both of the relation of Husserl to that tradition and of the role of Hegel in articulating a rendition of the tradition so powerful that it furnished the frame of reference infiltrating the thought of his most explicit critics. All Sartre's recent French critics would agree upon the significance of Freud, Marx, Heidegger, and Nietzsche for any critical enterprise. They have initiated a Nietzsche renaissance that has produced some of the most challenging interpretations of Nietzsche as a critical thinker to be considered more an object of emulation than of analysis. Derrida has provided an entire strategy of deconstructive reading that has caused a minor revolution (which in the United States has thus far been largely restricted to segments of the world of literary criticism).

An extreme and somewhat mechanical schematization of the strategy of the fine art of deconstruction might "present" it in the following terms: a continual reference to the texts of the tradition with their terms, analytic oppositions, and dialectical sublations; a "double inscription" of that tradition, which simultaneously uses its terms (the only ones we have) and critically sounds them out, thereby rendering explicit traditional assumptions that are often concealed, and placing the terms that articulate them *sous rature* (under erasure); an investigation of how the problematic language of the tradition contains submerged elements that place in question its own dominant motifs and desires (if not "fixations" or "fetishes"); an initial "moment" of reversal of hierarchical oppositions which provisionally gives

priority to the "oppressed" member of the hierarchy; displacement of the repeated terms of the tradition in which the "revolutionary" member of the opposition is denied sovereignty in
its turn and disclosed as "always already" inside its other;
the attempt to make room for new possibilities not governed
by the oppositions of the "old regime," yet actively forgetting
(therefore, in a certain sense, remembering) them; a constructive
affirmation of the disseminating play of "supplementarity,"
which gives rise to an active interpretation of the text and of
the world. Thus traditional notions are reinterpreted as recurrent functions of a differing "play," which repeats them in
continually displaced forms. The text becomes the scene of this
play—a scene where conflicting loyalties and offset tendencies
more or less blindly open up spaces that resist systematic closure.
Through "deconstruction" (or what Heidegger called "De-
struktion"), one may work to minimize the role of hollow,
incapacitating repetition and make room for a more creative
repetition: the regenerative transformation of traditional forms.

To crystallize the notions evoked in the preceding paragraph
and to make them applicable to the problems discussed in this
book, I shall single out Derrida's conception of supplementarity.
To privilege this "concept" (and even to call it a concept) is to
distort Derrida's thought, for supplementarity cannot be con-
ceptually defined, and its function is to question the status of
any central or dominant concept by revealing what it leaves out
or "represses." Hence, in Derrida's writings, one finds an intentional proliferation of "repetitive" terms that serve as substitutions for the word "supplementarity" and prevent it from attaining the sovereign status of a "master" concept or a key that
opens all locks. In its more extreme form, this terminological
proliferation comes with a textual shiftiness that seems to engender a bewildering and even monstrous *mimesis* (emulation
and parody) of the substitutive "free play" of symbolic systems.
In its more modulated form, Derrida's approach sets up a more
or less regulated interplay between structure and openness—an
interplay that brings an awareness of the possible resurgence of
dominant "centers" of discourse, if only in the minimal form of
thematizing the motif of the absence of center (or its analogues,

such as the death of God, problematics of language, breakdown of communication, crisis of existence).

Oversimplifying, one might say that supplementarity reveals why analytic distinctions necessarily overlap in "reality" and why it is misleading to take them as dichotomous categories. Analytic or binary opposites always leave an anomalous difference or remainder for which they do not fully account. In more positive terms, supplementarity directs attention to problematic areas where newer forms of conceptualization arise, at times to challenge the dominance of established forms. On the most general level, supplementarity refers to the undecidable or radically ambivalent interplay of excess and lack between the "same" and the "other." One (one of a pair of opposites, for example) is the same as its other but as "differed" or deferred. (The French term *différer* brings out this dual meaning. To mark it, Derrida coins the term *différance*, in which the anomalous *a* is apparent only in writing and not in speech.) The supplement is added to its "other" or "opposite" in a way that both exceeds it and simultaneously indicates a lack that needs to be supplemented.

Supplementarity and related notions, such as repetition and displacement, both signal the closure and enable the deconstruction of the system of values gathered around the ideas of "presence" and full, unproblematic "reality" (whose "true meaning" may be univocally represented, expressed, discovered, or invented). For they render problematic the relationship among signifier, signified, and referent (or, in more traditional language, word, meaning, and thing). And they make explicit the questions of the "textual" production of meaning, the referential uses of language, and the strategic nature of definitions of "reality." Supplementarity also reveals the theoretical basis of the technique or "game" of *l'un dans l'autre* (developed by the surrealists), through which one of a pair of putatively pure opposites is revealed as "always already" inside its other. Thus, for example, if one term is posited as designating the "origin" of a directed movement that leads to (or causes) the other, the supplementary status of the other displaces the origin and gives it, in its turn, a "derived" status. In this sense, anything analo-

gous to a "fall" has always already happened and been repeated; and the "paradise" of presence, purity, or spontaneity
(as, for example, in the form of a pure, free, spontaneous, prereflective consciousness fully present to itself) is a fiction that
comes after the "fall," only to be projected forward or backward
in time, logically in "ideal" space, or phenomenologically in
experience. More precisely, the very concepts "origin" and
"fall"—as well as that of pure opposites—are rendered problematic: the "origin" is never simple or absolute, for its place is
taken by the "originary" and "always already" situated play of
supplementarity itself. The attendant image of man is that of a
decentered being who, with more or less critical insight, takes
his beginnings and seeks his ends in a historical world where
absolute beginnings and ends are ideal constructs or functions
of a play of forces that man does not absolutely control. This
entire notion of relationships departs critically from a "logic" of
identity and difference that analysis formulates in terms of clear
and distinct opposites, and that dialectics attempts to "transcend" or "lift up" to a higher level (*aufheben, relever*) through a
"sublating," progressivist, and totalizing process.

Reason (*ratio*) itself might be seen as an attempt to ration and
limit the play of supplementarity. Analysis provides clear and
distinct ideas that define boundaries and confine ambiguity or
overlap to marginal, borderline cases. As far as analysis defines
polar, binary opposites, it constructs ideal types or heuristic fictions. When these opposites are perceived as "eidetic essences"
or projected onto the world as defining separate disciplinary or
life activities, one has the operation of a logic of surveillance and
control, if not of domination. Supplementarity does not obliter-
ate distinctions, and it cannot be identified with confusion or
"irrationalism." But it does situate dichotomies as functions of a
"logic" of identity and difference that serves to control the object.

Dialectics, in a sense, compensates for the excesses of
analysis. (If analysis may be seen on the analogue of a ritual of
purification, dialectics recalls an agonistic ritual process.) Dialectics takes analytically defined opposites and relates them in processes of becoming. As negative dialectics, it tracks forms of alien-

ation and attempts to explode them. In so-called "identity-theory," dialectical sublation may seek an ultimate reconciliation of opposites in a totality or harmonious whole that amounts to an end-game fiction. It thereby tries to make supplements entirely complementary by eliminating all problematic residues and remainders. By contrast, the notion of an open or unfinished dialectic—in so far as it is not entirely indentured to progressivist and totalizing motifs—converges in certain ways with a "logic" of supplementarity. It attempts to think through dichotomies and double binds and to prefigure a more creative interplay among aspects of the world. It recognizes, nevertheless, that structures of domination may always be resurrected, and thus insists upon the role of recurrent critique. To account for the very openness of a dialectical model, a notion of supplementarity may be necessary.[3]

How may these condensed introductory comments be developed, applied, and modified in an approach to Sartre's texts that is itself open to internal self-questioning? Most commentators on Sartre have recognized the limitations of an interpretive approach that presents him in terms of either simple continuities or discontinuities. Given Sartre's recent development and his related retrospective self-readings, a dialectical strategy with a predominantly political motif has been most tempting. This strategy can generate more or less numerous stages on Sartre's way. Or it may attempt to grasp one overall pattern of development that "totalizes" Sartre's itinerary and reveals how his later existential Marxism negates, preserves, and raises to a higher level of insight his earlier phenomenological existentialism. One may even hazard a dialectical synthesis of Sartre's existential Marxism and the thought of his critics in France—an enterprise whose initial plausibility (given Sartre's own later totalizing or syncretic quest for a historical and structural anthropology) falters when one realizes that his most forceful critics are placing in question the status of dialectics itself.

To delineate stages in Sartre's development, one could do worse than to select three and privilege one—a dialectical procedure in good form that has the virtue of approximating Sartre's own self-reading and the more or less authorized interpretation in Simone de Beauvoir's memoirs. Sartre's journey would be demarcated by radical conversions or identity crises that totalize his life or thought up to that point and provide the basis for a new original choice of being. (This is, of course, the model of development that Sartre employs to structure his existential biographies.) One crisis would come with World War II, when Sartre was jolted out of his apolitical individualism to discover History and the problem of commitment. Renouncing his quest for pure art, he then saw that the pen was not a sacramental object sanctified by the myth of literature. A second such crisis would come in the 1950s when the Resistance euphoria wore off and Sartre recognized the futility of a "third force" in politics—a futility symbolized by the failure of his own Rassemblement Démocratique Révolutionnaire. During this time, Sartre came to specify commitment in terms of Marxism and to believe that a united front of the Left in France must include the Communist Party. In the early 1950s, Sartre's opposition to the role of anticommunism in the Cold War was embodied in a series of long articles, "The Communists and the Peace," in which he went so far as to expound a Leninist vision of the Party as the objective expression of the proletariat. But his own sense of integrity and his growing awareness of the difference between the party line and Marxism prevented Sartre from being much more than an uneasy fellow "traveler without a ticket" vis-à-vis the Party in France. Events such as the invasion of Hungary in 1956 led him to outspoken criticism of the Party. But Sartre still tried to establish some sort of dialogue with it in the interest of proletarian revolution. Beginning in the late 1940s, he articulated a theory of committed literature in which the pen became a sword of social action that fended off propaganda but intervened politically in the interest of radical social change. His ideas on existential Marxism crystallized in his *Critique of Dialectical Reason,* prefaced by *Search for a Method* (*Question de méthode*). The third critical point—the privileged one—would be marked, of course, by Sartre's reaction to the events of the summer of 1968 in France, events heralded by his own earlier analysis of the group-in-fusion in the *Critique.* Nineteen sixty-eight was for Sartre analogous to what he believed the fainting fit at Pont l'Evêque was for Flaubert. But Sartre's apocalyptic moment led in the opposite direction from Flaubert's—not only away from Art for Art's sake but also from any inflated conception of literature (including that of the "committed" pen as sword) to a demystified understanding of man as a political animal. Nineteen sixty-eight, at least in retrospect, made Sartre realize that a Left was possible to the left of the Communist Party, which revealed itself during that year as a conservative force in French politics. And it brought the *prise de conscience* that made Sartre see the limitations of his earlier self as a classical intellectual with an unhappy consciousness. He now advocated the creation of the intellectual leftist and friend of the people—a role his advanced age enabled him to play only in marginal ways but which he urged the young to adopt. He seemed to pass the torch of authentic thought in France not to a Derrida or even to a Foucault but to Pierre Victor, a former Maoist leader and a young political activist who, along with Philippe Gavi, coauthored or cospoke with Sartre a new kind of book, *On a raison de se révolter* ("One Is Right to Revolt").

A more unified pattern of Sartre's development, which might include a delineation of stages as a subplot, could privilege the oriented movement from an early apolitical individualism to an existential Marxism reaching its practical fruition after 1968. Depending upon the interpretive emphasis and political commitments of the commentator, this movement might be seen as a progressive and promising journey toward a theoretical and practical basis for a *gauchiste* (if not more generally New Left) politics of liberation or as a negative and hollow passage from the activeless mind to mindless activism.[4]

Dialectical interpretations that emulate Sartre's own thought are not altogether wrong, and the elements of discontinuity they at least provisionally recognize in his development are significant. Moreover, a predominantly political motif is both inherently important and faithful to Sartre's recent self-understanding. But these interpretations harbor too many problematic features to be altogether convincing. Whether for purposes of praise or of blame, they go too far in accepting as gospel in the interpretation of Sartre his own self-commentaries or the readings of Simone de Beauvoir. What is needed instead is an entire strategy of reading in which Sartre's self-commentaries, which often function as retrospective intentions, are taken not as privileged texts but as parallel ones. Even if one is unable to elaborate an overall strategy for situating self-commentaries and cross-references in Sartre's works, one must recognize that these forms of discourse require interpretation and cannot be taken as unproblematic guides for commentary. Is Sartre altogether correct, for example, in his interpretations of *Nausea* and *Being and Nothingness* in *The Words* and interviews? More generally, can one unambiguously interpret the texts of the early Sartre as expressions of an individualistic and aesthetic view of the world? Does the cult of pure art as the individual's road to salvation ever find direct and affirmative articulation as the expression of Sartre's own voice in his early works? Is it possible that there was a significant discrepancy between Sartre's "ordinary life" and his texts on these issues, with his texts at times being more "advanced" in terms of his own later commitments? Does Sartre's later thought transcend individualism or does it in some sense instate it more forcefully as the complement to a growing social emphasis? And are there similar problems throughout Sartre's thought in the theoretical foundation for a radical politics and for the relation of art and politics?

Sartre, I think, remains the same while becoming different in ways which a dialectical model of interpretation can only partially account for. The model of "repetition" I would suggest for the interpretation of Sartre (and, by guarded implication, for the "reading" of history) focuses on continuities in discontinuities and discontinuities in continuities.

Continuities in discontinuities: There is, as I have already intimated, a basic continuity in Sartre's attempt to center thought on man conceived primarily in terms of free, conscious praxis in a situation, although in his later thought the range of freedom seems drastically narrowed and the situation made more historically and socially concrete. I would in no sense argue that continuity is, in the abstract, more important than discontinuity. The two exist side by side and interact in intricate ways; and at times they fail to interact and leave a blank or silence in the text (or in the life). Discontinuities, or ruptures, do exist in Sartre's thought, and they cannot be eliminated by an interpretation that places continuity in the foreground. To the extent that it functions to harmonize diachronic discontinuities, the notion of displacement becomes an ameliorative metaphor. What is repeated in the same is the different, and the different "is" different. There is, for example, a difference between religious belief in divinely revealed truth and atheistic secular humanism, even though both draw their categories and framework from the same metaphysical tradition. And there is a major difference between the explicit emphasis on the moral problem in the early Sartre and his later emphasis on politics. But the question I would like to raise is whether the diachronic discontinuity in Sartre's thought is radical enough and whether the "reinscription" of terms in a different context effects a sufficiently potent change of "problematic." It is not simply a question of finding Sartre's later themes in his early works or his early themes in his later works. It is rather that the more insistent emphasis on certain themes (the importance of society and political commitment, for example) and the use of different terms (such as alienation instead of bad faith, agent instead of subject, or praxis instead of consciousness) do not come with a sufficiently significant change in the structure of Sartre's thought—a change that would imply a more forceful rethinking of his earlier views. Sartre remains too much the same and does not change enough—at least as far as his writing is concerned. His life is a somewhat different story. Indeed, some of his most radical texts are his earlier works such as *Nausea*. And *Being and Nothingness* raises more probing questions than does the *Critique of Dialectical Reason*—not because of, but in spite of, the more explicit political emphasis of the later work. These observations, to the extent that they can be substantiated through a critical reading of the texts, should not be made to neutralize Sartre's later concerns, especially on the level of politics. But they should raise doubts about the theoretical foundation of the later work.

Discontinuities in continuities: Within the very continuities of Sartre's thought are discontinuities and forms of internal contestation. These might provisionally be labeled "synchronic" discontinuities in so far as one recognizes the interaction of the "synchronic" and the "diachronic" and does not take this binary pair as representing mutually exclusive or unproblematic opposites. For diachronic change may at least partially be seen in terms, not of simple rupture or break between synchronic structures over time, but of shift in position and function among tensely related and mutually contestatory elements. One problem in Sartre related to the more diachronic side of discontinuity is that the submerged tendencies in his thought do not become more forceful over time to function as a basis for more radical change in his framework. Indeed, at times his more submerged tendencies are further de-emphasized and his more dominant tendencies reinforced in response to his later critics. But one may perhaps contrast Sartre's "theoretical" works and "literary" writings in a partial manner. In his more theoretical, philosophical writings, internal alterity or self-questioning is largely "blind" or implicit. His decisive dedication to univocal language in philosophy tends to further his more dominant tendencies. If anything, the *Critique* is more self-certain in this regard than *Being and Nothingness*. The study of Flaubert, however, is somewhat ambivalent, and one may perhaps trace a growing self-doubt about certain key concepts—such as that of the status of a totalizing, original choice of being—through his existential biographies. "A Plea for Intellectuals" is rather a special case, for it contains some of Sartre's most subtle and challenging ideas about writing, language, and commitment. His own introductory note in *Situations VIII* tends to neutralize the text by situating it as the product of the classical intellectual rather than the friend of the people. But I think Sartre's own self-commentary should be resisted somewhat in this case.

In Sartre's "literary" works, self-contestation becomes simultaneously more indirect and more explicit. I find this to be especially true of *Nausea* (which Sartre himself considers his most successful piece of literature). Throughout Sartre's "literary" texts, the problem of the relation of purity, a logic of identity and difference, and totalization to that which endangers them, such as bastardy and the uncanny, is often explored with more insight than are analogous problems in his theoretical writings.

Or, another way of putting this is to say that Sartre's theories of literature and philosophy do not adequately account for his actual practice in writing. His philosophy, which strives for purity and a transparent, univocal language (the untinted medium of the for-itself or praxis), is the dramatic scene of relatively blind internal contestation. His literature, where he is willing to tolerate ambiguity, is often more explicit about problems of language and life, including that of ambiguity. One notion worthy of retention from Sartre's more theoretical writings nevertheless is that ambiguity must not render decision impossible—even if one argues that in certain ways the "goal" of decisive action is the furtherance of a cultural, social, and textual situation in which self-contestation and ambiguity of a certain kind are more effective and in which equivocation that functions to maintain structures of domination is demystified and at least partially incapacitated.

There is a larger question I would like to evoke in closing this introduction: that of the relationship between institutions and discourse—a question in relation to which the issue of intellectuals and texts is one small but not insignificant problem. Thought itself becomes institutionalized in texts that are "social facts" as objects of dissemination through teaching, commentary, and broader public circulation. Sartre's texts have been especially important in this regard throughout the world. How Sartre is read is an issue of historical and political interest. Reactions to him have often gone to the extremes of adulation and summary dismissal. Immediately after World War II, Sartre served as "guide to a generation." To say that he was widely read would be an understatement, and the marked centralization of French education and intellectual life made him an almost totemic figure subject to both emulation and ritual desecration. His own polemical bent was a recognition of this status and provocation to it. It is a seeming paradox that the most alienated intellectuals of modern society are among its most cherished institutions or fetishized objects. Sartre has not wanted to be taken as an institution. He is one, nevertheless. His refusal of the Nobel Prize did not de-institutionalize his status. It institutionalized him further as the writer-who-refused-the-Nobel-Prize—

a status eliciting through refusal more notoriety than would have been incurred by simple acceptance. Although the importance of structuralism from the late 1950s to the late 1960s dislodged Sartre from the center of French thought, his activities in the 1960s, culminating in his response to the events of 1968, brought a resurgence of interest in his work. (Indeed, in discussions of him, it is virtually impossible to distinguish among Sartre the man, Sartre the quasi-mythical idea-figure, and Sartre the writer.) More recently, the emergence of "poststructuralist" tendencies in Derrida and in figures like Foucault (who was never comfortable with the label of structuralism) has provoked another drop of interest in Sartre, for these recent tendencies seem "beyond" or at least apart from him. Sartre has gone his own way, often not comprehending more recent developments or oblivious to them. To some, the belief that Derrida is now the most important philosopher in France is synonymous with the idea that Sartre is hopelessly *démodé* and no longer of interest. Without Sartre as both path-breaker and critical foil, however, these more recent tendencies would not be what they are. For good and ill, Sartre has been, is, and will be on the horizon of modern thought. The point is not simply to forget him. The problem is how to remember and come to terms with him. It is to the resolution of this problem that the present study would like to make a contribution, however provisional.

Thus, I do not intend to write a descriptive history of Sartre's role in modern French thought. This project has already been undertaken and completed with a large measure of success, given the assumptions of the approach, by Mark Poster, for example, in his *Existential Marxism in Postwar France*. I shall not provide extended descriptions of the "essential" characteristics of the thought of Sartre's critics—notably Derrida and Foucault, who are especially pertinent for the approach taken in this study and who resist summarizing portraits in any event. I shall, rather, in a relatively restricted way use and, indeed, actively appropriate elements from Derrida's strategy of "deconstructive" reading and Foucault's history of discursive practices. (Given the topic and the scope of this study, the former will be much more prominent than the latter.) This perspective on the larger questions raised by an interpretation of Sartre's texts—a perspective simultaneously indirect and "engaged"—promises to offer a more active sense of what is at issue concerning history and theory in recent debates in France. I make no attempt, moreover, to be exhaustive and definitive, nor do I strive to "cover" all Sartre's writings or all the commentaries on him. Rather I treat selected texts in ways that may have more general consequences for a reading of Sartre that is allured by, and suspicious of, the totalizing motif with all that it implies. This study also avoids a purely thematic or topical approach by addressing itself to specific texts in a way that both respects their integrity and indicates why a certain idea of "integrity" is suspect. Finally, the extent to which my own more "participatory" and "dialogical" notion of the critical history of texts departs from conventional expectations about the nature of intellectual history emerges as an open question.

# 1

# Early Theoretical Studies:
# Art Is an Unreality

Imagination. Always "lively." Be on guard against it. When lacking it oneself, attack it in others. To write a novel, all you need is imagination.
                                    Flaubert, *Dictionary of Received Ideas*

The extreme beauty of a woman kills the desire for her. Indeed we cannot place ourselves simultaneously on the aesthetic level—where there appears this unreal "herself" that we admire—and on the realizing level of physical possession. In order to desire her, one must forget that she is beautiful, because desire is a plunge into the heart of existence—into what existence has of the most contingent and the most absurd.
                                    Sartre, *L'Imaginaire*

Regarding all aesthetic values I now avail myself of this main distinction: I ask in every instance, "Is it hunger or superabundance that has here become creative?"
                                    Nietzsche, *The Gay Science*

The work of art in Mallarmé is "just," but its justice is not that of existence; it is still an accusatory justice which denies life and presupposes failure and impotence. When Nietzsche speaks of the "aesthetic justification of existence," on the contrary, it is a question of art as "stimulant of life"; art affirms life, life affirms itself in art.
                                    Gilles Deleuze, *Nietzsche et la philosophie*

Sartre's early series of theoretical studies are rarely read today: *The Transcendence of the Ego* (1936–1937), *The Imagination* (1936), *Sketch for a Theory of the Emotions* (1939), and *L'Imaginaire* (1940). In preparation for the examination of Sartre's more famous and influential works, a brief and highly selective analysis of the early ones, explicitly addressed to the issue of continuity and discontinuity in Sartre's thought, is pertinent.

The analysis of imagination and emotion as structures or activities of consciousness is especially interesting in these early works. It fills gaps in the dominant line of argument of *Being and Nothingness* (1943), although more submerged but still forceful tendencies in the later work go beyond its limits. The early theoretical notions—especially in the case of *L'Imaginaire*—are situated and indirectly contested in *Nausea* (1938). And they are more directly challenged in Sartre's views on language, literature, and art in *What Is Literature?* (1947) and "A Plea for Intellectuals" (1965). But, in certain respects, Sartre returns repeatedly—as, for example, in the existential biographies—to notions or modes of conceptualization developed in the early studies, notably in the very important *L'Imaginaire*.

Sartre's early theoretical studies are organized around the phenomenological conception of consciousness. Consciousness is intentional, that is, it is always consciousness of something. The thing is the object of consciousness, but not its content. To see consciousness as itself a thing or as having contents is to fall into the naturalistic "illusion of immanence." Consciousness is a structure or an activity, which for Sartre is appropriately understood through the metaphor of an empty spontaneity. Indeed, in an important sense, which Sartre never takes as problematic, a series of metaphors structures the proper usage of "conscious-

47

ness" as a concept. (Consciousness is masculine, pure, limpid, clean, hard, active, mineral-like, erect yet devoid of content; its adventure is a flight from "feminine" passivity, maternal immanence, viscosity, "a stinking brine of the spirit," "moist gastric" intimacy, self-love, formlessness, mud, and indecision.) Consciousness as an activity that transcends the thing or object is, moreover, closely connected with human freedom. Sartre never makes theoretically explicit the precise nature of the relationship between freedom and consciousness: he often uses the two terms interchangeably. And these two terms are linked to a third: nihilation, or the ontological basis for processes of negation—a linkage explicated at length in *Being and Nothingness*, yet already crucial in *L'Imaginaire*.

Two relatively clear aspects of Sartre's early studies impugn common interpretations of his early thought. First, Sartre's early thought does, in one of its movements, directly relate freedom or consciousness to action and projects in the "real" world. The "mind" is not seen simply as activeless. Second, consciousness is not originally specified in terms of the individual. It is initially treated as impersonal, or at least as nonpersonal. It is individuated but in a sense initially contrasted, not with the social, but with the universal or generic. And it is always "mine" but in a sense specified in *The Transcendence of the Ego* as nonpossessive and purely designative. One explicit criticism of Husserl in this work is of his view of ego as the center and subject of consciousness, thereby giving consciousness a content. The ego for Sartre is not the subject or center of consciousness: it is the intentional object of consciousness in the world. Indeed, the early works of Sartre explode the notion of identity and individuality in the ordinary sense. As Sartre later put it in *Being and Nothingness*, the for-itself is what it is not and is not what it is. Sartre, in one important movement of his thought, does conceive consciousness as initially isolated in the world, but this isolation is not at first identified with that of the lonely or uncommitted individual.

One central equivocation in the early Sartre, however, continues throughout his works and allows, if it does not invite, systematic misreadings. There is a dominant tendency in his thought that presents freedom (or consciousness) as initially pure and total within itself and radically transcendent in relation to the world. In this sense, freedom—split off from the world—is initially isolated. A submerged tendency in Sartre's thought indicates that freedom is always already implicated in the world in a sense that undercuts and may give rise to the opposition between transcendence and immanence.

In his early theoretical works, Sartre's dominant tendency is especially powerful. In terms of it, freedom is conceived as having two basic "options." On the one hand, it can choose to direct itself toward perception, reality, action, desire, truth, and morality. On the other hand, it can attempt to escape this series of involvements in the "real" world and, in its negative purity, transcend them toward imagination, emotion, unreality, contemplation, artifice, error, evil, and art. The first series might be termed that of proper reactions to the world or proper uses of freedom and intentional consciousness. The second series is an object of suspicion and anxiety but also, paradoxically, a possible source of salvation (through art). At the most basic level, Sartre explicitly resists any ambiguous overlap or undecidable interplay between the two series of free choices or activities of consciousness even at the margin of borderline cases. But his texts do at times indicate the submerged and unspeakable intercourse or interplay of the two series in a manner that is not "raised to consciousness" as an object of theoretical reflection. In his early theoretical works, moreover, Sartre not only explicitly resists supplementary relationships; he also fails to discuss the possibility of complementary relationships through dialectical mediation and possible synthesis. Instead, he "relates" the two series through the nonrelation of segregation or a taboo on contact and relies on an extreme form of analysis to mark the divide. An analytic logic of identity and difference presents the only relationship between the two series as mutual avoidance or, upon contact and the impairment of purity, mutual annihilation. Sartre himself attempts to play the good shepherd of theoretical concepts that clearly separate the two series and prevent the encroachment of the one upon the other.

Sartre explicitly relates his enterprise in his early thought to Husserl and Descartes and in a sense repeats Husserl's own recapitulation of the Cartesian heritage—but in a form more uncompromising and *outré* than the endeavors of his predecessors, for Sartre makes no explicit allowance for exceptions or areas of permeability in his clear and distinct ideas. Subversive and misguided inclinations in Husserl and Descartes are duly observed and excoriated. Sartre will not wink where his predecessors nodded. His short but powerful essay "A Fundamental Idea of the Phenomenology of Husserl" begins with words calculated to produce a shock effect in the reader:

"He ate her with his eyes." This sentence and many other signs mark the illusion common to realism and idealism, according to which to know is to eat. French philosophy, after a hundred years of academicism, is still at this point. We have all read Brunschvicg, Lalande, and Meyerson; we have all believed that the Spirit-Spider [*l'Esprit-Araignée*] attracted things into its web, covered them with white spittle, and slowly swallowed them, reducing them to its own substance. [S. I, p. 29]

The rejection of what Sartre terms an alimentary philosophy, which presents consciousness as digesting contents, prefaces his own association of phenomenology with what might be called, by an extension of the metaphor, an emetic philosophy, which evacuates consciousness and throws it explosively into the world. For alimentary philosophy, consciousness is itself immanent in reality: it is sucked down by an alien "other," which makes it flesh of its flesh. For Sartre, consciousness is radically transcendent but in a sense that immediately presents it to the world. It has no contents or attachments to serve as barrier between its pure, empty spontaneity and the world. It is altogether *disponible*. The concluding words of this brief essay are as insistent as its opening lines:

If we love a woman, it is because she is lovable. Thus we are delivered from Proust. Delivered at the same time from "interior life": in vain do we seek like Amiel, like a child that kisses its own shoulder, the caresses and pamperings of our intimacy, since at last everything is outside, even ourselves: outside, in the world, among others. It is not in I know not what retreat that we discover ourselves: it is on the road, in the city, in the midst of the crowd, thing among things, man among men. [S. I, p. 32]

Sartre takes his distance from Husserl in criticizing the tendencies that betray the phenomenological project of liberation

by either filling in consciousness or diverting it from an orientation toward reality. In *The Transcendence of the Ego,* the transcendental ego as subject was rejected by Sartre precisely because it blocked the empty spontaneity of a wind-swept consciousness. And Sartre accepts the *epochè* or phenomenological
reduction only in so far as it does not simply bracket reality or
put it out of play but rather seeks to transform everyday life. In
*Being and Nothingness,* Sartre accuses Husserl of taking a turn
toward subjective idealism in seeking an intuition of ideal essences. In *The Transcendence of the Ego,* Sartre concludes by insist-
ing that for centuries philosophy has not experienced so realistic
a current as phenomenology and so intense a concern with
plunging man back into the world. A political, historical concern
with "real problems" is directly indicated: "It has always
seemed to me that a working hypothesis as fruitful as historical
materialism never needed for a foundation the absurdity that is
metaphysical materialism" (*TE,* p. 86). (This is, of course, the
theme that was later developed in the 1946 essay "Materialism
and Revolution.")

Yet the critique of Husserl is not without attendant difficulties
in Sartre's early thought. Sartre's rejection of the transcendental
ego and his purge of the "I" from consciousness still enable him
to assert that consciousness is "quite simply a first condition and
an absolute source of existence" (*TE,* p. 87). And the desire to
affirm a primary orientation toward reality fosters Sartre's extreme analytic tendencies, for he sometimes takes ideal types (or
eidetic essences) and projects them onto "reality" as inclusive
and exhaustive definitions of things in terms of categorial opposites or antinomies. This tendency marks his early analyses of
emotion, imagination, and perception (as well as his later
analysis of prose and poetry).

Before turning to these analyses, one may note Sartre's at-
tested affinity with Descartes. As Sartre expressed himself in an
interview of 1944: "In our country [*chez nous*], only one person
has profoundly affected my mind: Descartes. I place myself in
his lineage and proclaim my relationship to this old Cartesian
tradition that has been conserved in France."[1] But the criticisms
of Husserl in *The Transcendence of the Ego* were implicit criticisms
of Descartes, and Sartre—in expelling the ego from conscious-

ness—was engaged in displacing the final "o" from the *cogito*. Sartre attempts to explicate his relation to Descartes in an essay of 1945, "La Liberté cartésienne." Cartesian freedom and Husserlian intentionality are intimately linked in Sartre's mind, for the freedom of Descartes applies to consciousness in the world.

As Sartre sees it, freedom in Descartes is total but not absolute, for in Descartes, as in the Stoics, a crucial distinction is made between freedom and power. The purity and totality of freedom depend upon its clear distinction from power in the world. "To be free is not at all to be able to do what one wants [*pouvoir faire ce qu'on veut*] but it is to be able to will what one can do [*vouloir ce qu'on peut*]" (*S. I*, p. 294). Action, however restricted its field, is free to the extent that it is informed by the project of intentional consciousness. Freedom is total, but power is limited by the situation. One may note that this conception, which Sartre holds on a possibly dominant level of his thought, depends upon an identity between freedom and intentional consciousness and a dichotomy between freedom and the situation. The conception is placed in question to the extent that these associations are challenged. On this conception, moreover, freedom is related to power through an activist leap made in the interest of man's mastery of the situation. Sartre finds in Descartes "a magnificent humanist affirmation of creative liberty," which constrains us to take up "this fearful task, *our task par excellence:* to make truth exist in the world, to make the world be true . . ." (*S. I*, p. 296). Sartre, of course, objects to the Cartesian role of divinity as fail-safe. But—in a turn of thought that seems to confuse Heidegger with Feuerbach—he insists that the reliance upon traditional religious ideas does not detract from Descartes's ringing affirmation of man and freedom:

Little does it matter to us that he was constrained by his epoch, as by his point of departure, to reduce human free will to only a negative power to refuse itself to the point of finally giving in and abandoning himself to divine solicitude; little does it matter to us that he hypostatized in God this original and *constituting* freedom whose infinite existence he seized by the *cogito* itself: it remains that a formidable power of divine and human affirmation runs through and supports his universe. Two centuries of crisis will be necessary—crisis of Faith, crisis of Science—for man to recuperate this creative freedom that Descartes placed in God and for one to suspect finally this truth, the essential basis of humanism: man is the being whose appearance makes a world exist. But we do not reproach Descartes for having given to God what is our proper due [*ce qui nous revient en propre*]; instead we admire him for having, in an authoritarian epoch, laid the bases of democracy, having followed the requirements of the idea of autonomy to the end, and having understood, well before Heidegger in *Vom Wesen des Grundes*, that the unique foundation of being is freedom. [*S. I*, p. 308]

Thus, the task of human freedom is to repossess what was formerly "hypostatized" in divinity. In his early theoretical writings, Sartre explores the adventures of freedom through an analytic framework that is probably more demanding than Cartesianism in its insistence upon clear and distinct ideas. Analysis in the early Sartre functions as an extreme ritual of purification. Where Descartes, for example, allows for a possible confusion between the real and the imaginary, Sartre insists upon their radical discontinuity.[2] Perception for Sartre is informed by a logic of identity and difference, and it is geared to reality through a linkage with instrumental action that tests the real. Perception has no points of contact with imagination. Perception, imagination, and emotion are total, or totalitarian, structures of consciousness that can be experienced only alternately, not simultaneously. Their relation is purely diachronic, not synchronic. But all three are structures and activities of consciousness, which cannot be seen on the analogy of the thing or through the naturalistic "illusion of immanence" which would fill them with contents and implicate them in causal series. Sartre presents perception as central and guiding in its logical, adult relation to freedom and action in reality. By contrast, emotion and imagination are "perceived" in structurally analogous ways as escapes from reality and freedom—emotion as an evasion "from below" and imagination as one "from above." Both emotion and imagination are compared to magic, "prelogical" thinking, or childlike behavior. Both are what orthodox Freudians would call forms of substitute gratification and what Sartre later discusses in terms of the game of "loser wins." For both are prompted by some failure in reality and constitute inappropriate responses to real problems.

In one of the few significant studies of an important area of Sartre's thought, Joseph Fell makes observations that apply beyond the problem of emotion in the thought of Sartre:

> The question [is] whether instrumental [related to perception] and magical [related to emotion] attitudes are only *limiting cases* on a continuous scale whose intermediate points mark attitudes which are combinations or syntheses of the instrumental and magical attitudes. And are the corresponding perceptual fields which are intended by these attitudes likewise partially instrumental and partially magical, with wholly instrumental and wholly magical worlds representing only limiting cases? We said that in order for Sartre's theory to cover cases of delicate and weak emotion it would seem necessary for him to qualify considerably his apparently stark dialectical opposition of instrumental and magical ways of being-in-the-world. In presenting Sartre's theory of imagination I raised the question whether the following dialectical formulation was to be taken literally: "The image and the perception... represent the two irreducible attitudes of consciousness. It follows that they exclude each other." We concluded that weak and delicate emotions could not be regarded as emotions at all unless such statements were taken as descriptions of limiting cases, not formulas descriptive of *all* emotions or *all* cases of imagination. Yet such a conclusion seems contradicted by remarks such as this: "It is easy to see that every emotional apprehension of an object which frightens, irritates, saddens, etc., can be made only on the basis of a total alteration of the world."[3]

Fell himself strains to make his critical observations apply only to exceptions (such as "delicate" and "weak" emotions) requiring seemingly minor modifications that Sartre's theory might accommodate (by recognizing, for example, the status of his analyses as "descriptions" of limiting cases, not of all cases). But certain of Fell's comments fail to be contained in this framework of criticism. He astutely notices, for example, that Sartre's analysis of the emotions is radically contested by Sartre's own understanding of an emotion that is central in his thought— *angoisse*, or anguish: "[*Angoisse*] is reflective; it is neither transformative nor deceptive because it is recognition of the freedom of consciousness hidden by all other emotions; it may, certainly, be accompanied by bodily changes, it does not even seem to be a purposive act. It thus seems a thorough misfit, failing utterly to fall within the categories of Sartre's theory."[4]

One might add that the purifying reflection related to the recognition of anguished freedom can effect a radical conversion in being-in-the-world only if that freedom is lived on the prere-flective level and "is" an emotion. The very core of Sartre's early thought escapes the analytic categories of his dominant framework. Not only is it a question of "describing" limiting cases, it is also a question of "recognizing" the status of these limiting cases or analytically defined polar opposites as fictions more or less approximated in reality—a status that itself places in question any rigid categorial opposition between fiction and reality. The analytic type (which Fell curiously but revealingly refers to as the "stark dialectical opposition") is itself a pure form that attempts to center and master the "ambiguous" supplementary interplay that it simultaneously indicates and represses. It is not simply a question of "weak" and "delicate" emotions, but also one of possibly strong emotion (or imagina-tion) as the *proper* response to the situation—the status Sartre implicitly accords to *angoisse* itself. Sartre's equivocation on these matters "is" very much his equivocation about freedom (pure/impure, initially unengaged/always already engaged) and bad faith (escape from pure freedom and unproblematic reality/ escape from ambivalence itself). One might reformulate Fell's criticism by arguing that Sartre "describes" emotion and the imagination only in so far as they are responses in bad faith. But, given his own equivocation about the nature and status of his "descriptions," his own analysis is in "bad faith."

Perhaps the most important of Sartre's early theoretical studies is *L'Imaginaire* (badly translated both in title and content as *The Psychology of the Imagination*).[5] This work is a crucial sup-plement to *Being and Nothingness*, which largely assumes the theory of the imagination directly related in the earlier work to the problems of freedom and nothingness:

The imaginary represents at each instant the implicit meaning of the real. . . . And if negation is the unconditional principle of all imagina-tion, reciprocally it can never realize itself except in and through an act of imagination. One must imagine what one negates. [*Il faut qu'on ima-gine ce que l'on nie.*] In fact the object of a negation cannot be *real* since that would mean affirming what one denies—but no more can it be a total *nothing* because precisely one denies [or negates—*nie*] *something*. Thus the object of a negation must be posited as imaginary. And this is true for the logical forms of negation (doubt, restriction, etc.) as for its active and affective forms (defense, consciousness of impotence, of lack, etc.). . . . Thus the imagination, far from appearing as a factual characteristic of consciousness, is revealed [devoilée] as an essential and transcendental condition of consciousness. It is as absurd to conceive of a consciousness that could not imagine as to conceive of a consciousness that could not effect the *cogito.* [*L'Imaginaire,* pp. 238–39]

The dominant line of argument in *L'Imaginaire* may be seen as an attempt to disentangle in terms of clear and distinct analytic dichotomies the *noeud de vipères* embodied in this quotation. The ambiguous overlap of the imaginary and the real, of imagination and perception—indeed of affirmation and negation—are at times implicit in the language Sartre uses ("negation . . . can never realise itself"), but it is not recognized, and is in fact explicitly denied on the level of theory. In the interest of purity, a logic of identity and difference analyzes, controls, and guides a conception of the imagination and art. Sartre employs analysis to distribute "ambiguity" or the supplementary interplay of the same and the other (the imaginary is the same as the real but as differed) into discrete categories, or distinct boxes, of experience. Negation implies not the transformative reconstruction of its object but its "nihilation," the escape into the imaginary, and the postulation of a sharp divide. Life is one thing. Art is another. Reality is one thing. Imagination is another. Perception is entirely different from imagination. Perception is presented as excessively rich: we can always learn more about the perceived "real" object as we walk around it and acquire new perspectives on it. Imagination is poor. It gives its object all in one go, and it corresponds to a lack in reality created by freedom itself. Excess and lack are thus squarely placed on opposite sides of an unbreachable barrier. This "conception" of the imagination is indeed necessitated by Sartre's definition of imagination as an intentional structure of consciousness that "nihilates" reality and "presents" its object as not present, absent, or not existing. And imagination is related to the two faces of freedom that never come face to face. Imagination "is" freedom as a nihilating, empty spontaneity. It marks the paradox of freedom, for it liberates man from reality only to entrap him in a fatalistic world of escapist images that is poverty-stricken. Again, the silenced problems are those of overlap and mediation, supplementarity and dialectical relationship between "opposites"; Sartre himself seems unable to provide "viable" relationships among elements that threaten to constitute the world of hollowly repetitive fatal splits both explored and replicated in his early works. And again there are at least marginal, unexplored elements in the text that place his dominant view in question—for example, the fascinating case of the woman impersonating Maurice Chevalier in such a way that an interplay between perception and imagination is generated, which threatens to undermine or contaminate the decisive analytic opposition between the two.[6] But the most interesting part of *L'Imaginaire* is the concluding section, in which Sartre offers a sustained analysis of the relation of imagination to art—a problem that will continue to preoccupy if not haunt him in his later works. Toward the end of *L'Imaginaire*, Sartre presents seriously, but not explicitly as a means of salvation, the conception of art that he later presents toward the end of *Nausea* as a possible means of salvaging existence, although it then takes on an ironic quality. It is a conception of art derived from a rather literal reading of the theory of symbolist poetics: the aesthetic object is the rose missing from every bouquet. And it is a conception of art that Sartre later attributes to Flaubert and envisions himself as having outgrown.

What, then, is art in *L'Imaginaire*? As a product of the imagination, "the work of art is an unreality" (*L'Imaginaire*, p. 239). It negates reality and transcends it, not toward some heaven of real forms or essences, but toward an absence. The only point of contact between the real object and the aesthetic object of beauty is the material that serves as "analogon" for that imaginary derealization of the real. And this point, as Sartre interprets it, is a zero point that almost effaces itself. The relationship between the real and the aesthetic is purely analogical. Sartre's argument places a great deal of interpretive weight on the analogon as a feeble point zero of contact. It is a kind of sense datum in the real that somehow indicates the unreal. Sartre attempts to eliminate all ambiguity in the analogon's role as real reference point of the ideal but nihilating aesthetic object. There is a total divide between the sensible paint on the canvas and the painting as art, between the words on the paper and the poem as an aesthetic object, between the notes on the score sheet or even the performance of a piece and the other-worldly sounds of music:

> What is real, one must not tire of repeating, are the results of the strokes of the paint brush, the coating [*l'empâtement*] of the canvas, its grain, the varnish one has placed over the colors. But precisely all of that is not in the least the object of aesthetic appreciation. On the contrary, what is "beautiful" is a being that cannot be given to perception and which, in its very nature, is out of the world [*isolé de l'univers*]. . . . The painter has not in the least *realized* his mental image: he has simply constituted a material analogon such that each of us may seize this image if only he considers the analogon. But the image thus provided with an exterior analogon remains an image. There is no realization of the imaginary; at the very most one can speak of its *objectification* [*tout au plus pourrait-on parler de son* objectivation]. [*L'Imaginaire*, p. 240]

It is interesting that, in a significant slip, the English version (p. 247) translates the last phrase as "nor can one speak of its objectification," thereby transforming a weak affirmation into a strong negation. Given Sartre's conception of the analogon (which is far from clear and distinct), it is difficult to see how one can speak of the objectification or objectivation of the imaginary in the art object. In the distinction he makes between the analogon and the aesthetic object, Sartre repeats and displaces problems associated with the relationship between the world and divinity in theology or with the relationship between the *signans* and the *signatum* (signifier and signified) in the philosophy and theory of language. In Sartre's "iconoclastic" theory of the imagination, art functions as a secular, humanistic "surrogate" for a God that is not simply hidden but absent: it allows for a transcendental signified (a terminal concept, often identified with a referent, ultimately holding everything together in a meaningful way) that is purely imaginary. And the analogon generates theoretical problems "analogous" to those raised by any immanent sign in relation to a transcendent signified. The analogon is a purely external sign, or index, that must somehow remain purely external in relation to what it signifies but nonetheless function as a signifier pointing to the absent object. And the problems surrounding it create the anxiety of contamination. The objections raised to Sartre's early theory from more "immanent" conceptions of art (but does not modern art explore precisely the strokes of the brush, the texture and grain of the canvas, the varnish, as media of composition and as aesthetic objects?) often seem like pale shadows of religious debates.

The problems circulating around Sartre's theory of art are those found in his conception of freedom, for freedom is imagination as a nihilating consciousness. In his later works, Sartre returns to these problems, often in paradoxical or internally divided ways. One may note that in L'Imaginaire the drastic separation between the real and the imaginary, life and art, is applied to all forms of art and literature. It drives a wedge between morality and the aesthetic as well as between desire and the imagination. Commitment in art is out of the question: "It is stupid to confound morality and aesthetics" because "the values of the Good suppose being-in-the-world, aim at conduct in reality, and are subjected first and foremost to the essential absurdity of existence" (L'Imaginaire, p. 245). The moral problem is apparently to come to terms with the "rich" but nauseatingly ugly and absurd world given to us in perception. In relation to the "real" world, freedom in art is deadly. The aesthetic negates and transcends the nauseating absurdity of contingent existence, and it seems, at least implicitly, to indicate a possible path of "salvation" from the real world. But it does so at the price of furnishing an escapist illusion that carries with it a touch of evil. Indeed, Sartre interprets the feeling of letdown after an artistic performance in terms of the abrupt transition from a consciousness captivated by the imaginary to a renewed contact with reality that "provokes the nauseating disgust that characterizes the realizing consciousness" (p. 245). There is no mutually contestatory and possibly re-creative interplay between art and reality, only a passage from one to the other through the narrow gate of the analogon. Nor is art rooted in erotic experience or related to bodily desire even in terms of "sublimation." Sartre, rather, carries the divorce between desire and beauty to the point of swallowing the paradox that one cannot desire a beautiful woman—a perverse paradox that in effect presents all desire on the analogy of the impotent look of the *voyeur* gazing at frigid, glacial beauty.

In *What Is Literature?* Sartre tries to reverse fields by subtracting prose from complicity in pure art and by developing a theory of committed literature that demystifies the escapist illusion and plunges at least certain forms of literature into the "real world" of morality, desire, and politics. But he thus risks making a mystery of that which is literary in his conception of prose. And he will continue to ground his argument upon uncompromising analytic dichotomies that explicitly resist both supplementary interplay and dialectical mediation. His later turn to dialectics may in part be seen as an attempt to heal the wounds aggravated by his own extreme analytic tendencies.

One might argue that the deadly dichotomies of Sartre's early theoretical works replicated and reinforced the traits of the dominant culture against which he was revolting in other ways. The ugliness of reality is accepted and sanctioned as an ontological given, as is its divorce from aesthetic considerations. Art and life cannot possibly take on a relationship of mutual testing and affirmation. Sartre's conception of freedom seems to function as an ideology superimposed on extreme splits and contradictions presented in terms of a logic of mastery and repression. But the very uncompromising nature of Sartre's early thought has the ability to drive tensions to the breaking point of bewildering paradox if not of patent absurdity. Negative dialectics was already implicit in his early form of ultra-analysis. The idea of art as a pleasing escape from the cares of ugly reality seems acceptable up to a point. But when it is taken to extremes, its implications become too disconcerting for comfort. In so far as Sartre follows the analytic distinctions that structure common sense and have a familiar resonance in the metaphysical tradition, he seems to underwrite conventional attitudes and the "wisdom" of ordinary language.[7] But he never does this alone. He carries those distinctions to a point of opposition that evacuates them and, however blindly, brings out their fragility and proximity to shocking paradox. The familiar is defamiliarized, and the reassuringly recognizable opens onto the mad but extremely "logical" world of the paranoid schizophrenic. The important if obvious difficulty that Sartre is theoretically unequipped to confront in his early works is whether his approach to problems threatens to reflect both dominant tendencies and extreme reactions to them in a manner that provides little insight into critical and constructive alternatives.

# 2

# Literature, Language, and Politics: Ellipses of What?

Poetry. Entirely useless; out of date.
Prose. Easier to write than verse.
Literature. Idle pastime.

Flaubert, *Dictionary of Received Ideas*

It would be a most easy task to prove . . . that not only the language of a large portion of every good poem, even of the most elevated character, must necessarily, except with reference to meter, in no respect differ from that of good prose, but likewise that some of the most interesting parts of the best poems will be found to be strictly the language of prose when prose is well written.

Wordsworth, "Preface to Lyrical Ballads"

If the poet narrates, explains, or teaches, poetry becomes prosaic; he has lost the game. It is a matter of complex structures, impure but well delimited.

Sartre, *What Is Literature?*

*Prose and poetry.* — It is noteworthy that the great masters of prose have almost always been poets, too — if not publicly then at least secretly, in the "closet." Good prose is written only face to face with poetry. For it is an uninterrupted, well-mannered war with poetry: all of its attractions depend on the way in which poetry is continually avoided and contradicted. Everything abstract wants to be read as a prank against poetry and as with a mocking voice; everything dry and cool is meant to drive the lovely goddess into lovely despair. Often there are *rapprochements,* reconciliations for a moment — and then a sudden leap back and laughter. Often the curtain is raised and harsh light let in just as the goddess is enjoying her dusks and muted colors. Often the words are taken out of her mouth and sung to a tune that drives her to cover her refined ears with her refined hands. Thus there are thousands of delights in this war, including the defeats of which the unpoetic souls, the so-called prose-men, do not know a thing; hence they write and speak only *bad* prose. *War is the father of all good things;* war is also the father of good prose.

Nietzsche, The Gay Science

As Contat and Rybalka observe of *What Is Literature?* ("Qu'est-ce que la littérature?"): "To be better understood, this manifesto of committed literature [*la littérature engagée*] must be placed back into the atmosphere of the years from 1945 to 1948 and into a context of polemics."[1] Published almost as a "position paper" in *Les Temps modernes, What Is Literature?* also tried to respond to an immediate historical situation and to justify a contextual theory of writing and reading. It provides a generous theory of commitment that urges the writer to avoid manipulative propaganda as well as secure professionalism and to use his own freedom as an appeal to the freedom of the reader to become involved in the real issues of the day. Its polemical incentive partially accounts for its often one-sided controversialism, itself situated midway between committed political discourse and the provocative pedagogy of the good discussion leader. Sartre goes so far as to argue that the writer must forget about fleshless eternal verities in literature and see his work historically—indeed, as a "banana" that must be eaten on the spot. Only if the work is relevant can it be aesthetically valid. Formalism and Art for Art's sake are diversionary tactics that serve political reaction. Sartre himself at this time was trying to organize an independent Left in France, which was to capitalize on the spirit of the Resistance and rally together progressive forces for social change: his writing is linked to his own political involvement that was taking him out of the apolitical individualism of his prewar life and making him discover his own historicity.

The change from the position on art taken toward the end of *L'Imaginaire* could not be more blatant. Sartre is apparently arguing against his own early self as well as against others, and this

65

too helps account for his polemical and even exorcistic tone. In *L'Imaginaire*, art is not affirmed as the road to personal salvation, but it is seen as the pure product of an escapist imagination in a manner that seemed to lay a theoretical foundation for a vision of a saving cult of Art for Art's sake. This vision of art was uncommitted, at least in the normative political sense. Sartre has never renounced the notion of a bond between art and politics presented in the theory of *littérature engagée* of *What Is Literature?* But he has qualified, modified, partially transformed, and even displaced it. He came to believe, for example, that its forceful argument overinflated and, therefore, mystified the role of literature in the world, thereby functioning as a subtle ritual of degradation in relation to other activities—notably, more "direct" forms of political action. And the "argument from the banana" was itself a concealed variant of the game of loser wins, for the individual, who ostensibly turned away from eternal verities and immortalization, would be recuperated by these cavalierly rejected values and find his gift of self returned to him with profit: he would be immortalized as the committed writer.

Whereas the message of *What Is Literature?* seems relatively clear, although controversial, at least on the level of bald summary, the medium of its communication is less so. Sartre in this work is suspended between the rigid analytic framework characteristic of his early theoretical studies and a more dialectical approach related to his lived and textual discovery of history and political involvement. To a limited extent, the division between Part One and the rest of *What is Literature?* marks this tension in Sartre's thought. After the first part, the themes of history and dialectics become operative in a way that seems directly to anticipate his later work. And the tension in Sartre's thought also seems to mark a limit to the pertinence of the more immediate contextual explanation of it.

To learn what in his immediate sociohistorical context led Sartre into this impasse between analysis and dialectics, one must both raise and displace the problem of context to a higher level of generalization and relate it to the text in a more problematic way. One might refer the continued role of analysis to its place in the dominant metaphysical tradition and its function in the dominant bourgeois ideology and note its shifting but durable "love-hate" interaction with dialectics. Then one might perhaps return to the more immediate context and locate elements in it that furthered a forceful role for analysis and its "controversy" with dialectics. This approach would accept the relevance of Sartre's own later categories of interpretation and emulate his "progressive-regressive" method of tacking among levels in the understanding of a phenomenon. It would not tell the whole story, but it would not be without its usefulness for interpretation. One might argue, for example, that the role of the Communist Party in the postwar period provoked reactions among conservative elements that were "reflected" or inscribed in the works of writers who, despite their new-found political commitment, retained petty-bourgeois features in their approach to problems. In *Search for a Method*, Sartre himself partially accepted the more orthodox Marxist view that existentialism was a decadent petty-bourgeois ideology. But he objected that this interpretation must not be made to explain existentialism away and to eliminate what he held was of value in it (its insistence upon the lived and the concrete) and what in it must be related to regional histories of thought requiring a close, line-by-line reading of texts.

In Sartre's own thought, the problem of text and context becomes even more intricate when one moves from *What Is Literature?* (1947) to "A Plea for Intellectuals" (1965). By 1965, Sartre was still committed politically, in more insistent ways, if anything (as in his key role in the protest against France's war in Algeria). But his understanding of language, literature, and political commitment undergoes significant changes in the later work. And it is difficult to generate a plausible account of the relationship between the two works in terms of changes in the immediate sociopolitical context. (The problem is further complicated by the fact that "A Plea for Intellectuals" was first delivered as a series of lectures in Japan.) One might, however, speculate on the basis of some "internal" evidence in the text that an event in reading had something to do with the changes in Sartre's way of conceiving problems. And this event is related to the more general phenomenon of the rise of what is labeled "structuralism" as a force in French thought.[2] In "A Plea," Sartre builds on Roland Barthes's distinction between the *écrivant* ("literal writer") and the *écrivain* ("literary writer"). In so doing, Sartre attempts to confront constructively certain "structuralist" concerns relating to language in the light of his own theory of commitment. A specific text of Barthes, which Sartre does not mention, perhaps has special relevance for the change from *What Is Literature?* to "A Plea for Intellectuals": *Writing Degree Zero.*[3]

In this text of 1953, Barthes did not undertake a point by point refutation of *What Is Literature?* and his argument is not altogether incompatible with its interests, notably the concern for political and social commitment. Barthes's terse, allusive, and aphoristic essay performed subtle variations on themes common to himself and Sartre. It assumed in the reader a familiarity with a complex context of debate as well as sympathy with both modernist literature and leftist politics. The text attempted to negotiate the tense relationships among these elements to produce a configuration rather different from that generated by *What Is Literature?*

Using the ideas in *What Is Literature?* as an implicit critical point of reference, Barthes developed an approach that displaced its frame of reference and placed the problem of commitment in a different light. Instead of Sartre's binary opposition between prose and poetry, Barthes made a ternary distinction among style (the individual and even biological dimension), language (the universal dimension regulated by linguistic rules), and the form of writing or *écriture*, which both mediated and supplemented style and language. Writing for Barthes was the proper sphere of literature, but it could never be entirely fixated or accounted for in a totalizing manner. *Ecriture* was always "an ambiguous reality: on the one hand, it unquestionably arises from a confrontation of the writer with the society of his time; on the other hand, from this social finality, it refers the writer back, by a sort of tragic reversal, to the sources, that is to say, to the instruments of creation" (*WDZ*, p. 16). To the opposition between language and style was added a further opposition between society and the "inner" resources of art. *Ecriture* situated the writer betwixt and between overlapping realities, so that the "choice" of a form involved a choice of a social area into which the writer inscribed his language. But freedom in this process was never pure or total. It "began" as always already situated in history and tradition and "ended" by giving rise to a form that was bound to repeat itself:

It is under the pressure of History and Tradition that the possible modes of writing for a given writer are established; there is a History of Writing. But this History proposes—or imposes—new problematics of the literary language, writing still remains full of the recollection of previous usage, for language is never innocent: words have a second-order memory which mysteriously persists in the midst of new meanings. Writing is precisely this compromise between freedom and remembrance, it is this freedom which remembers and is free only in the gesture of choice, but is no longer so within duration. True, I can today select such and such mode of writing, and in so doing assert my freedom, aspire to the freshness of novelty or to a tradition; but it is impossible to develop it within duration without gradually becoming a prisoner of someone else's words and even of my own. A stubborn afterimage, which comes from all the previous modes of writing and even from the past of my own, drowns the sound of my present words. Any written trace precipitates, as inside a chemical at first transparent, innocent, and neutral, mere duration gradually reveals in suspension a whole past of increasing density, like a cryptogram. [WDZ, pp. 16-17]

History itself in this sense raises the problem of repetition, and this problem could not be seen solely in terms of an initially pure and total freedom that converted itself into a thing. Instead of Sartre's emphasis on content and message and radical de-emphasis of form ("Concerning form, there is nothing to say in advance and we have said nothing: each of us invents his own and one judges after the event" QL in S. II, p. 76), Barthes saw form as a crucial aspect of écriture and attempted to relate formal experimentation to radicalism with political and social implications. The seemingly revolutionary content of a work might be undercut by the use of manipulative stereotyped forms (such as those of social realism), and the seemingly escapist work might undertake critically probing ventures in the use of language. Whereas toward the end of Part One of his essay Barthes seemed to assert the specificity of modern poetry in contrast to both classical literature and all prose, in Part Two he seemed to take modern poetry as the vanguard expression of the state of crisis and the problem of language in all modern literature. The situation of modern literature involved a confrontation with the problematic in language and culture and an intimation of the possible, especially in terms of a utopia of language. Barthes accounted for the emergence of this modern literary context after about 1850 (in Flaubert and Mallarmé, for example) through a relatively loose Marxist analysis of changes in society and the economy. The force of his account lay in its exploration of the nature of literary change and its possible political implications rather than in the analysis of its putative socioeconomic causes.

In "A Plea for Intellectuals," Sartre in his turn did not respond point by point to Barthes. But his reading of Barthes apparently agitated his thinking enough to help effect a rethinking of certain problems and a significantly different approach. Any simple linear pattern of development from *What Is Literature?* to "A Plea for Intellectuals" is, however, out of the question. Sartre was already contesting Part One of *What Is Literature?* at the very time he wrote it, and other writings between the two texts continued the questioning process. Sartre soon saw "A Plea for Intellectuals" itself as inadequate from the perspective of "a friend of the people."

Having indicated the problem in relating *What Is Literature?* to "A Plea for Intellectuals," I shall now turn to a closer study of the earlier work. Part One of *What Is Literature?* is entitled "What Is Writing?" The "what" of writing is approached on the level of essence, or *eidos*. Sartre's answer to the question relies on a sharp categorical opposition between prose and poetry from the viewpoint of commitment in literature. On the side of poetry stand all the poetic arts: music and painting as well as verbal poetry—in brief, everything in art other than prose. On the side of prose stands prose alone. Within the homogeneous realm of prose, no further distinctions are deemed necessary for the purposes of a theory of commitment, as between genres or even between fiction and nonfiction. Only prose can be committed to changing the world in the interest of moral, political, and social justice. Prose's "other" cannot be committed or at least not in the same way. The substantive difference between prose and its almost residual "other" is seen by Sartre in the main body of the text as a total divide.

The two-faced nature of commitment in Sartre is played upon in his approach to prose's "other." From one perspective, freedom is pure and need not be engaged in the world of reality. Poetry seems to become identical with this sense of otherworldly freedom. It becomes the restricted repository of the theory of the imagination and art that was applied to all art, including the novel, in *L'Imaginaire*. The art of prose now escapes this theory to become covered by the theory of commitment. From this perspective, it is all right, proper, or even authentic for the poetic arts not to be committed or to be committed in a different way—a way that is never specified for the simple reason that it is impossible to specify it. Given the other face of freedom, however, the way the poetic arts are—indeed must be—committed can be specified. For freedom is always already engaged or committed in the world. The poetic arts, given Sartre's understanding of them, are "committed" to uncommitment or escape from reality into the realm of the imaginary. They are defeatist, in "bad faith," and cannot be authentic. They fall into the uncompromising realm of what would later be termed the "cop-out." The normative dimension implicit in this mode of "description" leads to the unavoidable condemnation of the poetic. Poetry is a degenerate flight from reality as seen from the perspective of the man of action and his verbal arm in the world of literature—prose.

Prose and poetry in Part One of *What Is Literature?* are apprehended in terms of purity and defined as pure opposites. The divide that marks a noncommunicative silence between them bristles with a series of hoary oppositions and contrasting metaphors (clear/obscure, sign/image, reference/self-reference, domesticated/savage, utilitarian/nonutilitarian, production/consumption, active/passive, success/defeat, male/female):

The poet has withdrawn in one stroke from the language-instrument; he has chosen once and for all the poetic attitude that considers words as things and not as signs. For the ambiguity of the sign implies that one can at one's will penetrate it like a pane of glass and pursue the thing signified, or turn one's gaze toward its *reality* and consider it as an object. The man who speaks is beyond words, near the object; the poet is on this side of words. For the first, words are domesticated; for the second, they remain in the savage state. For the former, they are useful conventions, tools that wear out little by little and that one throws away when they are no longer serviceable; for the second, they are natural things that grow naturally on the earth like grass and trees. [*QL* in *S. II*, p. 64]

"What" are at best two overlapping aspects or functions of language that allow of differences of degree and raise the questions, among others, of the interplay between continuity and discontinuity, the weighting of differences in any specific text, the thresholds between degree and quality, the dominance or mutuality of "prosaic" and "poetic" usages, are presented by Sartre in terms of pure identity and difference. Prose is the domesticated instrument or purely transparent medium of the free subject or agent in the world. Language in prose is like a pure pane of glass that reveals the world to the unclouded eye of the beholder. Perception through prose is immaculate, and praxis is close at hand. Indeed, "the 'engaged' writer knows that words are action" (p. 73). Poetry, by marked contrast, passes rough panes of glass between man and the sun of truth in the world—words that themselves become self-referential objects as they grow savagely from the pen of the poet and encase him in a verbal body or imaginary cocoon of words-become-things. Paradoxically, in poetry, what begins as an expression of pure freedom from reality becomes estrangement and entrapment in the in-itself of a purely imaginary world of words that mean nothing other than themselves. And the duty of the committed writer is to be eternally vigilant against the contamination of his liberty (and his action-oriented masculinity) by the obscure and ambiguous encroachment of the poetic.

Sartre's theory of pure prose as the tool of commitment threatens to reduce language to a purely instrumental and utilitarian, if not technical, level, and it mystifies that which is literary in the use of prose. It is the complement to an extreme notion of pure poetry developed on the theoretical level in symbolism, in the writings of Mallarmé and Valéry, for example. "In *symbolisme*," as Northrop Frye puts it, "the word does not echo the thing but other words, and hence the immediate impact *symbolisme* makes on the reader is that of incantation, a harmony of sounds and the sense of growing richness of meaning unlimited by denotation."[4] Or as Sartre himself sometimes puts it, poetry has *sens* (meaning) but not *signification* (referential or denotative usage). Instead of testing the theory of symbolism against the textual practice of symbolists in their poems in a manner that might reveal the interaction or deconstructive interplay of "prosaic" and "poetic" usage, Sartre accepts the theory of symbolism at face falue, identifies it as the spirit of modern poetry, and develops its antithesis in a theory of pure prose.[5]

The interaction between "prose" and "poetry" does occur in Part One of *What Is Literature?* but given the explicit theoretical refusal to recognize and account for it, it takes the form of uncontrolled equivocation rather than ambiguity, which, when recognized, can be partially controlled or at least played out *en connaissance de cause.* The most superficial reading reveals that the writing or use of language in Part One does not conform to the theory of language it propounds but, instead, more or less systematically transgresses its limits and founding oppositions. The writing is in no sense pure "prose," and it even seems to be more on the side of poetry—heavily allusive, evocative, connotative, persuasive if not cajoling, even lyrical, and replete with metaphors and obscure resonances. It shows that what the text tries to say cannot be taken at face value. The text both says what it does not want to say and yet in certain ways also manages to say what it does want to say but not exactly in the way it wants to say it.

What the principal text of Part One fails to thematize as a problem partially emerges as a supplement to the text in footnotes four and five. Footnote four forcefully summarizes the argument of Part One and adds to it in a problematic manner that indicates certain of its deficiencies. (The following extensive quotation from the note shows that its size alone threatens to capsize the principal text.)

Originally poetry creates the *myth* of man, while the prose writer traces his *portrait*. . . .

With the advent of bourgeois society, the poet puts up a common front with the prose writer to declare it unlivable. He continues to create the myth of man, but he passes from white to black magic. Man is always presented as the absolute end, but by the success of his enterprise, he sinks into a utilitarian collectivity. What is in the background of his act and will allow transition to the myth is thus no longer success, but defeat. By stopping the infinite series of his projects like a screen, defeat alone returns him to himself in his purity.... Human enterprise has two faces: it is simultaneously success and failure. The dialectical scheme is inadequate for thinking it through: we must make our vocabulary and the frames of our reason more supple. Some day I am going to try to describe that strange reality, History, which is neither objective, nor ever quite subjective, in which the dialectic is contested, penetrated, and corroded by a kind of antidialectic, which is nevertheless still a dialectic [*pourtant dialectique encore*]. But that is the affair of the philosopher; ordinarily one does not consider the two faces of Janus; the man of action sees one and the poet sees the other.... [In poetry] the defeat itself turns into salvation. Not that it gives us entry to some beyond, but by itself it shifts and is metamorphosed. For example, poetic language rises up out of the ruins of prose. If it is true that speech [*la parole*] is a betrayal and that communication is impossible, then each word by itself recovers its individuality and becomes an instrument of our defeat and a receiver [of stolen property, or "fence": *receleur*] of the incommunicable.... The communication of prose having failed, the very meaning of the word becomes the pure incommunicable.... The absolute valorization of defeat.... seems to me the original attitude of contemporary poetry. Note also that this choice confers upon the poet a very precise function in the collectivity. In a highly integrated or religious society, the defeat is masked by the State or recuperated by Religion; in a less integrated and secular society, such as our democracies, it is up to poetry to recuperate it.

Poetry is a case of loser winning [*qui perd gagne*]. And the authentic poet chooses to lose, even to the point of dying, in order to win. I repeat that it is a question here of contemporary poetry. History presents other forms of poetry. It is not my concern to show their connection with ours. Thus if one wishes absolutely to speak of the engagement [or commitment—*engagement*] of the poet, let us say that he is the man who engages himself to lose. This is the deeper meaning of that tough luck [*guignon*], of that malediction with which he always claims kinship and which he always attributes to an intervention from without; whereas it is his deepest choice, not the consequence but the source of his poetry. He is certain of the total defeat of the human enterprise and arranges to fail in his own life in order to bear witness, by his individual defeat, to human defeat in general. Thus he contests, as we shall see, which is what the prose writer does too. But the contestation of prose is carried on in the name of a greater success; and that of poetry, in the name of the hidden defeat which every victory harbors [recèle]. [Pp. 85–87]

This magnificent passage begins with a myth of origins that situates poetry and prose in an unspecified historical past. In relation to this point of origin, the transition to bourgeois society is marked by both continuities and discontinuities. The continuity is presented in humanistic terms: man is still the "absolute end" of poetry as well as of prose. But the success of poetry, which in some unexplained manner characterized its origins, turns into defeat. A reference is made to other possible historical forms of poetry (the epic?) whose relation to the "original" form is left blank (in contrast to Lukàcs's procedure in *The Theory of the Novel*). Except for a general notion of the social function of these other historical forms of poetry in an "integrated" society, their nature is unspecified and declared not to be Sartre's subject. At least by implication, however, periodization within history after the point of origin and other than in terms of a displacement of social function (poetry in place of state and religion) seems to be perceived predominantly in terms of radical discontinuity. (What does one make on this account of both parody and emulation of the epic in modern poetry?) The poet contests bourgeois society, but he does so by assuming his failure and playing the game of loser wins. His failure becomes the failure of language to communicate. In his poetry, he will, through a seemingly displaced or wayward religious gesture, convert failure into a sign of salvation in the negation and transcendence of an ugly bourgeois reality. By contrast, the prose writer will respond to the same situation through a form of activity vowed to success in changing reality itself (ultimately through socialist revolution). Sartre's own argument is grounded and, in a sense, legitimated by a rather "poetic" evocation of a genealogy situated somewhere between myth and fictionalized history. In a displaced religious gesture, the argument that valorizes prose, truth, realism, and action requires an appeal to its opposite in order to contrast itself with that opposite and found itself. This gesture provides a basis for the later turn in Sartre's thought toward dialectics and is related to its essential concepts (such as the totalizing, original choice of being).

The problem of the simultaneity and supplementarity of success and defeat, prose and poetry, is fleetingly evoked only to be elided. The force of dialectical desire is itself expressed in the paradoxical formulation of that which is antidialectical but still dialectical nevertheless. The indication of the inadequacy of the dialectical scheme is enunciated but it is unclear whether it is taken seriously. It does not in any event lead to a critical reflection on the train of thought in this footnote itself, which requires for its explication an appeal to notions such as supplementarity and repetition—supplementarity in relation to the principal text and repetition of those very poetic and mythical gestures which it is the ostensible function of the footnote to exorcise. And the reason why the principal text of Part One was not itself the "affair of the philosopher" is left a mystery.

Footnote five shifts the scene of the argument while seeming to be continuous with the preceding note. While note four mythologized and historicized with reference to unspecified possibilities of a more "successful" sort of poetry, note five stages the problem of prose and poetry on a universal philosophical level. And it qualifies the argument of the principal text in a self-contradictory way by admitting the ideal status of its eidetic, analytic types but denying the relevance of this status for its argument:

It goes without saying [*sic!*] that in all poetry a certain form of prose, that is, of success, is present; and reciprocally the driest prose always contains a bit of poetry, that is, a certain form of defeat; no prose writer, even the most lucid, *entirely* understands what he wants to say; he says too much or not enough; each sentence is a wager, a risk assumed; the more one gropes, the more the word singularizes itself; as Valéry has shown, no one can understand a word to its very bottom. Thus each word is used simultaneously for its clear and social meaning and for certain obscure resonances, I would almost say: for its physiognomy. The reader too is sensitive to this. At once we are no longer on the level of concerted communication, but on that of grace and chance; the silences of prose are poetic because they mark its limits, and it is for the purpose of greater clarity that I have been considering the extreme cases of pure prose and pure poetry. However, it need not be concluded that we can pass from poetry to prose by a continuous series of intermediate forms. If the prose writer tries to fondle his words too much, the *eidos* of "prose" is broken and we fall into nonsense [*galimatias*]. If the poet narrates [*raconte*], explains, or teaches, poetry becomes *prosaic*; he has lost the game. It is a matter of complex structures, impure but well delimited [*structures complexes, impures mais bien délimitées*]. [Pp. 87–88]

What is given with one hand is almost, but not quite, taken away with the other. The matter of measure and degree ("too much") is juxtaposed with the radical break ("however," "but"). The relationship between the two gestures is not explicated, nor is the general relationship among analysis, dialectics, and supplementarity. The contradictory movement in the phrase "complex, impure but well delimited"—a movement held together only by the force of grammar and of desire for unity—passes unnoticed in the text. It is significant that "A Plea for Intellectuals" liberates that which in Part One of *What Is Literature?* is confined to a footnote and elevates it to the status of a focal concern of the principal text itself.

At least three other texts by Sartre may be mentioned at this point, even without a fuller "intertextual" reading of them. They cannot be placed in a linear narrative or dialectical model of Sartre's development. They may be seen as texts running parallel to Part One of *What Is Literature?* and contesting its argument in terms of an intricate interplay of continuities and discontinuities at times more internally disparate than consistent. "Orphée noir" (1948, in *S. III*), an introduction to Léopold Sédar Senghor's *Anthologie de la nouvelle poésie nègre et malgache de langue française,* was published only shortly after *What Is Literature?* "Mallarmé (1842–1898)" was first published in 1952, at the same time as the study of Genet (and it paradoxically seems to see Mallarmé's poetry in terms of a more radically revolutionary impact than that attributed to Genet's work, even though Genet's work is seen as more "explosive" than that of Mallarmé in *Saint Genet*). And "Le Séquestré de Venise" (1958, in *S. IV*) was published at about the same time as *Search for a Method* (*Question de méthode* in the *Critique de la raison dialectique*).

"Le Séquestré de Venise" ("The Prisoner of Venice") argues that the paintings of Tintoretto demystified the illusions of the age and had a critical if not a revolutionary function in unmasking the bankruptcy of the ruling elite: "Tintoretto was born in a turbulent city; he breathed Venetian anxiety deep in his lungs, and it gnawed at him, until he could paint nothing else.... Bad luck [le malheur] had decreed that Jacopo should unknowingly bear witness to an age that refused to know itself" (S. IV, p. 342). Titian, by contrast, was lionized because his paintings had a conservative function. In this essay, painting is placed almost too clearly into a Marxist framework of ideology and its critique—although in the case of the painter the critique seems to be as unaware as the ideology. Nor are special conditions different from modern ones invoked. By contrast, the Renaissance is the seedbed of modern times. And Sartre's dramatic interpretation is an active, indeed an aggressively appropriating, one: he at least partially identifies with Tintoretto.

In "Black Orpheus" Sartre argues that situations exist in modern history that enable poetry to become the authentic voice of revolution. Black poetry of French expression is presented as having a genuine political incentive, although its rejection of analytic prose seems to appeal to sources of liberation analogous to those invoked by the surrealists whom Sartre severely criticizes in What is Literature? (The concept of négritude in "Black Orpheus" almost functions as a form of reverse discrimination through which only the blacks have, or are entitled to have, rhythm.) Sartre does see the poetic voice of black Africans as a force arising from a kind of defeat, or échec: that of blacks constrained to use an alienated medium—the language of the white other—as the means of protest against the domination of the other. But, in reference to black Africans, defeat does not engender an escapist game of loser wins; it becomes the basis of a poetry of revolution with implications that transcend the narrowly racial to acquire universalizing proportions. As Sartre himself formulates his intention in this essay:

I would like to show by what approach one finds access to this jet-black world and that this poetry which first appears to be racial is finally a song by all and for all. In a word, I address myself here to whites and I would like to express to them what blacks already know: why it is necessarily through a poetic experience that the black, in his present situation, must first take consciousness of himself and, inversely, why black poetry in the French language is, in our time, the only great revolutionary poetry. [*S. III*, p. 233]

To some extent Sartre believes that poetry becomes a medium of political protest when more effective and realistic means of social revolution are denied the oppressed. But the relationship between poetry and politics in "Black Orpheus" is not one of simple substitution of a surrogate for the real thing. Nor is this the status of poetry in the 1952 essay on Mallarmé, which in certain ways resembles "Black Orpheus." In this essay poetry is neither reduced to its social functions nor is it the object of purely formalistic analysis. Sartre recognizes what he terms the "negative work" that gives poetry a political dimension. Mallarmé plays the game of loser wins and he "is" in a sense the collection of his texts. But he is not involved in a one-way escape from an unlivable reality. For Sartre, Mallarmé saw the futility of total negation. In his poems he set up a mutual contestation of "opposites" (such as chance and necessity) that denied the possibility of pure annihilation of one by the other. "The irony of Mallarmé is born from the fact that he knows the absolute vanity and the entire necessity of his work and he discerns in it the couple of contraries without synthesis which perpetually engender and repel one another..." (*S. IX*, pp. 198–99). He was able to write in the tense space between political commitment and a fictive inscription of the absent sacred: his "real" work, the Book to come, was continually deferred:

He applied systematically to art what was still only a philosophical principle and would become a maxim of politics: "Make and in making make oneself" ["*Faire et en faisant se faire*"]. . . . He was entirely a poet, entirely engaged in the critical destruction of poetry by itself: and at the same time, he remained outside; a sylph of cold ceilings, he looked at himself . . . one day he was sent some sketches that pleased him; but he particularly liked one of an old magus, smiling and sad: "Because," he said, "he knew that his art was an imposture. But he also seemed to say: 'It could have been the truth.'" [*S. IX*, p. 201]

Sartre himself tried to express his attitude in an interview of 1960: "Mallarmé and Genet were both consciously committed. . . . Mallarmé's commitment appears to me to be as total as possible: social as well as poetic."[6]

One would like to give unity to Sartre's views on "poetry" and "literary" writing in general by arguing, for example, that in his later work he comes to recognize them as forms of praxis with possible revolutionary implications. But the complex and at times overlapping shifts in Sartre's thought fail to be captured by this interpretation. In *L'Idiot de la famille*, for example, he sees Flaubert's writing in terms largely defined by the analysis in *L'Imaginaire* and *What Is Literature?* One of the most subtle contestations of the theories of literature in the early Sartre is to be found in the writing of *Nausea* (1938). Nor can one find any simple unitary pattern in the three texts intercalated into our treatment of *What Is Literature?* at this point. Even *What Is Literature?* is not free of internal self-questioning.

Part Two of *What Is Literature?* is entitled "Why Write?" The argument develops in such a way that the definition of the "what" of writing in the first part fails to control the "why" of this part. Sartre makes no attempt to integrate the argument of Part One into that of Part Two, and the extent to which the dichotomy between prose and poetry is pertinent to Part Two remains dubious. Sartre's apparent intention is to have the argument of the second part apply only to prose, since the examples given are from the novel. But the argument develops on such a level of generality that it applies beyond the novel and at least undercuts distinctions between fiction and nonfiction. For Sartre in Part Two treats literature in the context of what he terms the aesthetic modification of the human project. What he actually seems to offer is a general theory of language and communication in the light of his conception of phenomenological ontology: "One of the principal motivations [*motifs*] of artistic creation is the need to feel ourselves essential in relation to the world" (*QL* in *S. II*, p. 90). "The final goal of art" is "to recuperate this world in giving it to be seen such as it is, but as if it had its source in human freedom" (p. 106). Sartre initially situates art in the context of a human project of appropriation and mastery of the world rather than in the context of an open, free play of the world in which man participates but does not master. But the "as if" indicates the role of fiction in the totalizing project of human freedom, and the tension between the two halves of the sentence related by the "as if" places in question any absolute dichotomy between realistic reference (giving the world to be seen as it is) and fictional reconstruction (but as if it had its source in human freedom). Indeed, after Part One, dialectical motifs—albeit of a restricted sort—tend to predominate in *What Is Literature?*

Beginning with Part Two, Sartre's focus is on the relationship among text, writer, reader, and world (or situation). The emphasis is on the circuit, although at crucial points the primacy of one or another element in Sartre's own text threatens to function as a circuit-breaker and to restrict the movement of the dialectic. At times the priority of an element may have a strategic function (such as the importance of proletarian revolution). At other times the function of an asserted priority is more dubious (such as the primacy of the reader over the writer in Part Two). But one clear implication of Sartre's concern with a circuit of exchange is that the text cannot be sequestered between the bindings of a book. It is contaminated by, and compromises one in, the "real" world. No sharp division is possible among art, morality, and politics. But Sartre's mode of affirming a relationship is often paradoxical: "Although literature is one thing and morality is a completely different thing, at the bottom [*au fond*] of the aesthetic imperative we discern the moral imperative" (p. 111). Art is not seen exclusively in terms of the escapist illusion of pure imagination. The role of the reader's identification with the characters of a story is a requirement of gripping art. But the reader freely lends his emotions to the characters in a story to bring them to life. If the story manipulates emotions by relying on sure-fire techniques of narration and stereotyped formulas, it betrays the role of freedom in art. And the relationship between nonescapist freedom and emotion, deemed impossible in Sartre's earlier theoretical writings, is itself supplemented by the role of aesthetic distance and alienation effects that had no place in a work like *L'Imaginaire*. The work of art as an appeal of freedom to freedom must allow room for critical reflection. Referring to the statement of Genet, Sartre terms this requirement the politeness the writer shows to the reader. In Part Two, Sartre thus makes some attempt to relate two seemingly opposed theories of art often associated with the names of Artaud ("theater of cruelty") and Brecht (alienation effects and critical distance). And, relying on the analogy of gift exchange, Sartre presents art as implicated in an open process of generous giving, taking, and rendering between writer and reader.

In Part Two, however, the dialectical process is restricted by the problem of the "other" precisely to the extent that Sartre is unwilling to admit alterity in relation to freedom itself and to relate supplementarity to an open dialectical process that does not privilege man as subject or agent. The writer is presented as a "projecting" subject in control of the process of writing. Thus he cannot read his own works or, if he does, it is only by assuming the position of the reader as a separate and distinct "other." In perception, we are told, the object is essential and the subject inessential; in writing, the subject is essential and the object inessential. The reader appears on the scene of the text almost as a *deus ex machina* and a master of ceremonies—the "other" who offers the writer a rather one-sided gift enabling him to feel essential in relation to his creation and to bring that creation to objective existence in the world. One has the intimation of a positive relationship between self and other of a sort indicated only by its absence in *Being and Nothingness*. Its price, however, is the invocation of the subject/object dualism, already declared irrelevant as early as *The Transcendence of the Ego*, and the restriction of the dialectic to a one-way gift exchange that assumes a status hierarchy and denies full reciprocity in the self and between self and other. Sartre, in effect, reverses the conventional status hierarchy between writer and reader by presenting the reader as primary in the creative process. But he does not extend this reversal to the point of questioning the principle of hierarchy itself—a gesture requiring fuller contestation of his own founding concepts and framework.

The third and fourth parts of *What Is Literature?* rely heavily on the themes of dialectics and historicity. They develop lines of argument basic to Sartre's later thought. The schematic periodization in Part Three of the history of literature, focusing on the relationship between writers and readers, was to remain a foundation of Sartre's later research, as in his studies of Genet and

Flaubert. His general conception of the nexus between literature and history continues as a leitmotif of his thought:

The world and man reveal themselves through *enterprises*. And all the enterprises of which we can speak reduce themselves to only one: that of *making history*. Thus we are conducted by the hand to that moment when we must abandon the literature of *exis* [being and consumption] to inaugurate that of *praxis*.

*Praxis* is action on history and in history, that is, as the synthesis of historical relativity and the moral and metaphysical absolute, with this hostile and amicable, terrible and derisory world that it reveals to us, that is our subject. I do not say that we have chosen these austere roads, and there are certainly those among us who carry within themselves some charming and desolate love story that will never see the light of day. What can we do? It is not a question of choosing one's epoch but of choosing oneself in it. [*QL* in *S. II*, p. 265]

Sartre at this point does not rely exclusively on absolute dichotomies. Neither does he render them fully problematic. And he insists upon posing the problem of choice in decisive terms:

The literature of production, which announces itself, will not make us forget the literature of consumption, its antithesis; it should not pretend to surpass it and perhaps it will never equal it; no one dreams of maintaining that it will enable us to reach the terminus and realize the essence of art. Perhaps it will disappear soon: the generation following us seems hesitant. . . . And even if this literature of *praxis* succeeded in installing itself, it would pass like that of *exis* and one would return to *exis* and perhaps the history of the next decades will record the alternation from one to the other. That would signify that men had definitively failed in another Revolution of an infinitely more considerable importance [than revolution in literature]. It is only in a socialist collectivity, in effect, that literature, having made a synthesis of *praxis* and *exis*, of negativity and construction, of doing, having, and being, would merit the name of *total literature*. In waiting [*en attendant*], let us cultivate our garden; we have enough to do. [Pp. 265–66]

The pattern is clear: alienation in the present; history as the alternation between opposing extremes; the totalizing possibility of synthesis in the future through revolution and the classless society. Structurally, we already seem to be in the world of the *Critique*. But here, waiting for the deferred totality, Sartre candidly beckons us to cultivate the literature of commitment and praxis. It is from this militant if somewhat Beckett-like position that Sartre formulates one of his most acerbic criticisms—that of surrealism. Toward the end of *What Is Literature?* surrealism is seen as *the* modern poetic movement, but the one that marks the bankruptcy of poetry in the West. It is a purely negative literature of consumption, which abandons rationality and loses itself in verbal games. Its desire to connect itself with politics is impotent and diversionary, for it undertakes only symbolic destruction and undermines distinctions that are necessary for decisive and effective political action: "For the proletariat, engaged in the struggle, needs at every instant, in order to bring its enterprise to a successful conclusion, to distinguish the past from the future, the real from the imaginary, and life from death" (p. 220). Indeed, Sartre lodges against surrealism complaints of a sort that Communist Party theorists and liberal critics like Raymond Aron would on one level join in addressing to him: surrealism is the utopian protest of unrealistic, total, abstract negation.

In an important footnote added later to *What is Literature?* Sartre attempted to respond to criticisms of his critique of surrealism. In so doing, he acknowledged the desire of surrealists "to affirm the rights of the human totality without excluding anything, even the unconscious." But for Sartre, they failed in realizing this desire because they lacked an authentic synthesizing idea—that of dialectical mediation and totality. To underscore this point, Sartre opposed Hegel and André Breton:

[The desire for totality] was the grandeur of the surrealist enterprise. Still one must note that the "totalitarian" idea is epochal; it is what animates the Nazi endeavor, the Marxist endeavor, and today the "existentialist" endeavor. One must certainly return to Hegel as the source of all these efforts. But I discern a grave contradiction in the origin of surrealism: to employ Hegelian language, I would say that this movement had the *concept* of totality (this is what very clearly springs from the famous saying of Breton: liberty, color of man) and that it *realized* something completely different in its concrete manifestations. The totality of man is in effect necessarily a synthesis, that is, an organic and schematic unity of all secondary structures. A liberation that proposes to be *total* must part from a total knowledge of man by himself (I do not try here to show that it is possible; one knows that I am profoundly convinced that it is). [*QL* in *S. II*, p. 320n.]

This passage raises many questions. Was the desire for totality really the grandeur of the surrealist "enterprise," or was this desire itself called into question by surrealism? Does not a notion of the unconscious have the effect of radically calling totality into question through a "recognition" of that which always defers an apprehension of the whole and liberates possibilities beyond the grasp of a totalizing synthesis? Is the concept of totality actually "what" springs from the disorientingly anti-racist saying of Breton? Can one cavalierly approximate on the level of animation the Nazi, Marxist, and existentialist endeavors? Does not the view of Hegel as the source of all these efforts invite an intellectual history *à la papa* (from Hegel through Marx to Hitler . . . and Breton)? What does one make of the demands for liberation of the body and for radical play that were so important for a theorist like Marcuse in *Eros and Civilization* (where the appreciation of the surrealists is drastically different from that of Sartre)?

Many of the problems of *What Is Literature?* are epitomized in Sartre's harshly authoritative reaction to surrealism. Whatever may have been the political and theoretical limitations of surrealism, one aspect of its attempt to confound or subvert conventional distinctions was a desire to render fully problematic dominant concepts and dichotomies (such as that between the real and the imaginary) and to open the way for radically new possibilities. For Sartre, "given the lack of the synthetic idea, [surrealism] organized only *tourniquets* of contraries" (p. 323n.). (One may perhaps translate *tourniquet* here as elsewhere in Sartre as "double bind.") Sartre refuses to recognize in surrealism even the partially valid "negative work" of poetry with political implications he was to see in Mallarmé. In *What Is Literature?* an explicitly dominant framework, suspended between analysis and dialectics, can present a strategy that contests oppositions only in terms of the "other" of defeatist, total negation. In "A Plea for Intellectuals," one finds both continuities and discontinuities with the framework of *What Is Literature?* and it is difficult to decide which are of greater importance in the text.

Sartre's argument in "A Plea" opens with a series of more or less conventional distinctions, but it develops them in relation to a conception of literature and commitment at times significantly different from that in *What Is Literature?* The "technician of practical knowledge," Sartre argues, confronts the problem of commitment in an indirect or external manner. The knowledge and skill of the "technician of practical knowledge," such as the physicist or doctor, are universalizing in nature. But the use of his knowledge and skill in a class society based on structures of domination is particularistic: it functions socially to benefit certain groups more than others. This contradiction generates an "unhappy consciousness" that may lead the "technician of practical knowledge" to assume the role of the intellectual and confront the problem of commitment. By contrast, the writer directly faces the problem of commitment, which is inherent in his work.

One cannot help but notice the dubiousness of the initial distinctions with which Sartre's argument gets off the ground. From a certain perspective, the situation of the "technician of practical knowledge" is analogous to that of the writer: he too confronts the problem of commitment in a direct or internal way, for he faces the problem of the practical ends to which his technical expertise or scientific knowledge is adapted. The strict separation between the technical or scientific, on the one hand, and the social or practical, on the other, is itself an ideological gesture that obscures their relationship and functions to underwrite the supposed neutrality of positivism. (This argument has, of course, been developed in the works of Jürgen Habermas, a recent exponent of critical theory in the tradition of the Frankfurt school.) Conversely, the writer may seek refuge in notions of pure technique or craft—and no one has been more insistent than Sartre in attempting to expose the ideological status of this attempt. Curiously, Sartre's argument begins by conceding in the "technician of practical knowledge" what he elsewhere castigates as mystification in the writer and by failing to recognize as a possibility in the writer that which he elsewhere ferrets out in its most minute manifestations.

But perhaps the most interesting section of "A Plea" is part (or lecture) three, "Is the Writer an Intellectual?" Here Sartre turns to the problem of language, ambiguity, and commitment. He starts by rehearsing an argument that in *What Is Literature?* served to disqualify poetry as a form of politically committed writing: "If beauty can be seen as a particular mode of unveiling the world, the role of *contestation* in a beautiful work of art would seem to be minimal and, in a certain sense, inversely proportional to its beauty" (*Plea* in *S. VIII*, p. 431). Without totally negating this line of argument, Sartre asserts in a self-questioning way that writers both seem to seek solitude in commitment to their art and, at least in certain cases, "*are committed* and struggle for universalization at the side of intellectuals if not in their ranks" (p. 431). And he employs this doubly inscribed and seemingly undecidable commitment to raise a question that he will not at first so much authoritatively answer as explore and, within limits, elucidate: "Is this to be explained by factors external to their art (the historical conjuncture) or is commitment a requirement [*une exigence*] that, in spite of all we have said above, is born from their art?" (p. 431).

Sartre approaches this question by confining his observations to "the contemporary writer, the *poet* who has declared himself to be a *prose writer* and lives in the post-World War II world" (p. 432). Defining the status of the contemporary writer in this way confounds and displaces the prose/poetry opposition of *What Is Literature?* Its place is taken by a more subtle distinction between technical and ordinary language overlaid by a distinction between literal and literary writers. The technical falls within the literal, and the literary is a more extreme manifestation of the ordinary. Sartre's earlier conception of prose itself represented a notion of literal, if not narrowly technical, language. By contrast, all literature is here discussed with reference to elements earlier confined to poetry. The poetic now fully contaminates all aesthetic uses of language.

Let us follow this reversal and displacement of perspectives on writing and language a bit more closely. A technical language is a "means of communication that will transmit a maximum of information and a minimum of *misinformation* ... it is conventional and specialized; new words are introduced corresponding to precise definitions; its code is, as far as possible, protected from the distorting influences of history" (p. 433). A specialist becomes *"master of his technical language"* (p. 435) as a means of knowing and mastering a segment of the world. Sartre recognizes the way in which technical languages borrow from the heritage of ordinary language, which leaves "a little of its imprecision" on all of them. This recognition might lead one to conclude that technical language has the status of an ideal that is virtual or fictive—an impossible but possibly heuristic ideal constructed within the heritage of ordinary language, which attempts to purify that language as an instrument of knowledge and technical control of the "other."[7] Sartre, however, does not develop this point but places his recognition between dashes (transformed into parentheses in the English translation) and classifies it as incidental in an observation about ordinary language:

Now ordinary language [*la langue commune*]—on which, moreover, are constituted numerous technical languages that conserve a little of its imprecision—contains a maximum of *misinformation* [*désinformations*]. That is to say, words, rules of syntax, etc., mutually condition one another and, having no reality other than this mutual conditioning, to speak is in fact to stir up [*susciter*] the entire language as a conventional, structured, and *particular* ensemble. At this level, its particularities are not pieces of information about the object of which the writer speaks; for the linguist they can become pieces of information about the language. But on the level of signification they are either simply superfluous or harmful: because of their ambiguity, because of the very limits of language as a structured totality, because of the variety of meanings history has imposed upon them. In short, the *word* the writer uses has a much denser *materiality* than, for example, the mathematical symbol that effaces itself before the signified. One might say that it [the word of the writer] wants simultaneously to point vaguely toward the signified and to impose itself as a *presence*, drawing attention to its own density. This is why it has been possible for people to say that to name is simultaneously to present the signified and to kill it, to swallow it in the verbal mass. The word of ordinary language is simultaneously *too rich* (it overflows by far the concept by its traditional age [*son ancienneté traditionnelle*], by the ensemble of violences and ceremonies which constitutes its "memory", its "living past") and *too poor* (it is defined in relation to the ensemble of language as a fixed determination of the latter and not as a supple possibility of expressing the new). In the exact sciences, when the new arises, a word to name it is simultaneously invented by some and rapidly adopted by all. . . . [The writer] prefers to utilize a "current" word and to charge it with a new meaning which is superadded to the old: in general, one might say that the writer has vowed to utilize the *whole* of ordinary language and nothing but it, with all the misinformative characteristics that limit its range. If the writer adopts ordinary language, it is thus not only in so far as language can transmit knowledge. To write is simultaneously to possess language ("The Japanese naturalists," one of your critics has said, "*conquered* prose from poetry") and not to possess it to the extent that language is *other* than the writer and *other* than men. [Pp. 433–35]

The writer is thus always already situated in a sedimented language marked by the supplementary play of excess and lack between signifier and signified, word and thing, which his project in writing does not entirely master. As the paradigm of the writer's phrase, Sartre chooses an example from Genet in which the crisscrossing of masculine and feminine genders creates an ambiguous play that transmits information only in a "bizarre" and "deforming" way: "Les brûlantes amours de la sentinelle et du mannequin." And to stress the way in which the writer "goes beyond" ordinary language by playing upon its problematic nature, he refers to a distinction drawn by Roland Barthes:

Roland Barthes distingushed between *écrivants* and *écrivains* [translated in the English edition as "literal writers" and "literary writers"]. The literal writer uses language to transmit information. The literary writer is the custodian of ordinary language, but he goes beyond it and his material is language as nonsignifying or as misinformation. He is an artisan who produces a certain verbal object by working on the materiality of words; he takes significations as means and the nonsignifying as end. [Pp. 436–37]

Sartre attemps to relate these considerations about the language of the writer to his own crucial concern for communication:

If writing consists in *communicating*, the literary object appears as communication *beyond language* through the nonsignifying silence which is enclosed by words although it is produced by them. Thus the phrase: "This is just literature" means "You speak in order to say nothing." It remains to ask ourselves what this *nothing* is, this silent nonknowledge that the literary object must communicate to the reader. The only way to conduct this inquiry is to go back from the *signifying content* of literary works to the fundamental silence which surrounds them. [P. 437]

I have quoted extensively from this section of "A Plea for Intellectuals" because I believe it contains some of Sartre's best insights about language, developed in dialogue with recent tendencies in French thought that Sartre often resists. These passages are not devoid of questionable elements, but such elements threaten to become preponderant when Sartre attempts to relate his insights about language to the problem of political commitment. For he does not inquire into the question of the relation of supplementarity or radical ambiguity to the dialectical project of totalization; he attempts to overcome or master the former by the latter through a reliance upon the later articulation of his dominant framework. Silence (or what Kierkegaard spoke of as "indirect communication") is pinpointed as the gap between the lived (*le vécu*) and the conceived (*le conçu*)—it demarcates the area designated in *Search for a Method* as that of rational, comprehensive nonknowledge of human being-in-the-world. The materiality of language is identified as the practico-inert. And ambiguity is domesticated and controlled by its insertion into the totalizing human project of making the world meaningful: "Without signification, there can be no ambiguity. How else could we speak of ellipses [*raccourcis*]? Ellipses of what? The essential task [*propos*] of the modern writer is to work on the nonsignifying element of ordinary language in order to reveal to the reader the being-in-the-world of a singular universal. I propose to call this: the quest for *meaning* [*la recherche du sens*]. It is the presence of the whole in the part" (pp. 449–50).

Radical ambiguity is reduced to manageable proportions, and the open play of the world is arrested by the essential question of the "what," which introduces the unifying project of dialectical totalization. This interpretive gesture threatens to repress and domesticate Sartre's insights into language rather than to situate them problematically in relation to the dialectical project and political commitment. Sartre provides no account of the way in which supplementarity is both the condition of possibility of the dialectical project and the continually displaced limit of the totalizing process, which keeps the dialectic open. When Sartre, including "A Plea for Intellectuals" in *Situations*, prefaces it with a warning to the reader—a warning that could almost be read as a "poison" label—he in effect represses the insights a second time. They become merely an expression of the "unhappy consciousness" of the "classical intellectual" and not the word of "the friend of the people." Yet the task of the friend of the people, unassumed by Sartre, might rather be seen in the attempt to relate political commitment to these insights about language in all their force and contestatory power. One may further note that the one use of language that Sartre passes over in silence or covertly situates *hors jeu* is philosophical or theoretical language—including his own use of language in this text. The status of philosophical or theoretical language is the core of Sartre's argument, which he cannot bring himself to contemplate in this text. For this self-reflexive gesture would have constrained a more intensive and internally self-questioning (but possibly affirmative) attempt to relate the elements of his argument other than exclusively in terms of a rather literal and repressive understanding of the dialectical project.[8]

# 3

# *Nausea:* "Une Autre Espèce de Livre"

Novels. Corrupt the masses. Are less immoral in serial than in volume form. Only historical novels should be allowed, because they teach history. Some novels are written with the point of a scalpel. Others revolve on the point of a needle.

Flaubert, Dictionary of Received Ideas

But could I not try in another genre?... It would have to be a book: I don't know how to do anything else. But not a history book: that speaks of what has existed—never can an existent justify the existence of another existent.... Another sort of book [*Une autre espèce de livre*]. I don't know very well what kind—but one would have to be able to divine, behind the printed words, behind the pages, something that would not exist, that would be above existence. A story, for example, such as cannot come to pass, an adventure. It would have to be beautiful and hard, like steel, and make people ashamed of their existence.

Sartre, Nausea

When we criticize something, this is no arbitrary and impersonal event; it is, at least very often, evidence of vital energies in us that are growing and shedding a skin. We negate and must negate because something in us wants to live and affirm—something that we perhaps do not know or see as yet.

Nietzsche, The Gay Science

O chestnut-tree, great-rooted blossomer,
Are you the leaf, the blossom or the bole?
O body swayed to music, O brightening glance,
How can we know the dancer from the dance?

Yeats, "Among School Children"

*Nausea* is the most intense and sustained "case" of critical, deconstructive writing among Sartre's works. It is significant that this form of "textual praxis" occurs most forcefully in a literary work rather than in a philosophical or theoretical one. Only at times in a theoretical work such as "A Plea for Intellectuals" does Sartre seem to account on an explicit level for what happens in the writing of a text such as *Nausea*. The novel's tendency to place in question extreme dichotomies between the literary and the philosophical or theoretical is one of its strengths. Indeed, its "textual praxis" contests the basic categories of Sartre's dominant philosophical framework and the theories of literature related to it. In this sense, *Nausea* may be situated in Sartre's "development" as an extreme and explosive point of internal contestation—a point that Sartre's texts perhaps never again attain.

That Sartre in his self-commentaries and cross-references ever fully realized what happened in the textual "trauma" of *Nausea* is questionable. His readings of *Nausea* tend to be recuperative or neutralizing. *Nausea* was presumably written during a period of apolitical individualism in Sartre's life, which he later saw as an existence in bad faith. The novel is often read as a direct expression or manifestation of that period in Sartre's life, especially when he, in writing it, is identified with Antoine Roquentin and is seen as espousing the view of art enunciated by Roquentin toward the end. Sartre has lent credence to this interpretation through his self-commentary in *The Words:*

I did not see straight. As long as this condition lasted, I felt I was out of trouble. At the age of thirty, I executed the masterstroke of writing in *Nausea*—quite sincerely, believe me—about the brackish, unjustified existence of my fellow men and of exonerating my own. I *was* Roquentin; I used him to show, without complacency, the texture of my life. At the same time, I was *I*, the elect, chronicler of Hell, a glass and steel photomicroscope peering at my own protoplasmic juices. Later [in *Being and Nothingness*], I gaily demonstrated that man is impossible; I was impossible myself and differed from the others only by the mandate to give expression to that impossibility, which was thereby transfigured and became my most personal possibility, the object of my mission, the springboard of my glory. I was a prisoner of that obvious contradiction, but I did not see it, I saw the world through it. Fake to the marrow of my bones and hoodwinked, I joyfully wrote about our unhappy state. Dogmatic though I was, I doubted everything except that I was the elect of doubt. I built with one hand what I destroyed with the other, and I regarded anxiety as the guarantee of my security; I was happy. [*M*, pp. 209–10]

Sartre here attempts to see himself writing *Nausea* as an aesthetic escapist or "knight of nothingness," who plays the game of loser wins. He attributes to himself in the past the self-serving ideology of antihuman hatred and resentment that he later imputes to Flaubert and his generation as the hidden, masked meaning of Art for Art's sake. In this gesture, self-commentary serves as retrospective intention, and the "auto-critique" that brings an accusation of guilt upon the earlier self functions to exorcise guilt in the present self. Sartre's account may or may not be accurate as a reconstruction of what went on in the mind of the biographical Sartre when he wrote *Nausea*. He may have identified with Roquentin on one level, only to distance himself on another level through a belief in the saving cult of pure art. But this account is at least somewhat questionable in relation to that more or less unitary creature of the shadows, that virtual presence—the implied author of the novel. And the account is altogether problematic in relation to the "textual praxis," or writing, of *Nausea*. It is that putative biographical Sartre—the apolitical individualist and ideologically mystified believer in salvation through pure art—who is placed on trial and contested in *Nausea* as a text.

In an interview of 1964, Sartre attempted to take his critical distance from *Nausea* in a more forceful way:

What I have regretted in *Nausea* is the fact that I did not place myself more completely into the affair [*dans le coup*]. I remained exterior to the difficulty [*le mal*] of my hero, protected by my neurosis which, through writing, brought me happiness. . . . I have always been happy. Even if I had been more honest with myself at that moment, I would still have written *Nausea*. What I lacked was a sense of reality. Since then I have changed. I have undergone a slow apprenticeship with the real. I have seen children die of hunger. In the face of a child who dies, *Nausea* has no weight [*ne fait pas le le poids*].[1]

Sartre begins this statement by regretting his aesthetic distance from Roquentin and the lack of a more complete identification with his hero. He offers a psychological explanation for this "inability" by referring to his neurosis, which by this time is largely identified with the game of loser wins. Again, what this self-commentary of a biographical nature adds to a reading of the novel is problematic. The latter part of the passage is especially disconcerting. The comparison of a text with the death of a child seems to posit an extreme either/or choice: kill the novel or kill the child. And the response to this choice is as facile as it is inadequate: the basic problem is the existence of a world in which crazy choices (or double binds) like this seem not only plausible but pressing. The goal is to create a world that enables decisions of a less murderous kind. Contat and Rybalka report a later reflection of Sartre: "Sartre told us in the course of an interview that his phrase was misinterpreted and that it was not a question of placing on the same level a work of fiction like *Nausea* and a child who dies of hunger. But it was important to pose the question: what does literature signify in a world that is hungry?"[2] Sartre apparently did not offer an answer. Perhaps the issue is not whether one can answer the question, but whether one allows it to be active in a more than rhetorical way. The textual and existential "space" agitated by this question gives to the discussion that follows an interrogative existence.

*Nausea* might be described as a novel antinovel or a deconstructed novel. In its "negative work" on traditional forms, it is like a missile antimissile. And its work (or play) of deconstruction overflows the novel form to engage philosophical and social traditions or, more generally, the structure of narration essential to sense-making or to the generation of meaning in the Western tradition. Frank Kermode in *The Sense of an Ending* terms this narrative structure apocalyptic. It makes sense of things by arranging events or experience in a beginning-middle-end structure, in which a middle passage is meaningfully integrated between an anticipatory beginning and a concordant ending. As an example of this structure, common to the novel and to life, Kermode offers the perception of the sound of a clock as tick-tock. He terms "tick" a humble genesis and "tock" a feeble apocalypse. The interval in the middle is meaningfully housed as other than mere noise by its insertion into the tick-tock structure, which thus makes sense of the middle passage. The good traditional novel provided interesting and involving *peripeteia* between the "tick" of its beginning and the "tock" of its ending. The modern novel, resonating with other features of modern culture, introduces tock-tick elements that take the story from the traditional house of meaning into occasionally uncanny wanderings in the desert. *Nausea*, for Kermode, is one of the most intriguing of these modern novels.[3]

Kermode's low-keyed example, of course, sends one back to the Bible as the paternal provider of the apocalyptic paradigm in our tradition (although Kermode would like to resist the element of continuity in Northrop Frye's notion of displacement and to stress the specificity of taking a narrative structure as fictive). This paradigm was repeated in displaced and different forms in the philosophical tradition. Nowhere was it more grandly formulated than by Hegel in the Preface to *The Phenomenology of Mind*: "The true is its own becoming, the circle that presupposes its end as its aim and thus has it for its beginning—that which is actual only through its execution and end."[4] When the apocalyptic narrative structure is self-consciously seen as fictive (or at least as involving fictive elements), as it is in a number of modern novels or in the philosophy of Nietzsche, difficulties arise for its relation to truth. Indeed, the very concept of truth is rendered problematic.

*Nausea* self-reflexively contains within itself a theory of the novel in terms of the beginning-middle-end structure, which applies beyond the "realm" of the novel and engages the entire problem of meaning and interpretation in our tradition. (To condense Aristotle's formulation in more Sartrean terms: plot repeats project or the structure of praxis.) And this theory of the (more than) novel is simultaneously "applied" and critically deconstructed in the writing of *Nausea* itself. On one level, *Nausea* presents the traditional elements of the novel (plot, characterization, setting or context, narrative point of view) and a theory of the (more than) novel, which "totalizes" them. These elements and this theory, however, are doubly inscribed and critically explored in the text. One recurrent technique of the novel— which by its ending almost attains the status of a repetition compulsion—is to set up an "apocalyptic" expectation of meaning only to have it frustrated or aborted. This technique, or narrative "double take," is related to the use of oblique and critical forms such as parody. At times one encounters self-parody, for Sartre's own "existentialist" views do not escape the acidic work and black humor of the text. In *Nausea*, radical ambiguity and supplementarity do forcefully contest the sense-making function of analytic oppositions and dialectical sublation. For the traditional narrative structure is an important "expression" of the dialectical overcoming of what the story organizes as the "analytic" divisions and trials of man in the middle. Perhaps one might more simply say that the apocalyptic narrative is the dialectic at work on the most unassuming and pervasive of levels, which "corresponds" to conventional sentence structure itself. To parody Plato: a good traditional story is a well-made sentence writ large. Or, in Hegelian language, the "tock" is the *Aufhebung* of the "tick."

In his *prière d'insérer* to the first edition of *Nausea*, Sartre himself (in a tone Contat and Rybalka describe as half-ironic and half-serious) furnishes a reading of the novel in terms of conventional plot and story line:

After having undertaken long voyages, Antoine Roquentin establishes himself at Bouville in the midst of ferocious solid citizens [*gens de bien*]. He lives near the station, in a hotel for traveling salesmen, and does a historical thesis on an adventurer of the eighteenth century, M. de Rollebon. His work often takes him to the municipal library where his friend the Autodidacte, a humanist, instructs himself by reading books in alphabetical order. In the evening, Roquentin sits at a table in the Rendez-vous des Cheminots to listen to a record—always the same one: "Some of these Days." Sometimes he goes upstairs to a room with the proprietress of the café. Anny, the woman he loves, has disappeared four years ago. She always wanted there to be "perfect moments" and exhausted herself at every instant in minute and vain efforts to recompose the world around her. They have left each other. At present Roquentin loses his past drop by drop; he plunges more every day into a strange and suspect [*louche*] present. His life itself has no more meaning: he used to believe he had beautiful adventures. But there are no more adventures; there are only "stories." He fastens himself to M. de Rollebon: the dead must justify the living.

Then begins his true adventure—an insinuating and sweetly horrible metamorphosis of all his sensations. It is Nausea. It grabs you from behind and then one floats in a lukewarm pool of time. Has Roquentin changed? Is it the world that has changed? Walls, gardens, cafés are suddenly taken with nausea. Another time he wakes up during a maleficent day: something is rotten in the air, in the light, in the gestures of people. M. de Rollebon dies for a second time: a dead man can never justify the living. Roquentin drags himself through the streets at will, voluminous and unjustifiable. And then, the first day of spring, he understands the meaning of his adventure: Nausea is Existence which unveils itself—and Existence is not beautiful to see. Roquentin still has a little hope: Anny has written to him; he goes to find her again. But Anny has become a heavy woman, fat and desperate. She has given up perfect moments as Roquentin has given up Adventures. She too, in her manner, has discovered Existence: they have nothing to say to each other. Roquentin returns to solitude, at the very bottom of this enormous Nature which collapses on the city and whose coming cataclysms he foresees. What to do? Call "help" to other men? But other men are solid citizens: they tip their hats to one another and do not know that they exist. He is going to leave Bouville. He enters the Rendez-vous des Cheminots to listen for a last time to "Some of these Days" and, while the record turns, he glimpses a chance, a slim chance of accepting himself.[5]

This schoolboy's or "naive" reader's *précis* is delightful in its reduction of a great novel to the level of existential soap opera. It reminds one of the film versions of *Madame Bovary*. One cannot tell whether Sartre is, in his summary, upholding traditional forms of reading or making a complete fool of the unwary reader. He offers us the Swiss cheese without the holes. Yet one must recognize that the reading offered in Sartre's blurb exists at some level in even the most "sophisticated" reader, and it is "faithful" to one level of the novel. But the directed, continuous narrative summarized by Sartre is not merely undercut or scandalized by a "structure" that is episodic, discontinuous, fragmented, gap-ridden, and strangely anecdotal. The bifaced plot structure is so inextricably intertwined with other doubly inscribed traditional elements that one cannot tell where one begins and another ends. Traditional construction and critical deconstruction overlap within and between levels in a way that sets up a disconcerting interplay of de-formed forms and monstrous possibilities that threaten to escape the containment of structures.

Let us turn briefly to the manner in which the text of *Nausea* erases traditional elements of the (more than) novel while allowing them to remain legible through a praxis of deconstruction and double inscription—a praxis that cannot be reduced to one or the other of the "opposites" involved but must be seen in terms of their sedimented, overlapping interplay. Aside from the linear/nonlinear plot, one may mention setting, characterization, and point of view.

On one level, the setting or context of the story is integrated into the text itself in realistic or naturalistic terms. One knows that Sartre as a young man was extremely interested in the use of realistic techniques in the works of American authors such as John Dos Passos. The realistic or naturalistic level of *Nausea* presents a portrait of French society of the Third Republic in a large provincial town (Bouville/Mudville/Le Havre) during the early 1930s. This world is quite recognizable to anyone with a minimal historical knowledge of the time and place. One may note, for example, the contrast drawn between the older patriciate living on the hill and the *nouveaux riches* of the boulevard. The lives of town fathers enshrined in the Bouville museum bear a striking resemblance to lives of leaders of the Republic. In brief, on one level there is a portrait of provincial mores that might interest the social historian. But the realism of the novel becomes *trompe-l'oeil* at a moment that cannot be unambiguously pinpointed, and this familiar world is subjected to telling distortions. The realism is itself suspiciously provincial. Certain contexts that would almost certainly have to be central in any empirical history are peripheral: the worldwide depression and the power takeover by the Nazis—indeed, the entire series of events that Sartre later attempted to use as the basis of his fiction in *Les Chemins de la liberté*. Perhaps even more important than the matter of selection is that of presentation. The portrait of *moeurs* is "distorted" through a use of caricature, parody, irony, and farce that is alternately brilliant and vicious. Within the novel itself, the portrait—as well as the statue and the graven face—is seen as the "representation" of the bad faith of bourgeois *salauds* or *gens de bien*, the only "solid" people in this world, but people whose solidity is based on the vacuous attempt to achieve the identity of a "thing."

The first level of setting or context shades into the second level: the world of the alienated intellectual's isolated consciousness, which brackets reality, lives the phenomenological *epochè*, is always on the verge of extreme experience, and can tell stories or interpret the world but not act constructively to change it. This is, of course, most ostensibly the world of Antoine Roquentin. In one sense, it seems drastically different from the world of the "solid" bourgeois whom Antoine hates. The very language of the novel on this level attempts to extricate itself from realistic representation as it attempts to escape from an ugly and meaningless reality. An enigmatic philosophical prose at times comes close to a strangely inverted lyricism in "representing" the workings of alienated consciousness: "Never have I had so strongly as today the sentiment of being without secret dimensions, limited to my body, to thoughts that arise from it like bubbles." (*N*, p. 54). At these times, language seems almost to go on holiday from the job-centered, work-a-day world of referential usage. It becomes what Sartre would later term "poetic."

But Antoine is not all that different from the hated bourgeois "other." He sees through the bad faith of others at the price of remaining blind to his own bad faith, for he seeks a freedom that is uninvolved and uncommitted in the world. Thought and language function for him as rituals of purification from reality: "I need to wash myself with abstract thoughts, transparent like water" (p. 85). His abstract freedom functions to alienate him from the bourgeois household of wealth, status, and power, but it keeps him on the same side of the tracks as the hated "other."

Antoine is a coupon-clipper, parasitic on the order he detests. He lives in a run-down hotel for traveling salesmen situated just this side of the bourgeois tracks. The tramway line—*Abattoirs/ Grands Bassins*—places him graphically as a marginal man in relation to the bourgeoisie but as a stranger to the people, if not its enemy. The working class has as vague a position in his consciousness as it has in that of the bourgeoisie. The workers are on the side of *Grands Bassins*—large pools—"toward the Factories of the black East" (p. 13). Antoine, however marginally, is on the side of the *Abattoirs*—the bourgeois slaughterhouses. Significantly, the working class, as well as Antoine's position in relation to it, is situated in the text in a fleeting but forceful way. And it is fairly clear that Antoine himself is part of the problem rather than the solution.

We have already moved to the level of characterization. Just as the discourse, or language, of the novel involves both realistic and antirealistic "opposites" without being reducible to either extreme, so the element of characterization is doubly inscribed in the text. In a certain sense, the characters become more or less familiar to us as individuals in the course of the narrative— notably the three whom Sartre mentions in his *prière d'insérer*: Antoine, Anny, and the Autodidacte. In another sense, however, characterization does not get beyond the letter *A*. The characters are excavated as individuals. Proper names become abstract, almost to the point of assuming the status of nominal references for sets of problems. And individuals come up against internal alterity as they become each other's alter egos. Antoine has difficulty keeping a grip on his "*I*": he moves toward the impossible limit of the pure, alienated, impersonal consciousness. The Autodidacte is not Antoine's simple opposite but his parodic alter ego—his distorted mirror image, the Pécuchet to his Bouvard. (A footnote tells us that the "real" name of the Autodidacte is Ogier P.) The Autodidacte embodies the exhausted values of the humanist tradition: the encyclopedic ideal, the myth of universal knowledge, the respect for intellectual authority, the cult of reading, writing, and the library. His ridiculous method of reading all the books of the library in alphabetical order is, in its reliance on the alphabet as a minimal sense-making code, as plausible or implausible as the historian Antoine's reliance on chronology to organize intelligibly the events of the past.

Antoine's recognition of affinity with the Autodidacte is blocked by his realization that the humanist-pederast lacks his degree of self-consciousness, and Anny is presented as even more lucid and more hollowed out than Antoine. After his mock-epiphanic encounter with the chestnut tree, Antoine follows Anny's letter by going to meet her. He experiences a "strong feeling of adventure" (p. 191). (It is interesting to note that Antoine seems more outgoing than the others in only two instances: his meeting with Anny and his attempt to help the Autodidacte in the library. The meeting with Anny is a frustrating fiasco. The failure of his gesture toward the Autodidacte is equally predictable and is indeed presented in the text as a foregone conclusion. His gesture is, moreover, highly ambivalent. In the library, Antoine had already been an involuntary but nonprotesting accomplice in the staging of the vicious scene that revealed the Autodidacte as a pederast. Antoine's seemingly outgoing offer of help breaks that earlier complicity with others and returns him to isolation, for it is and must be refused by the "other" who always sought his company but for the first time would like to be alone.) What Antoine seeks from Anny is not reconciliation but the sharing of a sense of loss in a scene of recognition that would identify her perfect moments with his adventures. She rejects this illusion of communion in a paradise lost. She attempts to survive herself without nostalgia. She is both more and less of a character than Antoine—as in the past she was the "man of action" and orchestrator of living theater.

We have now come to the level of narrative point of view and theory of the novel. Let us begin with the obvious point that Sartre canot be identified with Antoine in any simple way. *Nausea* poses the problem of autobiographical fiction in a complex, exploratory manner. One sign of this is what might be called an indeterminacy of narrative voice, which renders problematic the relationship among author (biographical or implied), fictive narrator, and text. The bulk of the text is presented as the diary of the fictive narrator Antoine, who tells his story in the first person and sometimes in a bewildering variety of tenses (present, past, conditional). One cannot, however, simply identify Antoine as a narrator or his diary as a diary, for both forms of identity are deconstructed in the text. The *o* of Antoine's *cogito* threatens to be decapitated or castrated as he loses hold of his "I." The narrator is dismembered and disseminated in the text. The thinking "I" becomes free-floating. And consciousness seems to pass into things. Indeed, it *almost* becomes irrelevant, and the text *almost* seems to write itself. Antoine Roquentin becomes "de l'abstrait"—almost the same as "an anonymous consciousness" (pp. 236–37). One may observe in passing that views of Antoine as an apolitical individualist are partially misleading, for it is individuality itself that is undermined as Antoine moves toward the impossible limiting "experience" of the pure, impersonal, alienated consciousness.

Sartre as implied author does not exist in this text as a full presence with an identity that may be portrayed. It is unclear to what extent Sartre as biographical author was aware of "what" was happening in the text "he"wrote. What is clear is the existence of marks or traces in the text that distance Sartre from Antoine and prevent any simple identification of the two. A number of elements, for example, intervene in the text before the appearance of Antoine's diary: the title of the "novel" (changed from *Melancholia* to *Nausea* at the suggestion of Gaston Gallimard, who was perhaps motivated by a commercial concern for a title that would sell); the dedication to "Castor" (nickname and code name for Simone de Beauvoir); the epigraph from Céline (a quotation from an author who sorely tested Sartre's later assertion that one could not write a good novel in defense of a bad cause like anti-Semitism). All of these prefatory elements tempt one to burst through the confines of parentheses and speculate further about the significance of their enigmatic presence. But let us begin in earnest with the editors' note.

"These notebooks were found among the papers of Antoine Roquentin. They are published without alteration" (p. 9). The editors' note inserts a rough pane of glass between the author and the fictional diary that is to follow. Its use seems to parody the more traditional function of the editorial intrusion to establish verisimilitude and reinforce the realistic illusion, for a recurrent theme of the text to follow is that of the deceptiveness of fiction. The footnotes to the undated pages continue the parodic note. Where the traditional footnote fills a gap in the text, these footnotes mark gaps that cannot be filled. The first note refers both to the scene of writing and to the problem of perception: "For instance, here is a cardboard box holding my bottle of ink. I should try to tell how I saw it *before* and how [fn. 1. Word left out.] now" (p. 11). The "mot laissé en blanc" seems to mark a blank space indicating a term of perception ("see it"). Unlike perception in Sartre's early theoretical works, in this text it is itself rendered problematic. It is not the immaculate offering of a full presence that gives the perceiver a simple grasp of reality. And the thing itself that is absent in a before-and-after sequence is the container that holds the fluid of the writer as a young man.

A second footnote seems to concentrate on the problem of realistic representation and art: "I must never [fn. 2. Word crossed out (*raturé*)—perhaps 'force' or 'forge'—another word added above is illegible (*un autre rajouté en surcharge est illisible*).] but carefully note and detail all that happens" (p. 11). The offset opposition between realism and something else that is crossed out and written over illegibly—possibly art or language in general, which requires the absence or deferment of its object—raises the entire problem of a deconstructive strategy that reinscribes the words of the tradition *sous rature*. The violence of the "forcing" and the artifice or counterfeit of the "forging" are another motif of the text to follow.

A third footnote refers to the uncertainty of time in these undated pages through which the diary makes its "beginning" on an infrachronological level below that of even the most minimal code. The final footnote of the undated pages tells us simply: "The text of the undated pages ends here" (p. 14). The last sentence of the text to which the note refers reads: "In one case only it might be interesting to keep a diary: it would be if. . . ." (p. 14). This last sentence is somewhat of a *piège à cons*. One is tempted to complete its ellipsis in one of two opposite ways, which perhaps amount to the same thing. One might say that it would be interesting to keep a diary if life made sense or was full of adventures that one could carefully note and detail (realistic representation). Or one might say that it would be interesting to keep a diary if life did not make sense and one could try to force and forge matters by papering and inking over its gaps through fiction. But one cannot unproblematically complete the ellipsis with a specified "what" that would give it an essential content to arrest its unsettling play. The last sentence of the undated pages makes the diary "proper" begin in a conditional, interrogative, and "improper" way, which contaminates and renders dubious the entire project of keeping a diary.*

Once the dated portion of the diary starts, two more editorial notes occur in the early pages (the second of which is actually signed by the editors), and then the footnotes disappear for no apparent reason. But, given their distribution in the text, one cannot use them to draw up a significant opposition between the undated and the dated pages. In a sense, the undated pages, which are a beginning that is not a "true" beginning, even on the basis of the minimal demands of the chronicler, set up the "entire" problematic of the text to follow.

The role of parody and irony as oblique strategies of deconstruction is almost bewilderingly insistent in the text from beginning to end. It is tempting to say that the entire philosophical and literary tradition resonates parodically in the text in both general and specific ways. I will return to the problem of the apocalyptic narrative paradigm. On a somewhat lower level of generality (but still implicated in the project of meaning and mastery), humanism is placed on trial. Humanism is associated with the Autodidacte's suspect tendencies toward pederasty. And in the course of Antoine's conversation with the Autodidacte (after which his feeling of nausea was at its strongest), virtually all variants of humanism are passed in review in a veritable carnival of commitment. Antoine refuses to label himself an antihumanist, for this label would present the Autodidacte with an opposite easily recuperated by a dialectical totalization that Antoine resists: "I don't want to be integrated or to have my beautiful blood fatten this lymphatic beast: I will not commit the

---

* "If I were a woman" would also complete the ellipsis. The penultimate sentence of the undated pages itself tells us that to keep a diary is to behave "*comme les petites filles.*" And Antoine's sexual identity will be very much in doubt in *Nausea*.

stupidity of calling myself 'antihumanist.' I *am not* a humanist, that's all" (p. 167). Indeed, Sartre's own existential humanism is parodied, but at times in so caricatural a form as to render the contestation relatively inconsequential. The Autodidacte, for example, tries to get Antoine to identify with the position of the author of *Is Life worth Living?* who argues that "life has a meaning if we want to give it one. One must first act, throw oneself into an enterprise. If one reflects later, the die is cast; one is engaged" (p. 159).

I have already alluded to the role in the text of Descartes's *cogito* and Husserl's *epochè*. Hegel and absolute knowledge could also be invoked. Early in the novel, Antoine is unable to pick up a soiled copy of a schoolchild's dictation entitled "Le Hibou blanc" ("The White Owl"). The dream of the philosophical tradition, expressed in the owl of Minerva, is fit only for a juvenile copyist's reinscription. It is also associated with the quest of the Autodidacte, who has a suspect relation to the schoolchild. The dream of absolute knowledge has lost its purity and exists only *sous rature*. In terms of hollow echoes of the literary tradition, one has the obvious cases of the relation of Proust's Vinteuil sonata to Antoine's "Some of these Days," counterfeiting in Gide to Antoine's fictionalizing, Joyce's artist as a young man to Antoine's forging, Valéry's Monsieur Teste to Antoine's cerebralism and alienation. Balzac has a function as a traditional "other" for Antoine similar to that of Michelet for Anny, because the use of secure narrative structures to organize events meaningfully is as important for the novels of the one as it is for the histories of the other. Indeed, the openness of *Nausea* makes it a kind of parodic Rorschach test, and one cannot tell unambiguously whether one is finding references in it or projecting them into it—so successful is it in soliciting or stirring up the tradition and in provoking the reader's desire to decipher possible references.

In the case of Flaubert, it is perhaps more fitting to speak of emulation rather than parody—to the extent that the two may be distinguished. Everything I have said about *Nausea* could be said *pari passu* about Flaubert's novels, which also put into practice an entire strategy of deconstruction and double inscription in relation to the literary and philosophical tradition.[6] One may ask whether Sartre understood Flaubert better in writing *Nausea* than in the more theoretical interpretation in *L'Idiot de la famille*. In *Nausea*, a proliferating series of elements invite "intertextual" readings with reference to the works of Flaubert: the petering out of editors' notes and the sputtering disappearance of the first person plural at the beginning of *Madame Bovary*—both of which resist becoming differential bases of thematic organization in interpreting the novel, indicate an undecidability of narrative voice, and work toward the limiting case of an anonymous text; the juxtaposition of the well-wrought page from Balzac's *Eugénie Grandet* with the senseless conversation in the café and the mutually destructive interplay of the language of seduction and agricultural discourses in the *comices agricoles* scene of *Madame Bovary*—both of which tend to reduce language to silence through static; the defamiliarized or "dehumanized" presentation of the Sunday ritual of bourgeois greeting and the fiacre scene in *Madame Bovary*; the meeting of Antoine and Anny and the encounter of Frédéric and Madame Arnoux toward the end of *The Sentimental Education*; the ambiguous trials of Antoine and the obscure temptation of St. Anthony, which seems to be simultaneously that of involvement in the world, and escape from it; the existence of "roquentin" as a common noun in Flaubert, becoming a proper name in *Nausea* only to move back to an abstract status; the decision of Antoine toward the end of *Nausea* that since he cannot live his fictions (and be like Madame Bovary), he will write about them (like Flaubert in Sartre's conception of him)—perhaps in the form of the impossible book about nothing, the *livre sur rien*. I shall terminate this possibly endless checklist by citing one more instance. *Nausea* perhaps most resembles Flaubert's *First Sentimental Education* in its exploration of the problem of autobiographical fiction and its explicit treatment of the theme of pure art as a road to salvation. But let us defer a discussion of Flaubert's *First Sentimental Education* until we confront Sartre's interpretation of it in *L'Idiot de la famille*.

Antoine's famous encounter with the chestnut tree is a "peak," or critical, experience that seems to totalize the narrative development, unveil existence, and provide the basis for Antoine's lucid choice of being. It is also, however, a repetition

of similar earlier experiences in encountering the "other," and it
is followed by the meeting with Anny and the "concluding"
decision of Antoine to become a writer. The section on the encounter with the chestnut tree includes both Antoine's attempt
to recuperate the "experience" as meaningful through a totalizing interpretation of it and the placing in question of that interpretive gesture. It is Antoine who would like to see the "vision"
of the chestnut tree as an epiphany to end all epiphanies and the
apocalyptic occasion for a narrative to end all narratives. But the
text resists his initiative as does the tree itself.

Antoine's "experience" with the chestnut tree is recounted in
the past tense: the existence of language marks the absence of
that which it would refer to, capture, or evoke. Referring to the
experience, the text speaks of an illumination, a frightening and
obscene nudity, a strange excess, a horrible ecstasy, an atrocious
*jouissance*. We are in the realm of the uncanny, the strangely
disconcerting, the fascinating and repulsive, the sacred pure
and impure, the incestuous desire, the ambiguous interplay of
excess and lack between the same and the other. Antoine attempts neatly to distribute ambiguity by placing excess securely
on the side of things and lack on the side of words: "Words
vanished and, with them, the signification of things, methods of
use, the feeble reference points which men have traced on their
surface" (p. 179). Categories arise to stabilize the situation: "The
word Absurdity is born at present under my pen . . ." (p. 181). It
is rejected by Antoine on the pretext that in the garden he
"thought without words, *on* things, *with* things" (p. 181). Yet, in
the face of this evocation of phenomenologically unmediated
vision or a pure beholding of things, something paradoxical
happens in the text. At precisely this point, a substitutive series
of metaphors arises to show how Antoine thought "on" things:
"Snake or claw or root or vulture's talon, what difference does it
make" (pp. 181–82). In the language used, an uncanny transfer
occurs: excess moves to the side of words and lack to the side of
things. Even earlier in the text appears: "It was like a floating
analogy, almost entirely elusive [*insaisissable*] with certain aspects [*situations*] of vaudeville" (p. 180). (The language and
grammar of this sentence are as elusive and floating as the anal-

ogy they evoke, and it is even unclear what the "it" refers to.)
What Antoine would like to see as a surplus on the side of the
thing or signified and a deficit on the side of language shifts in
an enigmatic way to a surplus on the side of signifiers and a
deficit on the side of the thing or signified. A monstrous proliferation of metaphors is paradoxically poured into the hole of
being in order to show how language falls away in the face of
existence unveiled.

When the category of contingency comes on the scene, Antoine accepts it. Nausea is specified as the feel of meaninglessly
contingent existence stripped of sense-making structures that
domesticate and humanize it. And naked contingency is contrasted with necessity—the necessity of mathematics, music,
and fictive narratives that would emulate them. In identifying
Nausea with contingency and defining the "vision" of the tree
as a beholding of raw contingency, the language of the novel
approximates a perhaps unself-conscious parody of a flat-footed
philosophical treatise: "The essential is contingency. I mean
that, by definition, existence is not necessity" and so on (p. 184).
Anticipating the terminology of *Being and Nothingness*, one
might say that the experience of the tree is analyzed in terms of
an encounter of the pure in-itself with the pure for-itself—a
confrontation of radical contingencies. But just as this interpretation in *Being and Nothingness* is an appropriation of the more
ambiguous problem of transphenomenality, so in *Nausea* the
stabilizing moment of categorial fixation is exceeded—and its
overflowing is more powerful than in *Being and Nothingness:*
"How long did this fascination last?" (p. 185). And as the text
goes on to discuss this "atroce jouissance," it is unclear whether
the question that opens the paragraph refers to the "experience"
of the tree or the categorial attempt to encompass and control it.

Toward the end of the passage on the chestnut tree is a supreme paradox. Intentionality itself moves from the side of consciousness to the side of things. The sense-making structures
and words that have been revealed as distant from an existence
stripped bare of the illusion of immanent meaning nevertheless
infiltrate things and harbor a strange complicity with them:
"Then the garden smiled at me. I leaned against the gate and

watched for a long time. The smile of the trees, of the laurel, *meant* something; that was the real secret of existence. I remembered one Sunday, not more than three weeks ago, I had already detected everywhere a sort of conspiratorial air" (p. 190). Given the revelation of existence as radically contingent and meaningless, the smile of the park—which repeats an earlier experience—should be as impossible as the smile of the Cheshire cat. This ineradicable sedimentation of meaning in things is for Antoine more bothersome than the seemingly overwhelming vision of radical contingency. It poses a riddle that cannot be solved by pure categorial opposites and clear and distinct ideas. And its existence is here related to the scene of writing: "That little sense annoyed me: I *could not* understand it, even if I could have stayed leaning against the gate for a hundred and seven years; I had learned all I could know about existence. I left, I went back to the hotel and I wrote" (p. 190).

The Autodidacte took seven years to read half the library of Bouville. It is noteworthy that a century more is seen by Antoine as insufficient to understand what is at the root of the problem of understanding. And Antoine is more puzzled by the residue of meaning in things than he is by radical contingency, which itself enables an unproblematic opposition between the thing and consciousness. His worrying this problem ends the section on the chestnut tree with stress on radical ambiguity rather than on radical contingency. And it is the former that is linked here with the project of writing, which is later described as a way of deferring Nausea (p. 241). Nausea itself in this light is not the feel of radical contingency but that of vertiginous ambiguity in the interplay of "opposites" that cannot be definitively stabilized or fixated as pure opposites. And *Nausea* cannot be read simply as a novel "about" the problem of contingency.

These considerations help to appreciate the way in which the text of *Nausea* does not entirely conform to the opposites it situates and explores. (It may, of course, be observed that the "feeling" of nausea is itself neither purely mental nor purely physical but is a threshold or liminal feeling.) This nonconformity applies to the "binary" opposites constituting the theory of the novel that *Nausea* includes, applies on one level, and deconstructs on another. The theory of the novel self-reflexively included as an internalized critical apparatus in *Nausea* is repeated and displaced in various guises. It is ("nonidentically") there in Antoine's adventures and Anny's sequence of annunciatory signs, privileged situations, and perfect moments (beginnings, middles, and endings). It is there in the song "Some of these Days," which in the course of the novel shifts from being a metaphor for life to being one for art. And it is there most elaborately in Antoine's theoretical reflections, which contrast life and art. The meaningful concordance of beginning and end sought in "real-life" adventures is possible only in the stories of art. Life is on the side of radical contingency and mere chronicity. Art or narration is on the side of the meaningful but fictive integration of time through sense-making structures:

True beginnings appear like the sound of trumpets, like the first notes of a jazz tune, brusquely, cutting short boredom, tightening up duration.... For the most banal event to become an adventure, it is enough to begin narrating [*raconter*] it. This is what fools people: a man is always a teller of tales; he lives surrounded by his stories and the stories of others, he sees everything that happens to him through them; and he tries to live his own life as if he were telling a story.

But you have to choose: live or tell.

Nothing happens while you live. The scenery changes, people come in and go out, that's all. There are no beginnings. Days are tacked on to days without rhyme or reason, an interminable monotonous addition.... Neither is there any end.... And then everything looks alike.

That's living. But everything changes when you tell about life; it's a change no one notices: the proof is that people talk about true stories. As if there could possibly be true stories; things happen one way and we tell about them in the opposite sense.... In reality, it's by the end that one begins. The end is there, invisible and present, and that is what gives to words the pomp and ceremony of a beginning. [Pp. 59–63]

Narration effects a fictive transubstantiation of existence that brings to life a meaningful structure. What is crucial is that *Nausea* itself does not choose between living and telling as extreme opposites. It critically reveals the functioning of fictions of narration on the level of pure interpretation in traditional stories. And it tells about mere living in a paradoxical gesture that undercuts itself. For it is life as narrated in this text that is said to be mere contingency and to differ totally from narration. The text itself mediates and supplements these distinctions, which are shown to be pure opposites only on the level of pure fiction. The theory of the novel is dismantled as it is expounded. It is also dismantled as it is applied. And, at least indirectly, the question arises: Can life be different from the way this text presents it?

The technique of the text in deconstructing the traditional narrative is to set up a beginning that brings with it an expectation of a certain ending, which the text itself frustrates. Suspense is built up and narrative premonition is stimulated only to be aborted or let down. At times, this work, generally known as a bleak novel, is at least momentarily funny in the way it plays with the reader's expectations. Here, for example, is a passage relating the unlikely trinity of humanism, heroism, and cheese:

> The Autodidacte laughs openly but his eyes stay wicked:
> "You are too modest, Monsieur. In order to tolerate your condition, the human condition, you, as everybody else, need much courage. Monsieur, the next instant may be the moment of your death, you know it and you can smile: isn't that admirable? In your most insignificant actions," he adds sharply, "there is an enormous amount of heroism."
> "What will you have for dessert?" the waitress asks.
> The Autodidacte is quite white, his eyelids are half-shut over his stony eyes. He makes a feeble motion with his hand, as if inviting me to choose.
> "Cheese," I say heroically. [P. 171]

The repeated use of the aborted apocalypse makes of *Nausea* an extended lesson in reading novels. By its end, the reader is almost programmed to expect an expectation of meaning to be frustrated. This inverted expectation cannot but contaminate the way we read Antoine's project to salvage his existence at least retrospectively through art.

The kind of novel that Antoine projects writing, toward the end of *Nausea*, falls within both the conception of art presented in *L'Imaginaire* and the theory of the novel formulated earlier in *Nausea* itself. It will negate and transcend existence. It is on the side of necessity with music and mathematics in stark contrast to life and contingency. Antoine, in proposing this project, has not really changed: he is still in quest of a pure form of freedom that escapes from complicity in the world.

The build-up to this novelistic project is staged with such a blaring fanfare of trumpets that the reader whose reading habits have been formed by *Nausea* must remain suspicious. Antoine's project is preceded by a series of surrealistic images of a world upsetting all conventional expectations. The song "Some of these Days" is surrounded by a myth of origins that sanctifies its creation by a Jewish composer and a Negress singer: "That's the way it happened. That way or another way, it makes little difference" (p. 245). The words in which Antoine formulates his project are broken and awe-struck (like those of Stephen Daedalus in *Portrait of the Artist as a Young Man*). There is an almost unbearable surplus of expectation, suspense, and meaningful plot. Antoine may seriously intend his project. Sartre as author may share his intention. But the text does not. Given the nature and the context of Antoine's novelistic project in the text, it must be "ironized," at least in part. The last great narrative apocalypse cannot entirely escape the repetitive pattern of deflation that the praxis of *Nausea* has itself generated. The last paragraph of *Nausea* would seem to confirm these comments, for it is markedly anticlimactic: "Tomorrow it will rain in Bouville" (p. 248). And a point of anecdotal interest fits in with the interpretation of the novelistic project suggested here. Antoine's use of the song "Some of these Days" is somewhat fraudulent. It was recorded not by a Negress but by Sophie Tucker—the last of the white red-hot mamas. It is not *echt* but *ersatz*. (Sartre, by the way, refers to Sophie Tucker in the story "The Childhood of a Leader.")[7]

*Nausea* is not the kind of novel that Antoine projects writing. Another sort of book situates his project, deconstructs it, and provides a perspective for interpreting or "reading" it. *Nausea* does not go to the extreme of pure fiction that negates and transcends life in a totally inhuman gesture that mystifyingly seems to save the self by damning others. It does not furnish the novel that is analogous to the band of steel or the little diamond-shaped suffering that is out of this world. Rather

*Nausea* situates and necessarily casts doubt on these extremes as pure fictions. And it provides a notion of at least one level of critical praxis in general—one that questions a total dichotomy between life and fiction and that might conceivably be extended to include a more affirmative notion of interaction and play. By and large, Sartre himself does not read *Nausea* along the "deconstructive" lines I have suggested. *A fortiori*, he does not build upon this sort of reading in his conception of critical praxis. Indeed, in his later theoretical works, he often attempts to exorcise Antoine's quest for pure art from himself, projects it onto others (notably Flaubert) whom he criticizes, and opposes to it a quest for the true novel presented in the totalizing terms rendered radically problematic by *Nausea* itself.[8]

# 4

# From *Being and Nothingness* to the *Critique*: Breaking Bones in One's Head

Philosophy. Always snicker at it.

Flaubert, Dictionary of Received Ideas

A good idea cherished secretly by each of them. They hide it from one another. From time to time they smile when it occurs to them, then at last communicate it simultaneously: *To copy as in the old days.*

Flaubert, Bouvard and Pécuchet

Naturally, I'm not taken in. I'm quite aware that we repeat ourselves. But this more recently acquired knowledge undermines my old certainties without quite destroying them. My life has a few supercilious witnesses who won't let me get away with anything; they often catch me falling into the same ruts. They tell me so, I believe them, and then, at the last moment, I feel pleased with myself: yesterday I was blind; today's progress lies in my realizing that I've stopped progressing. . . . In short, I fix things up: though undeceived, I fool myself in order to keep feeling, despite the fact that old age is creeping up on me, the youthful exhilaration of the mountain-climber [*l'alpiniste*].

Sartre, The Words

"Mankind" does not advance, it does not even exist. The over-all aspect is that of a tremendous experimental laboratory in which a few successes are scored, scattered throughout all ages, while there are untold failures, and all order, logic, union, and obligingness are lacking.
1. My endeavor to oppose decay and increasing weakness of personality. I sought a new *center*.

2. Impossibility of this endeavor recognized.

3. Thereupon I advanced further down the road of disintegration—where I found new sources of strength for individuals. We have to be destroyers!—I perceived that the state of disintegration, in which individual natures can perfect themselves as never before—is an image and isolated example of existence in general. To the paralyzing sense of general disintegration and incompleteness I opposed the *eternal recurrence.*

Nietzsche, The Will To Power

The plurality of *the meanings* of History can be discovered and posited for itself only upon the ground of a future totalization—in terms of the future totalization and in contradiction with it. It is our theoretical and practical duty to bring this totalization closer every day. All is still obscure, and yet everything is in full light. To tackle the theoretical aspect, we have the instruments; we can establish the method. Our historical task, at the heart of this polyvalent world, is to bring closer the moment when History will have *only one meaning,* when it will tend to be dissolved in the concrete men who will make it in common. . . . Without living men, there is no history. The object of existentialism . . . is the individual, alienated, reified, mystified, as he has been made to be by the division of labor and by exploitation, but struggling against alienation with the help of distorting instruments and, despite everything, patiently gaining ground.

Sartre, Search for a Method

The supplement is always unfolding, but it can never attain the status of a complement. The field is never saturated.

Derrida, "White Mythology"

I have been trying to interpret Sartre's thought in terms of a model of repetition: continuities in diachronic discontinuities and discontinuities in synchronic continuities. The basic continuity is that of a philosophy centered on man who, in his intentional consciousness and free praxis, creates meaning and value in the world. This perspective is based on a form of thought that is both analytic and dialectical. The danger in this perspective is that a concept of pure and total human freedom will function as an ideology masking a logic of control and domination from which the only exit is the blind and terroristic hope for a violent apocalypse. The basic discontinuity in continuity is the existence of more or less submerged tendencies in Sartre that contest his dominant perspective by decentering man and construing freedom as more radically at play in a world where it and its correlates (project and counterfinality) do not fully define the situation. *Nausea* has a somewhat eccentric or acentric position in Sartre's thought because in it his submerged tendencies to some extent surface in a forceful and disconcerting way. In Sartre's more theoretical studies, the problems of supplementarity and repetition—played out in the deconstructive strategy of *Nausea*—do not receive theoretical articulation as "contestants" vis-à-vis analysis and dialectics. The entire problem of a deconstructive critique of tradition tends at best to remain implicit, often in misleading ways. And the interaction between centering and decentering tendencies in Sartre's thought is not explicitly thematized as a problem. Instead, the centering approach tends to dominate, and it is increasingly seen in terms of a totalizing dialectical project. The relationship between *Being and Nothingness* (1943) and the *Critique of Dialecti-*

119

*cal Reason* (1960), Sartre's two major philosophical treatises, offers a testing ground for the approach of this book.

Their relationship has been the occasion for reading Sartre in terms of his own self-readings and dominant ideas: it is often seen as a dialectical or narratively teleological one, in which *Being and Nothingness* is the "beginning" and the *Critique* the "end" of a meaningfully oriented and progressive story. The *Critique* is thus the *Aufhebung* of the earlier work, negating, conserving, and raising its argument to a higher level of insight. Contat and Rybalka formulate this interpretation in the following manner:

> Sartre returned only on rare occasions and always incidentally to *Being and Nothingness*: he never placed in question its essential conclusions. A note in the *Critique of Dialectical Reason* (pp. 285–86), moreover, explicitly links the problematic of the second great philosophical work to that of the first, while clearly indicating the expansion and development he brought to it and warning against erroneous interpretation to which *Being and Nothingness* might give rise. In an important interview of 1965, he reproached himself with having used in this work too literary a language and with having thus exposed himself to misunderstandings. One must also note the expression "eidetic of bad faith" employed by Sartre in 1961 (cf. *Situations IV*, p. 196) to designate *Being and Nothingness*. This formula clearly marks the limits of the work: in a first stage, Sartre founds his phenomenology of consciousness on the analysis of forms of behavior through which individuals, envisaged through a psychological and moral perspective, manifest their fundamental alienation, but he does not yet account for the historical and social causes of this alienation and this is precisely what he will attempt to do in his later work....
>
> To link very schematically *Being and Nothingness* and the *Critique of Dialectical Reason,* one might say that the problem Sartre attempts to solve in the second work is the following: how can we understand that History, the product of the free *praxis* of man, turns against its agent and is changed into an inhuman necessity that makes of man the object of the historical process? The essentially psychological perspective of *Being and Nothingness* is thus enlarged in the *Critique of Dialectical Reason* into a historical and sociological perspective that should allow one to account for the existence of *alienated* freedom.[1]

Contat and Rybalka, despite the apparent dialectical theme of their own "description" of the relationship between the two works, nonetheless add that "the principal difficulty that must be removed today, it seems to us, is whether or not there is an 'epistemological break' between *Being and Nothingness* and the *Critique of Dialectical Reason*."[2] Fredric Jameson's influential interpretation has no difficulty in removing the difficulty:

It is clear, however, that if the above description is correct, it will not logically be possible to describe the *Critique* as a radical break with the position of *Being and Nothingness*. The fact is that in genuinely Sartrean fashion the new book has *changed* the old; *Being and Nothingness* can no longer be read in the same way after its appearance. The idea of logical inconsistencies between the two positions is a static one: it is more satisfactory to think that the *Critique* comes to complete *Being and Nothingness* in certain basic areas where it remained abstract or insufficiently developed; and that this act of completion, lifting all the problems onto a higher dialectical plane, ends by utterly transforming the very appearance of the earlier system.[3]

I should like to argue that both an attempt at dialectical reconciliation and an analysis in terms of an "epistemological break" are inadequate and that they must at least be supplemented by a notion of repetition. What is repeated and displaced is a dominant framework or problematic: one moves from an "eidetic of bad faith" to what might be termed a negative dialectic of alienation. And what is not explicitly articulated as a problem for theoretical reflection in either work is precisely the issue of repetition and that which accompanies it (such as supplementarity, a "logic" of the same and the different, internal alterity). The changes from one work to the other are often substitutions of terms within a similar framework (practico-inert for in-itself, praxis for for-itself, among others). And the passage from one work to the other brings losses as well as gains. The theoretical self-contestation in *Being and Nothingness* is in certain ways more powerful; at least on an explicit thematic level, the mode of dialectics in the *Critique* is more secure, if not dogmatic and mechanical. These considerations should not be made to deny the significance of discontinuities between the two works, especially in the shift from a concern with phenomenological ontology and morality to a concern with history, politics, and society. But they do situate these shifts and raise questions about their theoretical basis.[4] The "richness" in Sartre's development from

*Being and Nothingness* to the *Critique* conceals an essential poverty, whereby Sartre's thought more or less blindly replicates the structures of bad faith or alienation he castigates in the "external" world. The only perspective on alienation continues to be one "from the inside."

*Being and Nothingness* is generally acknowledged to be Sartre's greatest philosophical work. It is, I think, also one of Sartre's most troubled texts, a veritable textual jungle (it might even be read as a philosophical systematization of a paranoid-schizophrenic world view). From the perspective of this study, these two qualities are not incompatible, for the troubled nature of the text is related to forms of internal self-questioning that are part of its greatness. There is an interplay between a centering analytic and dialectical movement and a decentering supplementary movement in *Being and Nothingness*. The centering movement, however, tends to dominate and the decentering movement to be submerged and inadequately articulated. Hence, the interplay between the two is relatively blind and is not an explicit problem thematized and explored "self-consciously" in the text.

In examining the argument of *Being and Nothingness*, let us attempt to pay attention not only to thematic content but also, to a certain extent, to the way in which the text is made. The Introduction is perhaps the most intricate and difficult section. Its argument circles around the perennial problems of philosophy: which comes first, the chicken or the egg, or how does a philosophical argument get off the ground? Is there an absolute beginning and end to philosophy, or are there multiple beginnings and endings always already situated in a network of more or less compelling or exhausted traditions and institutions of discursive practice? In the Introduction, Sartre's project is identified as one of phenomenological ontology. He distinguishes his approach from that of Husserl, in which pure phenomenology presumably leads to subjective idealism, and from that of Heidegger, in which pure ontology presumably leads to a captive objectivism oblivious of the problem of subjectivity and consciousness. Sartre tacks "dialectically" between phenomenology and ontology in a manner that he believes does justice to both objective and subjective poles. He also attempts to distinguish between phenomenological ontology and metaphysics—especially in the Conclusion, which on this level resonates with the Introduction. Phenomenological ontology describes the structures of being as they inform phenomena. Metaphysics is explanatory in that it poses the question of the "why": it attempts to account for the origin of that which phenomenological ontology approaches on a descriptive level. In the course of Sartre's discussion, however, these somewhat strained distinctions tend to break down and even prove misleading. The overlap between phenomenology and ontology, phenomenological ontology and metaphysics, generates problems that the distinctions cannot altogether handle.

The Introduction begins with a statement of progress: "Modern thought has realized considerable progress by reducing the existent to the series of appearances that manifest it" (*EN*, p. 11). This phenomenological move has eliminated the dualism between phenomenon and noumenon and has dissipated what Nietzsche termed "the illusion of worlds-behind-the-scene" (p. 12). (It is interesting that the first nominal reference in *Being and Nothingness* is to Nietzsche.) The avoidance of the Kantian dualism has not eliminated all problems, however. In an intricate discussion, Sartre seems to suggest, in a very exploratory manner, what might be termed a displacement of problems. A further distinction or set of distinctions is generated: that between the finite and the infinite and that between the phenomenon of being and the being of the phenomenon. The phenomenon reveals itself and has meaning. But being, while not a noumenon, does not directly reveal itself; it is the condition for the revelation of the phenomenon. Any finite phenomenon or perspective [*Abschattung*] does not exhaust the infinite series of phenomena or perspectives founded in the being of a phenomenon. Being is transphenomenal and both "overflows and founds the knowledge one takes of it" (p. 16).

In a similar manner, consciousness is "the dimension of the transphenomenal being of the subject" (p. 17). Consciousness of an object is simultaneously self-consciousness, but reflection that knows consciousness as "having already been there before" (p. 17) cannot totally objectify and seize consciousness.

Consciousness is intentional: "All consciousness is consciousness of something" (p. 27). The transcendent status of this "something" is the basis of what Sartre terms the ontological proof. Consciousness is a being whose essence implies the existence of its object as a being other than consciousness. The nonconscious being that is the object of consciousness is transphenomenal in that its being is never exhausted by perspectives on it. Consciousness is itself transphenomenal in that the reflexive attempt to posit it as an object never exhausts it: "Consciousness is a being for which it is in its being [a] question of its being in so far as this being implies a being other than itself" (p. 29).

The final section of the Introduction identifies this being other than consciousness as the in-itself. Consciousness is described as able "to transcend the existent not toward its being but toward the *meaning* of this being," and "the meaning of the being of the existent, in so far as it reveals itself to consciousness, is the phenomenon of being" (p. 30). Meaning is thus placed on the side of consciousness and is identified with the revealed phenomenon. Being-in-itself is what it is—a meaningless massiveness that is full positivity and knows no alterity (p. 33). Alterity is all on the side of consciousness. The in-itself is what might colloquially be called the "thingy" thing, brute existent, or raw material. Moreover, the in-itself is identified as radically contingent and as "de trop pour l'éternité." (*De trop* might be translated as "excessive" or "superfluous.") With reference to the in-itself and the for-itself, Sartre speaks of "two incommunicable regions" or "two types of being" (p. 31). He justifies the work to follow as an attempt to answer the questions generated by problems left unresolved in the Introduction, such as that concerning "the profound meaning of these two types of being" (p. 34).

The rest of the work might be described in less linear and progressive terms as a repetition and displacement of the textual movement of the Introduction. Sartre begins Part One with considerations that seem to present the Introduction as a false start. What is the textual movement of the Introduction? The Introduction offers in more traditional language and condensed form the problematic of the work—including its central equivocation—in which, for the most part, Sartre is concerned with specifying the role of consciousness in terms of freedom, nihilation, and the for-itself. Consciousness on a prereflective level is immediate, spontaneous, and lived. It is always already beyond the situation of which it is conscious through its projects that require a nihilation of the given. But consciousness is also ("nonpositional") self-consciousness as it is ("positional") consciousness of the object as "other." In reflection, consciousness attempts to take a position on itself but it can never achieve a "metaconscious" angle of self-vision: reflection is recognition at a distance. Nor is consciousness identifiable with knowledge. It is the foundation of knowledge but it is never exhausted by concepts. Knowledge is a realization related to intentional projects in the world. It should be emphasized that prereflective consciousness is situated on the level of what Sartre later discusses as lived experience [*le vécu*] and that it is contrasted with conceptual knowledge for which it is the basis. Moreover, consciousness through perception is directly related to action in the "real" world. "Perception is naturally surpassed toward action; better yet, it can be revealed only in and through projects of action" (p. 386). Consciousness is not entirely seen in terms of the individual. The individual intervenes in Part Three in a relatively arbitrary manner from the viewpoint of theory. Before that point in the text, consciousness is individuated in a sense contrasted with the universal, not with the social. The basic theoretical difficulties of *Being and Nothingness* are not to be found on these levels; and they are at times aggravated in the thought of the later Sartre. What is the relationship between freedom and the situation or between the for-itself and the in-itself? Is freedom (or intentional consciousness or the for-itself or praxis) "originally" pure and total, and does it unilaterally define the meaning and value of the situation or the world? Or is it always already situated and limited by situations in which it takes its beginning and seeks its ends in ways that cannot be derived from a simple or single origin or creative act?

The treatment of transphenomenality suggests a relationship between consciousness and being (or between the for-itself and the in-itself) in terms of an overlapping interplay between excess (*de trop*) and lack (*manque*). The for-itself is added to the in-itself in a way that indicates a lack in the in-itself which the for-itself simultaneously marks, creates, and attempts to fill. The for-itself is in this sense the in-itself as "differed," or displaced. And, in this sense, the for-itself is not pure and total freedom. It is "characterized" by an internal alterity, for it is the same as its "other" but as differed. It is always already situated in a field sedimented with meaning and nonmeaning. "Originary" ambiguity saturates the relationship between the for-itself and its "other." To use Sartre's own formulation later in the text, "The situation, the common product of the contingency of the in-itself and freedom, is an ambiguous phenomenon in which it is impossible for the for-itself to discern the contribution of freedom and the brute existent" (p. 568). This formulation both uses and places in radical question the distinction between freedom and the in-itself as well as the very concepts of pure, total freedom and the brute existent. Nor can freedom be seen as the origin of the meaning of the situation. Free, intentional consciousness may elaborate analytic distinctions to orient itself in the world, and it may attempt a totalizing interpretation related to praxis. But these efforts do not entirely master the situation, and they rely upon the use of fictions that cannot be totally disjoined from an unproblematic conception of reality. The clear distinction between the in-itself and the for-itself is as fictive as their desired but impossible reconciliation in the ideal totality or wholeness of the in-itself-for-itself.

The concluding movement of the Introduction, however, inaugurates the approach that will tend to be dominant in the body of the work. A sharp analytic distinction separates the in-itself and the for-itself: it permits an entire series of comparable divisions in the ensuing argument. The in-itself is pure identity. The for-itself is pure difference, or total negativity and freedom. The alterity of the for-itself is in no sense internal. Its alterity is alienation from the in-itself. Internally, the for-itself is pure and total freedom, or nothingness. Ambiguity is distributed in a clear and distinct way that allows only for equivocation and contradiction. The for-itself is the origin or source of all meaning and value in its definition of the situation. And it is conceived in terms of pure paradox. Man is condemned to be free. This pure and total freedom is an empty spontaneity that approximates blind will and allows only for a "leap" into commitment. When this freedom is conceived in terms of the person or the individual (a gesture that comes in Part Three and carries into Part Four), it brings with it the existential pathos of total responsibility: "From the instant of my upsurge into being, I carry the weight of the world by myself alone without anything or anyone being able to lighten it. . . . I am responsible for everything, in effect, except for my responsibility itself, for I am not the foundation of my being. . . . I am condemned to be wholly responsible for myself" (p. 641).

The notion of pure and total freedom paradoxically tends to obscure its own foundation in a logic of mastery and domination that denies playful ambiguity and affirms alienated oppositions or fatal splits. Each of a pair of opposites is internally a totality that expels all alterity onto the "other." It is forbidden to recognize sameness in the other or otherness in the same. The one is the scapegoat for the other. And there is a total divide between the for-itself and the in-itself as well as between contingency and necessity. Both the for-itself and the in-itself are originally contingent. The for-itself undertakes a totalizing, dialectical appropriation of being to recuperate itself and master the situation in light of the supreme desire or end of being in-itself-for-itself or God. But the higher totality, which Christianity placed in divinity and Hegel in Absolute Knowledge, is for Sartre an impossible dream. Man defined in terms of the ultimate project or supreme fiction of being in-itself-for-itself is a useless passion. He cannot join the two radical contingencies into the one necessary totality or wholeness that is the final end of all his projects in the world.

This tension between a notion of freedom as pure and total

and a notion of freedom as always already situated is basic to the hesitations, equivocations, and paradoxes of Sartre's text. The distinction between phenomenological ontology and metaphysics functions to divert attention from it. When Sartre terms his work a study in phenomenological ontology, he seems to place himself in a position to offer a purely descriptive account of the structures of being or the way things are. Of course, his concepts, problems, and framework are heavily indebted to the metaphysical tradition. And the tension in his text is a reworking of a tension in the tradition itself, which reveals how his thought is already situated in a context from which he tries to free himself. The renewed displacement of a tension between submerged supplementarity and the internally subverted attempt to master it through analysis and dialectics is perhaps the nonlinear story of that tradition. But denial of a relation to the tradition simply enables the tradition to repossess one's own discourse in a relatively blind way. Sartre, for example, presents the quest to be in-itself-for-itself as a simple ontological given rather than as a project situated within the Western metaphysical tradition. Thus, when he suggests a move beyond that project and the double binds or fatal splits that both motivate and frustrate it, he can do so only in the mode of apocalyptic pronouncement. He does not undertake a sustained "deconstructive" reading of that tradition, which would attempt to situate his own discourse in relation to it. And the interplay between a centering movement of appropriation and a decentering movement of contestation in his own discourse remains relatively unaccounted for and uncontrolled.

Part One of *Being and Nothingness* begins with the indication of a frustrated apocalypse that makes one think of *Nausea* or, more generally, of the narrative structure of the detective story: the Introduction made a false start and led the philosophical inquiry astray. A seeming clue to the solution of problems was misleading:

Our inquiry has led us to the heart of being. But it has also led us into an impasse, since we have not been able to establish the connection between the two regions of being that we have discovered. No doubt this is because we have chosen a bad perspective to conduct our inquiry. Descartes found himself faced with an analogous problem when he had to deal with the relations between soul and body. Then he advised us to look for the solution on the field of fact where the union between thinking substance and extended substance was effected, that is, in the imagination. His advice is valuable; to be sure, our concern is not that of Descartes and we do not conceive of the imagination as he did. But what we can retain is the reminder that it is not proper [*il ne convient pas*] first to separate the two terms of a relation in order to try to join them together again: the relation is a synthesis. Consequently the *results* of analysis can not be covered over again by the moments of this synthesis. [*EN*, p. 38]

Sartre here senses that his own analytic turn threatens to repeat the mind/body dualism of the metaphysical tradition. And to avoid this threat he draws a rather indirect lesson from a "founding father" of that tradition who is often seen as the most extreme exponent of the mind/body dualism. Sartre, however, does not look to the imagination as both mediation and supplement of the relationship between mind and body—a role it enigmatically plays in Descartes. Nor does he attempt to provide a theoretical articulation for the problem of transphenomenality in terms of supplementarity and "originary" ambiguity and present the repression of this problem as a source of the impasse. He turns rather to a dialectical formulation and somewhat surprisingly uses Descartes's authority to enunciate the idea that it is appropriate to begin with an original synthesis. Analysis can never be congruent with this synthesis and its "moments." The Introduction led to an impasse because it was analytic and abstract. To find a way out, one must locate "the concrete [that] can only be the synthetic totality of which consciousness, like the phenomenon, constitutes only a moment" (p. 38). The quest for this synthetic totality leads immediately to humanism. "The concrete is man in the world with that specific union of man with the world that Heidegger, for example, terms 'being-in-the-world'" (p. 38).

As an "example," Sartre identifies Heidegger's *Dasein* with human reality—an identification more or less plausible on the basis of a certain reading of *Being and Time*, which Heidegger subsequently took extreme pains to dispel. *Dasein*—the problematic locus for an inquiry into being that exceeds human reality and situates it—is unproblematically interpreted by Sartre as identical with human reality. To escape the impasse generated by certain classical analytic distinctions, Sartre looks to another classical analytic distinction—that between the abstract and the concrete. And the concrete is man. Man becomes the new beginning for Sartre's inquiry.

But new impasses are in store, and the sphinxlike enigma seemingly resolved by the answer "man" is regenerated in the textual drama that ensues. Man is conceived by Sartre in relation to the theological and metaphysical tradition. He is the fundamental desire or original project to be God as wholeness, concrete synthetic totality, or in-itself-for-itself. But defined in these terms, man is an ontological failure: he succeeds in realizing only a missing God. In a radical secular displacement of the theological tradition, the hidden God becomes the missing God (*le Dieu manqué*). Man is revealed in the course of *Being and Nothingness* not to be the concrete synthetic totality with which Sartre appears to take his new beginning at the outset of Part One.

In Chapter I of Part One, Sartre inquires into man in terms of consciousness as the origin of negation, and consciousness as a pure nihilating spontaneity is equated with human freedom. In Part Two, the for-itself (related or equated with freedom and consciousness) is explicated in terms of its structures and its relation to temporalization. The for-itself "makes time" in its open but futile dialectical quest to appropriate self and world in realizing the impossible totality. Two things remain equivocal beginning with the turn to man at the outset of Part One: (1) What is the relationship between man and the for-itself? (2) Are there alternatives to the original human desire to become a totality—a project that for Sartre must end in failure?

These equivocations emerge most forcefully in the second chapter of Part One—Sartre's famous discussion of bad faith. Here as elsewhere in the text, Sartre for the most part treats man as if he were identical with freedom, consciousness, or the for-itself. And freedom itself is presented in an equivocal or two-faced way: in a possibly dominant sense, it is seen as pure and total in contradiction to the meaningless in-itself; in a submerged sense, it is discussed as always already implicated or situated in the world.

Given its displaced theological resonance, bad faith might be conceived as secularized pious fraud. It is an escape or evasion from freedom and anxiety, which takes the form of self-deception. To the extent that freedom is pure and total, however, man is necessarily in a condition of bad faith, which becomes analogous to the Fall. The primary form of bad faith that receives theoretical articulation in Sartre is that in which man in his freedom tries to become a thing (or the for-itself an in-itself). This was the bad faith of the solid bourgeois in *Nausea*. In *Being and Nothingness*, it is the bad faith of the waiter who identifies entirely with his role. From this perspective, even good faith is in bad faith, for in it one seeks sincerity as a state in which one is totally coincident with oneself and has the solidity of the thing. Two other key examples of bad faith in *Being and Nothingness* point to a form of it that does not attain theoretical articulation in the early Sartre—perhaps because it was too close to Sartre's own frame of mind. The case of the woman who distractedly leaves her hand in the hand of a seducer and the case of the homosexual who rejects the other's designation of him through this label are analogous to the attitude of Antoine Roquentin in *Nausea*. In these cases, the question is not of an escape from freedom but of an identification of the self in terms of a pure freedom not really implicated in the world. Or, if there is an escape from freedom, it is from a freedom that is itself not pure and total but already at play and at stake in existence. This freedom is radically ambiguous in the way it overlaps the world. And in so far as Sartre's own analysis presents freedom as originally pure and total, it is itself in bad faith from this point of view.

Sartre's dominant tendency does attempt to represent freedom as internally problematic (the for-itself is what it is not and is not what it is) but as originally pure and total within itself. This dominant tendency is forceful in Sartre's effort to distinguish himself from Freud. Bad faith is of course Sartre's replacement for the unconscious. Why does Sartre reject the unconscious and insist that everything in human behavior is conscious? He offers two unproblematic reasons: the unconscious may be taken as a myth; or it may be seen positivistically as a causal determinant that reduces man to the level of a thing. Freud, it is true, does at times oscillate between these seemingly opposite poles of the explanatory spectrum in discussing the unconscious. More problematic is Sartre's nonrecognition of the most revolutionary aspects of Freud's notion of the unconscious, which seem to provide theoretical articulation for certain of Sartre's own submerged tendencies. In these aspects, the unconscious is not a causal or mythical entity behind the scenes, controlling consciousness and potentially open to full reappropriation by the ego in quest of identity and mastery. It is not a full "text" present beneath the text of consciousness but what is radically "other" yet within the same text as consciousness. This internal alterity can not be directly known and its possession is always deferred or displaced. It is the "other" in the self that eludes full control by reflexive consciousness. And one may be blind to it in full daylight. In a sense, it bespeaks the "originary" ambivalence of freedom in the world. As Jacques Derrida formulates this "notion" of the Freudian unconscious:

The unconscious is not, as we know, a hidden, virtual, and potential self-presence. It is differed—which no doubt means that it is woven out of differences, but also that it sends out, that it delegates, representatives or proxies; but there is no chance that the mandating subject "exists" somewhere, that it is present or is "itself," and still less chance that it will become conscious. In this sense, contrary to the terms of an old debate, strongly symptomatic of the metaphysical investments it has always assumed, the "unconscious" can no more be classed as a "thing" than as anything else; it is no more of a thing than an implicit or masked consciousness. This radical alterity, removed from every possible mode of presence, is characterized by irreducible after-effects, by delayed effects. In order to describe them, in order to read the traces of the "unconscious" traces (there are no conscious traces), the language of presence or absence, the metaphysical speech of phenomenology, is in principle inadequate.[5]

In my own "description" of the unconscious, I intentionally used language that Sartre in *Being and Nothingness* applies to prereflective consciousness and later to lived experience. On one level, it might seem that the difference between Sartre and

Freud is purely terminological. Freud seems to identify consciousness with knowledge and to appeal to a notion of the unconscious to account for "what" escapes this identity. Sartre distinguishes sharply between consciousness and knowledge and discusses in terms of prereflective consciousness what Freud treats in terms of the unconscious. This formulation is plausible, but only on one level. Sartre's resistance to Freud's theoretical notion of an unconscious is related to his internal resistance to giving theoretical status to his own submerged tendencies, which radically place in question the idea of a pure and total freedom of man in the world.[6] On an explicit level, Sartre tends to present bad faith in terms of a masked consciousness and to employ the language of phenomenology in discussing it. When the for-itself is personalized, this approach justifies a notion of the total responsibility of the individual (a great metaphysical investment).

Sartre's own discussion of bad faith seems to bring his text into a bind or blind alley, where bad faith is not only "the immediate and permanent menace of every project of the human being" (p. 111), but also a necessary outcome of the mere contact of freedom with the world. The first of Sartre's two apocalyptic footnotes in *Being and Nothingness* functions to provide relatively ungrounded hope not only for man but for the movement of Sartre's text as well: "If it is indifferent whether one is in good or in bad faith, because bad faith recaptures good faith and slides to the very origin of the project of good faith, that does not mean that we can not radically escape bad faith. But this supposes a self-recovery [*une reprise*] of the corrupted being by itself which we shall call authenticity, the description of which has no place here" (p. 111). The last phrase of this note might lead one to believe that the description of authenticity finds a place somewhere else in Sartre. Indeed, Sartre's intention was to provide it in a sequel to *Being and Nothingness* on ethics and, more "concretely," in the fourth volume of *Les Chemins de la liberté*. These projects, which were to give content to the apocalyptic promise, miscarried: the concept of authenticity or its analogues remained empty. The basic equivocation in the conception of the relationship between man and consciousness (or freedom) was apparent in the last sentence of Part One, which prefigured the sections to come: "In the light of these remarks, we can now approach the ontological study of consciousness inasmuch as it is not the totality of the human being but the instantaneous kernel [*le noyau instantané*] of this being" (p. 116).

"The instantaneous kernel": Sartre can formulate the elusive relationship between man and consciousness only by appealing to an extremely enigmatic metaphor. In the conceptual edifice built in the light of this bewildering metaphor, Sartre often identifies man and consciousness or freedom, and he continues to equivocate about the status of freedom itself. In Part Three, moreover, a further equivocation is added to that between pure, total freedom and situated freedom. Until Part Three, the for-itself is not discussed in personal or individual terms. Indeed, it is impersonal or prepersonal, as in Sartre's earlier conceptions of consciousness. In Part Three, the for-itself becomes personal in a theoretically problematic way. The personalization or individualization comes with a perhaps dominant emphasis on pure and total freedom that rejects internal alterity and allows for a notion of total individual responsibility. Beginning with the third part, *Being and Nothingness* becomes in large measure a book "about" the individual—but it does so in the same gesture through which it becomes a book "about" the social other.

In Part Three, the "other" surges onto the scene. Solipsism is not disproved in any purely logical manner. The "reef of solipsism" is avoided by textual navigation, which points to the ontological presence of the "other" as it is revealed phenomenologically in an experience such as that of shame. But the "other" in Part Three is presented in terms of total alterity analogous to the presentation of the in-itself at the end of the Introduction. The separation between self and other replicates that between the for-itself and the in-itself. An "other" can only be an in-itself for my for-itself. If I recognize an "other" as a for-itself, it is at the cost of having my own for-itself reduced to the status of a subservient in-itself. In view of the Medusa-like "look" of the "other," interpersonal relations are a zero-sum game whose rule is petrify or be petrified. This view informs the discussion of "concrete relations with others," which must necessarily take the form of conflict. Before the appearance of the "other," my body is not other to me; it is part of my lived subjectivity on a prereflective level. My body becomes other to me and a basis is laid for an experiential mind/body dualism only with the up-surge of the "other," which enables or constrains me to take the perspective of the "other" on myself and feel the alterity of my body. The latent "schizophrenic" split between prereflective and reflective consciousness is materialized, and it is supplemented by a "paranoid" relation to others. Before the "other" appears on the scene, my for-itself is presumably the center of my world. It is the encounter with the "other" that radically decenters my world and causes a hemorrhage of the world away from me and toward the "other." The master/slave dialectic of Hegel receives a powerful rendition in Sartre's account of interpersonal relations. But for Sartre it does not allow of reconciliation in a mutual recognition of the self in the "other." The dialectic of self and "other" remains open at the price of total war.

It is important to repeat the assumption of Sartre's famous analysis of "concrete relations with others," which finds its dramatic summation in the play *No Exit* (*Huis clos*): Hell is other people. Not only is the concrete individual identified with the for-itself for the purposes of the analysis. The for-itself is pre-sented as pure and total freedom, which allows of no internal alterity or overlap with the "other." I am not seen as always already decentered by an "other" within me. Nor am I both the same as and different from the "other." Scapegoating (such as the scapegoating of the Jew in one of Sartre's related analyses) is not interpreted as a mode of defense in which the denial of the "other" (the Jew) in me is related to the repression of me (the anti-Semite) in the "other." Sartre's analysis itself scapegoats the "other" by projecting all alterity onto it in order to preserve the integrity of the for-itself. His own textual praxis doubles the equivocations and double binds of the alienated relationships he tracks. And the synchronic dimension of the argument in *Being and Nothingness* disappears, to give way to a deceptively pure diachronic development. Before the disorienting "look" of the "other," I am in control of the situation. Prereflective consciousness, reflection, and alterity are not simultaneous structures that generate comparable threats both within and without the self. My loss of mastery and the decentering of the "I" are derived from the upsurge of the "other." And again, the impasses of the text related to its own unthematized equivocations allow for only apocalyptic hope, which comes once more in a boltlike footnote: "These considerations do not exclude the possibility of a morality of deliverance and salvation. But this can be attained only at the end of a radical conversion of which we cannot speak here" (p. 484).

It is immediately after this footnote that Sartre offers his analysis of the group. Perhaps the most striking characteristic of this analysis is its unacknowledged theoretical uncertainty and *ad hoc* use of the category of the ontological, which implicitly renders dubious its distinction from the empirical. Sartre in Part Three has virtually identified pure and total freedom with the for-itself of the person or the individual. In his analysis of the group, he extends this theoretically unfounded identification to allow for a distinction between the first person singular and the first person plural as well as between the status of the first person plural as subject and its status as object. Instead of providing a theoretical justification for these asymmetries, he masks the absence of justification by asserting a further asymmetry between language and thought: "'We' can be subject and, in this form, it is assimilable to a plural of 'I.' And, certainly, the parallelism between grammar and thought is in many cases doubtful; perhaps one must even revise entirely the question and study the relation of language to thought in an entirely new form" (p. 484).

Sartre asserts that the "we-subject," unlike Heidegger's *Mitsein* or being-with-others, lacks ontological status. The experience of community exists, but it is a purely psychological phenomenon—"a purely subjective '*Erlebnis*'" (p. 502). Sartre observes that, in modern society, community is unstable and the idea of human solidarity functions in the bourgeoisie as a means of denying both its own internal anarchy and its class conflict with the proletariat. These considerations would seem to lead to the problem of social structure and ideology. But in this text they become the pretext for an *ad hoc* invocation of the category of the ontological, which thereby loses a critical dimension. In contrast to the "we-subject," the "us-object" is given a reality that is more than psychological. (The "us" is like the "me" but the "we" is not like the "I.") And the notion of the "third" ("le tiers") is employed to show how the group, such as the exploited pro-letariat, is unified by the objectifying other (pp. 487ff.). But there is no notion of praxis whereby the us-object may become a we-subject with other than psychological status. And the us-object is itself different from the we-subject only up to a point. The limiting us-object of humanity as a whole remains an empty concept, for it requires unification by the missing God or the absolute third. "The limiting-concept of humanity (as the total-ity of the us-object) and the limiting-concept of God imply each other and are correlative" (p. 495). There is no indication of the possibility of a universalizing social project that totalizes in the name of man but remains dialectically open (Sartre's later exis-tential Marxism). These observations complicate considerably the problem of the passage from *Being and Nothingness* to the *Critique*. A minimal reservation is that this passage cannot be seen in terms of a simple model of movement from indi-vidualism to social theory via the use of the presumably new concept of the "third" in the later work.[7] A basic point is that the intervention of the individual in Part Three of *Being and Nothing-ness* is problematic, and the theoretical problem is compounded by the discussion of the group.

The treatment of language in the third and fourth parts of *Being and Nothingness* is hardly "entirely new," but it provides the foundation for Sartre's later objections to a certain kind of structuralism. It is significant that a sustained discussion of lan-guage comes so late in the text and in such an ancillary way. The problem of language is not, for example, raised in the Introduc-tion. There is no argument to justify the privileging of the prep-ositions "for" and "in" to designate "regions" of being. One might argue that the introductory discussion of transphenom-enality might give rise to a notion of the "between-itself" re-lated to the problem of "originary" ambiguity.[8] When language is treated, it is not related to the problem of ambiguity. Instead, language is presented as mastered by the notions of the for-itself and the in-itself. In Part Three, a discussion of language is inserted between the topics love and masochism in "concrete relations with others": language is an instrument of seduction (pp. 440–41). The theoretical basis of a conception of language as the expression of the for-itself in relation to the other becomes explicit in Part Four. Language is the living expression of truth as the intentional meaning of the projecting for-itself. By contrast, language appears as an impersonal structure governed by laws only when it is dead and considered an inert in-itself:

> But if the sentence pre-exists the word, then we are referred to the speaker [*discoureur*] as the concrete foundation of discourse.... Words... are only the traces of the passage of sentences, as highways are only the traces of the passage of pilgrims or caravans. The sentence is a project that can be interpreted only in terms of the nihilation of a given (the very one which one wishes to *designate*) in terms of a posited end (its *designation* which itself supposes other ends in relation to which it is only a means).... The sentence is a moment of the free choice of myself.... People in considering speech take it *once it is dead*, that is *once it has been spoken*, and breathe into it an impersonal life and a force, affinities and repulsions that one in fact borrowed from the personal freedom of the for-itself that speaks. [Pp. 598–99]

This metaphysics of meaning reduces language to the opposition between a living truth of the intentional, projecting for-itself and a deadly counterfinality of rule-bound structure (*parole* and *langue* in another formulation of the metaphysical opposition)—an opposition that language both generates and overflows. In this conception, Sartre does not see language as simultaneously decentering the speaking subject and enabling the speaking subject to attempt to center language on himself and his projects. He unproblematically presents language as centered on the intentional subject or agent.

Part Four does, however, offer a textual movement that raises problems analogous to those fleetingly evoked in the introductory discussion of transphenomenality. They can be seen by following Sartre's somewhat harried pilgrimage from the project for an existential psychoanalysis through play to viscosity.

Existential psychoanalysis represents Sartre's attempt to apply his basic concepts in a method that remains central in his later works and that he later tries to integrate with Marxism. In *Being and Nothingness*, the formulation of the project for an existential psychoanalysis (which Sartre already relates to a study of Flaubert as well as to one of Dostoevsky) rests on a militantly "centering" concept of dialectical totalization. But the assumption of total unity in the life of a person leads not to the Freudian unconscious but to the original choice of being that apocalyptically condenses and totalizes a life. Existential psychoanalysis explicates the specific way a free being chooses to be or to live the impossible project of attempting to be God. Everyone freely falls into the repetitive pattern of a will to fail by attempting to appropriate the world, recuperate the self, and be justified as a necessary in-itself-for-itself:

> It is a matter of finding again, under the partial and incomplete aspects of the subject, the veritable concreteness of his impulse toward being, his original relation to himself, to the world and to the other, in the unity of *internal* relations and of a fundamental project.... What best captures the fundamental project of human reality is that man is the being who projects being God.... The *principle* of this psychoanalysis is that man is a totality and not a collection; consequently, he expresses himself entirely in the most insignificant and the most superficial behavior—in other words, there is not a taste, a mannerism, or a human act that is not revealing. [Pp. 649–650, 653, 656]

The "totalitarian," if not inquisitorial, premise about the nature of a life reveals "the truth of man" (p. 654). The fundamental choice that is the instantaneous kernel of a life is a "radical decision" that represents "the veritable psychic irreducible" (p. 647). The original choice of being replaces the Freudian complex. Like the complex, it is "totalitarian" and "anterior to logic"—it "gathers up in a prelogical synthesis the totality of the existent and, as such, is the center of reference for an infinity of polyvalent significations" (p. 658). The original choice of being is thus a transcendental signified—an ultimate meaning of a life, an origin and an end—which gives the essential sense of various and seemingly disparate or ambiguous phenomena. But unlike the complex, it is a choice—the prelogical choice of a paradoxically pure, total freedom, which is not deliberate but for which one bears total responsibility. (The centering totalization that Sartre earlier rejected on the level of Husserl's transcendental ego he now affirms on the level of prereflective consciousness or lived experience—a level on which the individual may not have self-conscious control but does presumably have total responsibility.) "A being does not collapse into dust and one can discover in it this unity—of which substance is only a caricature—and which must be a unity of responsibility, a loveable or hateful unity, blamable or praiseworthy, in brief personal" (pp. 647–48). In the face of this prereflective intentional unity and total moral responsibility, the original choice of being raises the question: saved or damned.

To interpret this frame of reference as a secular displacement of a radical Christian viewpoint (Calvinism, Jansenism) would be superfluous. To call it exaggerated would be an understatement. With reference to its later applications in Sartre's existential biographies, it is perhaps pertinent to note that existential psychoanalysis with its assumption of unity (the original choice of being) within unity (the totalization of a life) is involved in a quest for origins that invariably becomes fictive and even mythical as it conveys the "truth" about man. The problem is that the form of discourse that tracks down the appropriative quest of a putatively free being is itself appropriative of that being and resists elements in the other that contest (perhaps intentionally or self-consciously) the totalizing intentionality of the man-who-would-be-God. Nowhere is the tendency of Sartre's pure and total freedom to become the ideological mask for a "totalizing" logic of appropriation and surveillance more evident than in the project for an existential psychoanalysis. Perhaps the unintended lesson of that project is that the one engaged in it is involved in what might be called a game of winner loses. The existential house of being becomes a panopticon in which the analyst plays a godlike game in his totalizing "look" at the other. A specific analysis of the manner in which this occurs will have to be deferred to our discussion of Sartre's "concrete" existential biographies.

The section of *Being and Nothingness* on existential psychoanalysis is followed by a brief discussion of the relation of knowledge to appropriation. All knowledge is appropriation—

an observation that reflects back on the project for an existential psychoanalysis and the role of the analyst's "helping hand" in bringing the individual to self-knowledge. Indeed, the theme of appropriation becomes insistent in Part Four, and it is directly related to the fundamental project to recuperate self and world. The for-itself in its relations with the "other" invariably behaves like a capitalist during the stage of primitive accumulation: its project is one of limitless appropriation in conflict with the "other." But within a few pages of the section on existential psychoanalysis, a brief discussion of play intervenes and seems to disrupt momentarily the theme of appropriation.

Sartre contrasts play with the spirit of seriousness, but the contrast depends upon the opposition between subjectivity and objectivity. Seriousness is objective: it attributes more reality to the world than to oneself and to oneself in the degree to which one belongs to the world. Materialism is a serious doctrine, and revolutionaries are serious people. They "know themselves on the basis of the world that crushes them and they want to change this world that crushes them." All serious thought is "a dismissal of human reality in favor of the world." The serious man gives himself the solidity of the rock and is thus in bad faith. "Marx posited the first dogma of the serious when he affirmed the priority of the object over the subject and man is serious when he takes himself for an object" (p. 669).

By contrast, "play, like Kierkegaardian irony, releases subjectivity." "What," Sartre rhetorically asks, "is a game if not an activity of which man is the first origin?" The game is the subjective expression of human freedom. "As soon as man apprehends himself as free and wishes to use his freedom, whatever his anguish may be, moreover, his activity is play" (p. 669). The goal of man in play is not to possess but "to attain himself as a certain being, precisely the being who is in question in his being." In play the desire to do is still reducible to the desire to be, but the being in question is "absolute freedom which is the very being of the person." The seemingly authentic playful project has freedom as its foundation and goal. It therefore "merits a special study. Indeed, it differentiates itself radically from all other projects in that it aims at a radically different type of being" (p. 670). For Sartre, the study of the relation of the playful project to the project of being God belongs to ethics, and it presupposes that one has "first defined the nature and the role of purifying reflection (our descriptions have so far aimed only at 'complicitous' [or 'accessory': *complice*] reflection" (p. 670).

I have summarized most of Sartre's page-and-a-half discussion of play, which looks forward both to the Conclusion of *Being and Nothingness* and to the unwritten book on ethics. It also seems to resonate with the initial reference to Nietzsche, but the notion of play in all its disseminating dimensions is not developed in a Nietzschean fashion. In however transient a manner, the discussion of play does seem to disrupt the appropriating movement and provide some notion of an alternative to the fundamental project to be in-itself-for-itself or God. Nevertheless, the brief discussion of play is caught up in Sartre's equivocations. It is based on the subject/object dichotomy, in which play is placed on the side of subjectivity. Sartre's analysis is controlled by narrowly humanistic assumptions about origins. It seems to exclude a revolutionary project mindful of the importance of play. And play is contrasted with a form of bad faith (seriousness as thinglike identity) in a way that equates it with what is another form of bad faith (pure freedom of the human being or person). Indeed, when Sartre discusses irony earlier in the text, it occurs in the opening paragraph of the section on bad faith. Irony is termed one of "those subtle behaviors" that "lead us further into the inwardness of consciousness": "In irony a man annihilates what he posits within one and the same act; he leads us to believe in order not to be believed; he creates a positive object but it has no being other than its nothingness" (p. 84).

Sartre develops this rather conventional conception of irony in a more interesting manner in a piece on Kierkegaard, "L'Universel singulier" (*S. IX*, pp. 152–90). In *Being and Nothingness*, irony is associated with bad faith. The correlation of play with irony cannot but incriminate play. The basic point is that both play and irony are seen in extremely restricted ways. They do not refer to the play of the world and to man's implication in that play, which decenters the humanistic, god-derived project of appropriation. They are, instead, grounded in human subjectivity or pure freedom and come at the expense of the "other" (the serious man in play and all others in irony). This is a relatively safe play in which man is not fully at stake. And this conception of play does not foster what Nietzsche termed "gay science" or "joyful wisdom."[9]

Sartre in *Being and Nothingness* doubts whether the game itself is "pure of all appropriative tendency" (p. 670)—or what Nietzsche would term will to power. But Sartre, unlike Nietzsche, is in no "position" to explore the interplay between decentering playfulness and centering appropriation in an open and self-questioning way. After the evanescent evocation of play, his discussion returns to the dominant theme that all projects of doing or having are reducible to forms of appropriation based on the fundamental human project to be a totality. Within a few pages, however, the pilgrimage of the for-itself in the world is interrupted by another perilous phenomenon—the viscous, or the slimy (*le visqueux*). The for-itself threatens to sink into this slough of despond.

The discussion of the viscous refers one to an originary ambiguity that signals danger both for sharp analytic distinctions and for the totalizing project of appropriation or mastery in the world. In the viscous, the for-itself is compromised in its freedom, and its purity is contaminated. As in the case of transphenomenality—but in a less sublimated way—there is a threat that may expropriate the free appropriator. The viscous has neither the transparency of water (a metaphor for the for-itself) nor the solidity of rock (a metaphor for the in-itself): "Immediately the viscous reveals itself as essentially fishy [*louche*], because its fluidity exists in slow motion.... Viscosity is the agony of water" (p. 699). Sartre's heavily metaphoric, or "literary," discussion of the viscous is as anxiety-ridden as the experiences he treats. The liminal or threshold status of the viscous, with its intimation of incestuous complicity with the "other," conjures up in Sartre an almost uncanny discourse—one convulsed paragraph runs on for five dense pages (pp. 697–702). In it, Sartre associates the themes of loss of mastery, limits to appropriation, revenge of the in-itself on the for-itself, metamorphosis, antivalue, death, and the sexual threat of the feminine to the masculine.

The viscous "is a soft, yielding action, a moist and feminine sucking; it lives obscurely under my fingers, and I sense it like a dizziness. . . . It draws me to it as to the bottom of a precipice." The clammy, clamping trap of the viscous leaves its sticky traces on the assertive and projecting for-itself. The revenge of the in-itself is a "sickly sweet, feminine revenge, which will be symbolized on another level by the quality 'sugary.' Indeed, "a sugary sliminess is the ideal of the slimy [or viscous]; it symbolizes the sugary death of the for-itself (like that of the wasp which sinks into the jam" (pp. 696 ff).

If we consider the viscous, we notice (although it mysteriously conserves *all* its fluidity in slow motion; one must not confound it with purées where a beginning fluidity undergoes abrupt breakages, abrupt stoppages, and where the substance, after beginning to *flow*, fluffs abruptly ass-over-heels) that it presents a constant hysteresis in the phenomenon of transmutation into itself: honey that flows from my spoon into the honey contained in the earthenware jar begins by sculpting the surface; it detaches itself in relief and its fusion with the whole presents itself as a collapse, a resurfacing that appears simultaneously as a *deflation* (one thinks of the importance for infantile sensibilities of the little man made from the gold-beater's skin [bonhomme de baudruche] that one "blows" like glass and that deflates in letting escape a lamentable groan) and as a *display*—the flattening of the full breasts of a woman who stretches out on her back. [Pp. 699]

I have tried to preserve some of the flavor of this passage in the translation, for it is a striking instance of the frenzied outburst of tortured images in the account of the viscous—an account that at times verges on grotesque self-parody. The encounter with the viscous is extended into a discussion of the desire to plug up holes, which, for Sartre, exerts its allure even on the child in a manner whose sexual significance will appear only retrospectively. The woman is condemned to be in the form of a hole: "The obscenity of the feminine sex is that of everything that 'gapes open.' . . . Woman senses her condition as an appeal because she is in the form of a hole" (p. 706). This invidious distinction closes the discussion of the viscous, providing Sartre with the occasion to stress the importance of the existential analysis of "immediate and concrete existential categories" (p. 706). The fascination with the viscous is arrested by recalling man's original project—a call to order that ends Part Four:

> Every human reality is a passion in that it projects losing itself so as to found being and by the same stroke to constitute the in-itself, which escapes contingency by being its own foundation, the *Ens causa sui*, which religions call God. Thus the passion of man is the reverse of that of Christ, for man loses himself as man in order that God may be born. But the idea of God is contradictory and we lose ourselves in vain. Man is a useless passion. [P. 708]

Sartre continues this train of thought in the Conclusion. In the light of the spirit of seriousness where man attributes thinglike solidity to his values, "all human values are equivalent (for they all tend to sacrifice man in order that the self-cause may arise) and... they all are in principle doomed to failure. Thus it amounts to the same thing whether one gets drunk alone or is a leader of nations" (p. 721). It should be noted that these comments apply to man only with reference to the spirit of seriousness and the fundamental project to be in-itself-for-itself. The basic problem in *Being and Nothingness* is whether Sartre can suggest a viable alternative to this project other than in the purely apocalyptic, empty terms of authenticity, purifying reflection, and radical conversion. The final words of *Being and Nothingness* return to this problem:

> Hitherto... the theme that made the unity of all choices of possibles was the value or the ideal presence of the *ens causa sui*. What will become of freedom if it turns its back upon this value? Will freedom carry this value along with it whatever it does and, in its very turning back upon the in-itself-for-itself, will it be reapprehended from behind by the value it wishes to contemplate? Or will freedom, by the very fact that it apprehends itself as a freedom in relation to itself, be able to put an end to the reign of this value?... A freedom that wills itself freedom is in fact a being-which-is-not-what-it-is and which-is-what-it-is-not, and that chooses as the ideal of being, being-what-it-is-not and not-being-what-it-is. This freedom chooses then not to *recover* itself but to flee itself, not to coincide with itself but to be always at a distance from itself. What are we to understand by this being that wills to hold itself in respect, to be at a distance from itself? Is it a question of bad faith or of another fundamental attitude? And can one *live* this new aspect of being? In particular, will freedom by taking itself as an end escape all

*situation*? Or, on the contrary, will it remain situated? Or will it situate itself so much the more precisely and the more individually as it projects itself further in anguish as a conditioned freedom and accepts more fully its responsibility as an existent by whom the world comes into being? All these questions, which refer us to a pure and not a complicitous reflection, can find their reply only on an ethical plane. We shall devote to them a future work. [P. 722]

These questions, which refer to the problem of a critique and a possible "overcoming" of tradition, also point backward to the work the reader has just completed. In that work, these questions not only received an equivocal answer; often they were also inadequately formulated—and in the Conclusion the attempt to distinguish sharply between ontology and metaphysics tended to obscure the problem of a deconstructive reading or immanent critique of the metaphysical tradition as well as the problem of the indebtedness of Sartre's own discourse to that tradition. In Sartre's later work, the moral problem is related to the problem of politics and social action. Is existential Marxism an answer to the questions that end *Being and Nothingness* or, indeed, is it a dialectical transformation of both questions and answers, which reformulates them on a higher plane of theory and practice? Are the questions and answers repeated and displaced, and does Sartre remain the same while becoming different?

It should be useful to begin by reviewing briefly some of Sartre's own specific attempts to situate *Being and Nothingness* in relation to his later thought. In a 1961 essay on Merleau-Ponty, Sartre put forth a notion of what had to be done to overcome the difficulties of *Being and Nothingness*. With particular reference to Merleau-Ponty's position on problems of peace and war, Sartre asserted that one must investigate the *tourniquets* that mark the limits and extent of historical action and that make men victims and accomplices in alienated processes despite good faith. Then he added in a footnote: "Not, as I did in 1942, by an eidetic of bad faith but by the empirical study of our historical fidelities and the inhuman forces that pervert them" (*S. IV*, p. 196). In an interview of 1970, Sartre commented extensively on his progress since the writing of *Being and Nothingness*. He asserted his fidelity to the notion of man as freedom in a situation: "The idea that I have never stopped developing is that, in the last analysis, a person is always responsible for what one has made of him" (*S. IX*, p. 101). But "*Being and Nothingness* retraced an interior experience without any relation to exterior experience—which had become historically catastrophic at a certain moment—of the petty-bourgeois intellectual that I was" (p. 102). Although *Being and Nothingness* was written after the disaster of France in World War II, that historical and collective experience did not have an impact on the book because it was not internalized as Sartre's own experience and made a result of his own praxis. After the war, he passed through another individualist myth—that of heroism—but nonetheless came finally to "true experience, that of society" (p. 101). A stronger historical sense of the situation was related to a diminution of the range of freedom. It now became "this little movement that makes of a totally conditioned social being a person who does not give back the totality of what he or she has received from conditioning" or "this little displacement [*décalage*] in an operation whereby an interiorization re-exteriorizes itself in an act" (pp. 101–02). "There was no idea in *Being and Nothingness*" of the mediating relation of interiorization and exteriorization between the individual and society— "relations of production, the family of one's childhood, the historical past, contemporary institutions" (p. 103). Sartre still rejects Freud's unconscious either as "an ensemble of mechanistic determinations" or as a "mysterious finality" (p. 106). But he believes that his notion of the lived [*le vécu*] in contrast to the conceived [*le conçu*] marks a real progress in accounting for phenomena that concerned Freud without resorting to Freud's notion of the unconscious. "This term [*le vécu*] . . . designates neither the refuges of the preconscious, nor the unconscious, nor the conscious but the field on which the individual is constantly submerged by himself, by his own richnesses, and where consciousness has the wiliness [or ruse—*l'astuce*] to determine itself by forgetfulness [*l'oubli*]" (p. 108). Indeed, for Sartre commenting on himself, "this conception of the lived is what marks my evolution since *Being and Nothingness*" (p. 112).

This self-commentary specifies certain nodal points in a model of "dialectical overcoming" that relates Sartre's early work to his later work. It is partially accurate and partially misleading. The phrase "eidetic of bad faith" is, I think, valuable as a characterization of *Being and Nothingness*, but everything depends upon its interpretation. To term *Being and Nothingness* the account of a purely interior or individual experience—a book "about" the inner self of the isolated individual—obscures some of the most interesting problems in it. Sartre's works after *Being and Nothingness* are, it is true, more directly and extensively concerned with political, historical, and social issues. But it is difficult to accept Sartre's account of the theoretical foundations of his change in emphasis. The notions of interiorization and exteriorization (certainly present in Freud and others) are, by and large, indicative of advances in social psychology. They may readily function ideologically to mask or obscure the more fundamental issue concerning the very understanding of freedom in a situation, because their mediating role is based on a split between "inside" and "outside," which at best leaves equivocal the question of whether freedom is seen as "originally" pure and total. And Sartre's exaggerated conception of the importance of the notion of *le vécu*, or lived experience, conceals the extent to which it is a terminological substitution for his earlier notion of prereflective consciousness, which "covered" the same range of problems. If one accepts Sartre's estimation of the theoretical and philosophical importance of the notion of the lived in his later works, one would have to argue that the early Sartre understood practically nothing about the nature of the phenomenological enterprise. It is difficult to assess Sartre's claim that in his later works the range of freedom becomes more restricted. Certainly, as the political, social, and historical context comes to be conceived in a more detailed and theoretically relevant way, the situation of freedom becomes more "concrete" and empirically informed. In *Being and Nothingness*, however, freedom seemed paradoxically to be both total and self-effacing or self-nugatory—nothing in effect, but the nothing that made a world of difference in meaning and value. Whatever the range of freedom, the theoretical issue that remains problematic in the later Sartre is the very conception of freedom in its relation to the situation. Sartre's attempt to characterize *le vécu* in his 1970 interview hardly clarified this issue.

On the problem of the impact of World War II, one may at least complicate matters by quoting Sartre against Sartre by quoting Sartre against Lukàcs:

> One needs a great deal of [time] to write a theoretical work. My book *Being and Nothingness*, to which he directly refers, was the result of study begun in 1930. . . . By the winter of 1939–40 I had already worked out my method and my principal conclusions. . . . Lukàcs has the instruments to understand Heidegger, but he will not understand him; for Lukàcs would have to *read* him, to grasp the meaning of sentences one by one. And there is no longer any Marxist, to my knowledge, who is still capable of doing this. Finally, there has existed a whole dialectic—and a very complex one—from Brentano to Husserl to Heidegger: influences, oppositions, agreements, new oppositions, misunderstandings, distortions, denials, surpassings, etc. All this adds up to what one could call an *area history*. Ought we to consider it a pure epiphenomenon? According to what Lukàcs says, yes. Or does there exist some kind of movement of ideas, and does Husserl's phenomenology—as a moment preserved and surpassed—enter into Heidigger's system? In this case the principles of Marxism are not changed, but the *situation* becomes much more complex. [*Search*, p. 39]

This statement on the proper method for intellectual history explicitly relies on the dialectical model that I have been in part contesting. It comes from the work in which Sartre makes his boldest and most forceful attempt to forge an existential Marxist approach to problems, *Search for a Method* (*Question de méthode*). And it suggests that to appreciate Sartre's comments on *Being and Nothingness*, one must raise the further question of the nature of Sartre's later thought not only in relation to his early works but also in relation to itself. Sartre's later writings do not form a homogeneous whole. They are marked by "internal" self-contestation and by "external" tensions in relation to one another—features that render dubious the idea that even his later works are entirely intelligible in accordance with a dialectical model of totalization. One sign of this is the fact that his self-commentaries apply much more to a work like *Search for a Method* than they do (to the extent that they do at all) to the principal text of the *Critique of Dialectical Reason*. If one expects the *Critique* to overcome *Being and Nothingness* in the direction indicated by Sartre's footnote in his 1961 essay on Merleau-Ponty, one will be sorely disappointed. *Search for a Method* provides methodological guides for "the empirical study of our historical fidelities and the inhuman forces that pervert them." But the *Critique* is a study of social ontology and formal sociology—an attempt to delineate the abstract structures of historical intelligibility. I think it very much repeats the structure or problematic of *Being and Nothingness* in so far as a dialectic of alienation replaces an eidetic of bad faith. And there are even some losses in the process that are not dialectically reappropriated. The theoretical work that would perhaps follow more directly from *Search for a Method* was deferred to a second volume of the *Critique*, which would presumably have taken the reader into the field of "concrete" history. This second volume proved to be one more unfulfilled expectation of Sartre's intellectual life. In certain ways, he sees his study of Flaubert as filling this gap and providing the follow-up to *Search for a Method*.

It is perhaps paradoxical but nonetheless theoretically interesting that *Search for a Method* and the *Critique* were published as one text or at least between the covers of the same book, and that Sartre felt constrained to confront the problem of their relationship. The juxtaposition of these two works, which are often taken by commentators as the foundation for a unified field theory of existential Marxism, poses the theoretical problem of the role of dialectics in the later Sartre and, by extension, of the role of dialectics more generally. Are these two works integrated internally and related to each other by a dialectical model of intelligibility? This problem threatens to displace the question of the nature of the relation of the early to the later Sartre: if the later Sartre is not unified or "totalized" dialectically, it becomes less plausible to see a dialectical relationship between his early and his later thought. One is perhaps even led to doubt the validity of the periodization or schematization of his writings in terms of an early and a later stage.

Let us briefly rehearse the argument and inquire into the textual development of *Search for a Method*. The work is divided into four parts: Marxism and Existentialism; the Problem of Mediations and Auxiliary Disciplines; the Progressive-Regressive Method; and the Conclusion. The relationship among these parts is problematic with reference to the explicit theme elaborated in the text—that of dialectical totalization. For among the parts, there seem to be elements of a dialectical progression and, at times more insistently, of repetition and displacement. Repetition is especially obvious in the relationship between the sections on mediations and on the progressive-regressive method, which seem to be about the same set of problems seen from slightly different angles. One blatant sign of repetition is the use of Flaubert as a recurrent motif. One can not plausibly argue that the discussions of Flaubert (one—interrupted by a digression— in the section on mediations and three in the section on the progressive-regressive method) fall into a dialectical pattern of development. What the text *does*, does not entirely conform to what the text *says* about the proper or appropriate form of reasoning. Rather, it transgresses its own rules of method.

The underlying theme of the introductory section on Marxism and existentialism is made explicit in the Conclusion. Existentialism is an ideology or a fragment of knowledge that initially fell outside the totalizing dialectic of Marxism but now seeks to be integrated and ultimately dissolved within Marxism. Existential Marxism, taking account of the contribution of existentialism, will raise that contribution to a higher level of insight and thereby bring existentialism into the truth. The specific contribution of existentialism was its emphasis on the concrete reality and lived experience of human beings, which must be approached on the level of comprehension. Human praxis in history is itself a unifying, totalizing, dialectical movement of thought and action, which provides a basis for theoretical knowledge in the existential comprehension of lived, concrete experience. In the introductory section, the approach of existential Marxism is presented as the outlook of Marx himself and Marxism is declared to be a young philosophy—the philosophy of our time—which has yet to be adequately developed and which can be itself transcended only in the apocalyptic reign of freedom. What might be termed the original existential Marxism of Marx stands as a protestation against its distortion in the hands of Engels, the theorists of the Second International, and contemporary thinkers like Lukàcs and the theorists of the Communist Party in France. This distortion came through the institution of Marxism as a positivistic theory of causal determinism that relied on abstract schemata and prefabricated models for the *a priori* explanation of human events. In the process, the very specificity of the event was lost. What fell outside official Marxism provided the rationale for the emergence of existentialism: the concrete and the lived as vital elements of human praxis. Aside from his own hermeneutic return to Marx, Sartre presents himself in relation to official, dogmatic Marxists in a role analogous to that of Kierkegaard responding to Hegel. In a critical reaction to Hegel's totalizing and totalistic system of conceptual knowledge, Kierkegaard affirmed the irreducibility and specificity of what is lived through and suffered. Kierkegaard pointed to the "scandal" that was sublated in the Hegelian system: "He looks everywhere for weapons to aid him in escaping from the terrible 'mediation'; he discovers within himself oppositions, indecisions, equivocations which cannot be surpassed: paradoxes, ambiguities, discontinuities, dilemmas, etc." (*Search*, p. 11). For Sartre, Kierkegaard "obstinately fixed his stand on poor, frozen paradoxes ultimately referring to an empty subjectivity" and sought refuge in the leap of faith toward God (p. 12). For Sartre, by contrast, Kierkegaard's valuable assertion of "the incommensurability of the real and knowledge" (p. 12) becomes the basis (or the pretext) for an open dialectical approach, which resists the Hegelian closure of Absolute Knowledge. Totalizing praxis seeks mediations between the lived and the conceived, the real and the known. An existential Marxism built on these foundations overcomes the one-sidedness of both subjective, individualistic existentialism and dogmatic, conceptualistic Marxism.

Certain questions may be raised, however, which, while not invalidating Sartre's project, do situate it in a certain way. Does Sartre "sublate" Kierkegaard too readily, by identifying his "position" with subjectivism, the leap of religious faith, and sterile paradoxes? Was not Kierkegaard pointing to what Sartre himself would like to ignore or repress—and what even Kierkegaard attempted to sidestep when he presented religion as the unproblematic point of view for his work as an author? Did not Kierkegaard textually explore the problem of repetition in a way that threatened to expropriate him as author, make impossible any identification of his texts with a dogmatic "position," and raise doubts about the foundations of a totalizing dialectic, however open and unfinished? (One might perhaps raise analogous questions about the texts of Marx himself.) The question of the relationships between existentialism and Marxism is in a sense the same as the question of those between the lived and the conceived, comprehension and explanation, indirect communication and direct knowledge. And there are indications in *Search for a Method* that the relationships in question must, at least in part, be seen in terms of a supplementary interplay that permits a process of mutual grafting not entirely accounted for by a notion of dialectical totalization. Indeed, the very openness of the dialectical method may depend for its intelligibility upon supplementary and repetitive relationships that both invite a project of dialectical totalization and limit it. An open dialectical approach that renounces the imaginary ending of totality may be nothing other than an enterprise that enigmatically merges with repetition. In so doing, it tends unknowingly toward the more hollow forms of repetition to the extent that it fails to raise the explicit question of more creative possibilities, for example, in relation to institutional life.

The last paragraph of the section on existentialism and Marxism is itself enigmatic, if not paradoxical, for it leads to the section on mediations by enunciating a notion that tends to be neither mediated nor supplemented in Sartre's dominant approach:

"The mode of production of material life generally dominates the development of social, political, and intellectual life." . . . Marx's statement seems to me to point to a factual evidence which we cannot go beyond *so long as* the transformation of social relations and technical progress have not freed man from the yoke of scarcity. We are all acquainted with the passage in which Marx alludes to that far-off time: "This reign of freedom does not begin in fact until the time when the work imposed by necessity and external finality shall cease; it is found, therefore, beyond the sphere of material production proper" (*Capital,*

III, p. 873). As soon as there will exist *for everyone* a margin of *real* freedom beyond the production of life, Marxism will have lived out its span; a philosophy of freedom will take its place. But we have no means, no intellectual instrument, no concrete experience which allows us to conceive of this freedom or of this philosophy. [P. 34]

This apocalyptic pronouncement begs for a confrontation with the problem of mediations, especially with reference to existing and possible institutions—a confrontation that Sartre never furnishes. The problems of apocalypse and scarcity will both be taken up again in the *Critique* but in a rather different sense not dialectically related to this passage. In the *Critique*, the apocalyptic moment of the group-in-fusion is inserted into the infernal circle of project and counterfinality rather than offered as a way of breaking it. And scarcity is seen on an ontological level, which equates alterity with alienation in a manner amenable neither to technical nor to the most broadly conceived social solutions.

Before turning to the problem of the relation of *Search for a Method* to the *Critique*, one may note that the difficulties in the former work emerge most forcefully in its Conclusion. The intervening sections on mediations and the progressive-regressive method attempt to encircle the same set of problems: the project, the situation, and mediations between them. In the conclusion, Sartre returns to the more theoretical foundations of an existential Marxism evoked in the introductory section: the importance of man and the distinction between the lived and the conceived:

Within this living universe, man occupies, *for us*, a privileged place. First, because he is able to be historical; that is, he can continually define himself by his own *praxis* by means of changes suffered or provoked and their internalization, and then by the very surpassing of the internalized relations. Second, because he is characterized as the *existent which we are*. In this case the questioner finds himself to be precisely the questioned, or, if you prefer, human reality is the existent whose being is in question in its being. It is evident that this "being-in-question" must be taken as a determination of *praxis* and that the theoretical questioning comes in only as an abstract moment of the total process. [Pp. 167–68]

In a footnote, Sartre elaborates on the first reason why man should be taken as privileged:

Man should not be defined by historicity—since there are some societies without history—but by the permanent possibility of living *historically* the breakdowns which sometimes overthrow societies of repetition. This definition is necessarily a posteriori; that is, it arises at the heart of a historical society, and it is in itself the result of social transformation. But it goes back to apply itself to societies without history in the same way that history itself returns to them to transform them—first externally and then in and through the internalization of the external. [P. 167]

Sartre seems oblivious to the dangers of a "species-imperialism" that centers everything on man, especially when it is defined in terms of historicity as limitless change in the interest of human projects. His footnote narrows the imperialistic assumption of his approach to invidious ethnocentric distinctions within humanity, for he privileges certain societies over others on altogether dubious grounds. Indeed, his conception of the way history returns to "societies without history" threatens to employ the notion of "internalization of the external" as a euphemism for colonialism and imperialism. And the projection of limiting cases onto phenomena obscures the basic problem of the actual and desirable relationships between historicity and repetition in all societies, including modern ones.

For Sartre, historical praxis is the lived experience of man as an existential agent. It is "known" only indirectly through "rational nonknowledge" in comprehension or understanding, in contrast to causal explanation. (Sartre employs *compréhension* very much in the sense in which those involved in the *Methodenstreit* in early twentieth-century Germany used the term *Verstehen*.) Comprehension of lived experience is the basis of communication with the other: although it is nonconceptual, it is the foundation of all concepts and scientific knowledge of the human. The emphasis on comprehension of lived experience is the specific contribution of existentialism to Marxism. The role of comprehension reveals why the dialectical process of totalization must remain open and can never attain totality or the closure of Absolute Knowledge. But at this point a problem arises for dialectical totalization that Sartre does not explicitly articulate. It is analogous to the problem of transphenomenality in *Being and Nothingness* in that it refers one to supplementarity

and displacement. Lived experience, which is the very foundation of dialectical totalization and marks its limit, paradoxically
falls both inside and outside the process of dialectical totalization that it originates. Its "position" vis-à-vis the dialectic is
logically scandalous and undecidable. In this sense, the dialectical totalization both gets off the ground and reaches a continually displaced limit in a fashion indicating that it is not its own
foundation but requires reference to another "principle" both to
enable it to begin and radically to contest it. Sartre's attempt to
center everything on the human project of dialectical totalization
is "in question in its being" in a manner more fundamental than
that which he is willing to entertain explicitly. The dialectic is
open or unfinished because its "foundation" or "origin" is not
intelligible in terms of dialectics.

Turning from *Search for a Method* to the *Critique*, one finds that
the sustained concern for lived experience is no longer in the
foreground of Sartre's investigation. To the extent that the
*Critique* founds the dialectic, it does so with reference not to
lived experience but to conceptual knowledge. Nor are the
mediations between the two the center of Sartre's attention. His
attempt to relate the two works curiously seems in its formulation more "critical" in the Kantian sense than dialectical.[10] At
the very outset of the *Critique*, Sartre offers it as the philosophical or theoretical grounding or condition of possibility for the
methodology of *Search for a Method*: "Everything we have established in *Search for a Method* flows from our agreement on principles with historical materialism. But in so far as we present this
accord as a simple option, among other possible options, we
have done nothing. Our conclusions remain conjectural: we
have proposed certain adjustments in method. These are valid
or at least debatable only if dialectical materialism is true"
(*Critique*, p. 115). In this formulation, the relationship between
the two works is not dialectically demonstrated. The unargued
assumption is that the methodology of *Search* requires a dialectical theory as its ultimate foundation (or "truth") and that the
*Critique* provides it. The validity of this assumption is not immediately self-evident. And, aside from the nondialectical na-

ture of Sartre's own formulation of the problem of relationship, there are other indications that the relationship between the two works raises difficulties for an unsupplemented dialectical model.

The nature of thought in the two works is dissimilar in a way that cannot be explained through the distinction between method and philosophical demonstration: the problem cuts across this distinction and addresses the issue of the nature of critical theory. *Search for a Method* begins with a specific context or historical situation of which it attempts to provide an immanent critique—the nature of contemporary Marxism. In this sense, it resembles Marx's texts, especially *Capital*, which begins with the problem of the commodity form. By contrast, the *Critique* begins in a more abstract and absolute fashion with a discussion of analysis and dialectics, followed by a postulation of a theoretical starting point for rendering intelligible the historical process. It by and large brackets the problem of lived experience for the purposes of the analysis and deals in ideal types or limiting cases, among which it sets up a relatively restricted form of dialectical relationship. It resembles not so much a text by Marx as more or less philosophical exercises in formal sociology, such as Dilthey's *Einleitung in die Geisteswissenschaften* or Weber's *Gemeinschaft und Gesellschaft*. The nature of the Marxism of the *Critique* is dubious enough to have generated considerable controversy, especially with reference to the problem of scarcity. And the question of mediations is developed only in very limited ways. The entire problem of relating *Search for a Method* to the *Critique* is crystallized in Sartre's own doubt about how physically to situate the two texts in relation to each other—a doubt that surfaces, appropriately enough, in the Preface to the entire "book." The very first words of the Preface are:

The two works that compose this volume will appear, I fear, of unequal importance and unequal ambition. Logically, the second [the principal text of the *Critique*] ought to precede the first for which it aims at constituting the critical foundations. But I feared that this mountain of pages would then appear to give birth to a mouse: was it necessary to agitate so much air, to use up so many pens and to fill so much paper in order to arrive at a few methodological considerations? And since, in fact, the second work issued from the first, I preferred to keep the chronological order which, in a dialectical perspective, is always the most meaningful. [*Critique*, p. 9]

What is silenced in this "explanation" (which explains nothing) is the possibility that *Search for a Method* may be neither head nor tail in relation to the *Critique*—that it may have in relation to it a supplementary and not a dialectical "position." Indeed, why does the *Critique* need a methodological companion piece in the position of either preface or appendix (the two are in the same position "logically") if it is true that dialectical totalization spawns its method as it philosophically goes along in an all-encompassing process of becoming? The problem confronting Sartre is somewhat similar to that facing Hegel in the Preface to the *Phenomenology of Mind*. A preface on method is a theoretical impossibility given the assumptions of a dialectical philosophy. Hegel writes what amounts to an antipreface. But even the preface that questions its own existence does, by existing, contest the dialectical totalization it introduces, for it falls outside the spiral of totalization it simultaneously affirms.[11]

The principal text of the *Critique*, read in terms of its explicit theses and reconstructed in a simplified dialectical format, seems relatively straightforward. As Mark Poster puts it: "Though the *Critique* did not include a table of contents to clarify its overall plan, it had a remarkably coherent internal structure. Tracing the intelligible structure of need, Sartre began with the individual and ended with social relations, all encompassed in a magisterially enunciated dialectical network."[12] But, on other levels, the *Critique* is not unproblematic even with respect to its own explicit intentions. The textual development conforms to the notion of dialectical totalization only in the most questionable of ways. I shall not trace in detail the repetitions, oblique movements, gap-shooting leaps in thought, that even the most superficial reading of the *Critique* can reveal. But it is significant that Sartre did try to account for the involuted and tortured "style" of the work by arguing that it reflected the totalizing movement of the dialectic itself and that any departures from the dialectic were of purely anecdotal interest. In answer to a question about the writing of the *Critique*, Sartre asserted in an interview of 1965:

First, one must be frank. I could certainly have written better—these are anecdotal questions—the *Critique of Dialectical Reason*. I mean by that that if I had reread it once more, in cutting it and tightening it up, it would not perhaps have such a compact aspect. Thus, from this point of view, one must nonetheless take account of the anecdotal and the individual. But except for this self-criticism, it would nevertheless have very much resembled the work that it is because at bottom each sentence is so long, so full of parentheses, of quotation marks, of "inasmuch as's," etc., only because each sentence represents the unity of a dialectical movement. [*S. IX*, p. 75]

In providing a dialectical rationale for the nature of his writing, Sartre reduces stylistic considerations to the most elementary editorial level. Paradoxically, he excludes the relevance of biographical elements that he deems so important in the case of others. The disconcerting problem avoided by Sartre is that, in the writing or textual praxis of the *Critique*, it is often difficult to distinguish what is due to dialectical totalization and what stems from varieties of repetition that displace and contest the dialectical model. Indeed, the well-known conditions under which he produced the *Critique* lend psychological plausibility to a relatively mechanical model of repetition in interpreting its relation to his earlier works, notably *Being and Nothingness*. For Sartre worked in a way that indicated the cathartic retelling of an old story, one that the notion of radical conversion in the writing of the *Critique* did more to conceal than to reveal. [13]

The initial sections of the *Critique* on analysis and dialectics attempt to argue that dialectical reason includes analysis in its totalizing movement. When analysis falls outside the dialectic, it becomes abstract and ideological in its attempt to apply to man the methods adapted to the study of things. Natural science is the proper sphere of analysis. In relation to man, analysis is appropriate only to the study of inert or dead totalities, whose full comprehension requires reinsertion into the dialectial totalization that is their ultimate source of meaning and intelligibility. In this sense, analysis in the sciences of man (as employed, for example, in structuralism) is suited solely to the investigation of counterfinalities that can be fully understood only with reference to intentional projects of an inherently dialectical sort.

Much of Sartre's energy in these opening sections is devoted to an attack on the idea of a dialectic of nature as developed by Engels and later theorists (pp. 115–62). Sartre argues not only that knowledge of nature is based on human constructs but also that man never knows nature as intimately as he knows his own reality. A dialectic of nature makes human history dependent upon the laws of the exterior world and offers no comprehension of human activity from the inside. The knowledge of matter is different enough from that of man to require specifically different principles for the investigation of human reality. In any case, the advocates of a dialectic of nature paradoxically impose human ideas on nature and then attempt to derive a knowledge of man from the laws of nature. The Marxist dialectic is for Sartre specifically human and depends upon the dialectical nature of human praxis. In the sphere of history, the dialectic applies simultaneously to the ontological object of knowledge (the social history of man) and to the epistemological subject (man himself). Only on these grounds can one establish the dialectical intelligibility of history that Marx himself never provided on a philosophical level, but which is necessary for Marxist method in the human sciences and for Marxist revolution.

Yet Sartre's own discussion of analysis and dialectics is itself paradoxical in its reliance on analytic oppositions (man/nature, inside/outside) and neo-Kantian assumptions to provide the basis for dialectics. His arguments recapitulate those of the advocates—including Windelband, Rickert, Dilthey, and Weber—of a cultural and social anthropology, or *Geisteswissenschaft*, separate and distinct from natural science during the German *Methodenstreit* early in the century. In terms of *Being and Nothingness*, the criticism of a dialectic of nature parallels the earlier critique of the spirit of seriousness and causal determinism (or the reduction of man to the status of a thing having a nature). The apparent paradox is that a dialectical approach presumably "begins" with a synthetic totalization concerned with the interactions of man and nature and overcomes sharp analytic oppositions such as those between nature and culture, matter and man. Nature in Sartre's discussion is initially perceived as radically other on the disjunctive model of the in-itself in *Being and Nothingness*. And no problem of transphenomenality interposes itself to suggest a relationship between alterity and supplementarity. Nature in the first instance is brute matter or mere thing. All knowledge of it is a projective construct of the human being. And the dialectic is specifically human and applies to human history as the direct or indirect story of intentional human projects. The dialectic of nature is at best derivative and, in any case, irrelevant for the comprehension of human affairs.

This narrowly analytic conception of the basis of dialectics informs the investigation of human history in its formal structures of intelligibility or conditions of possibility. Sartre begins by privileging the putatively "translucent praxis of the organic individual" in a manner comparable to the dominant treatment of the for-itself in *Being and Nothingness*. The difference is that in the *Critique* Sartre starts by individualizing or personalizing the for-itself; the dialectic is possible because the praxis of the organic individual is itself dialectical: "If one refuses to see the original dialectical movement in the individual and in his enterprises in producing his life, in objectivating himself, one must give up the dialectic or make it the immanent law of history" (*Critique*, p. 101).

Initially, individuals separated from one another confront brute, meaningless matter. Their free, intentional, translucent praxis is in this confrontation stolen from them in ways that generate counterfinality. At this point in the discussion, scarcity intervenes. The appropriation of scarce matter by competing individuals makes each man *excédentaire* (excessive, expendable, supernumerary) for the other. Scarce matter creates a lack defining competing needs in a way that makes others *de trop*. Thus, lack (in the form of scarcity) and excess (in the form of the expendability of the other) are distributed in Sartre's analysis in a nonoverlapping, clear and distinct manner that generates the total conflict, or "antagonistic reciprocity," of self and other. Violence itself is for Sartre interiorized scarcity. In this fashion, scarcity first appears in the *Critique* with a status entirely divorced from the problem of institutions. It is the ontological origin of class conflict in an institutional framework. Through this notion of ontological scarcity, alterity or otherness (and in consequence objectivation or objectification) seem to become identified with alienation. Sartre is relatively explicit on this point, including the way in which it in one sense makes his analysis approximate to that of Hegel rather than that of Marx (p. 285). In Sartre, alterity is associated with alienation of an "original" sort and distinguished from exploitation in history, which it ontologically grounds. (This is plausible only in the context of a logic of identity and difference in which alterity is dissociated from sameness and supplementarity.) In Marx, relations of alterity and processes of objectification are distinguished from alienation, which is associated with exploitation. (This suggests an important role for supplementarity in the thought of Marx.) In Sartre, alterity and objectification are more than alienation's condition of possibility. They must bring alienation, and man must be an alienated freedom. Sartre is altogether explicit (especially in *Search for a Method*, p. 180) that freedom cannot be seen as pure or original in the sense of historical or even logical priority. But, within Sartre's own perhaps dominant framework, freedom is pure and total in its necessary initial or original opposition to the in-itself or the practico-inert. It is in this sense that alterity is the necessary *and sufficient* condition of alienation, if not initially identified with it. And, given Sartre's rejection of the Hegelian happy ending in a total reconciliation of opposites that overcomes alterity, it is difficult to see how revolution could conceivably overcome the most fundamental kind of alienation.[14]

The confrontation of the individual with matter produces worked-over matter as the result of praxis. This worked-over matter is a primary form of the practico-inert. The practico-inert might be seen as a "baptized," or named, in-itself of the second order. In *Being and Nothingness*, this derivative in-itself was at least implicitly present but not given a distinctive name, or discussed to the same extent or granted the same importance. (In the earlier work, it referred, for example, to one's past as the facticity of the for-itself which the for-itself had to be in the mode of not being it—an essence or dead possibility that one had to face up to in an ongoing totalization or temporalization.) In the presence of the practico-inert, individuals are serialized and related to each other by noncooperative antagonistic reciprocity.

The group-in-fusion arises as an apocalyptic way out of the hell of serialization and atomization. The group begins with objectification by a third, as in *Being and Nothingness*. But in the *Critique*, the group attains the status of a group-in-fusion (or what *Being and Nothingness* termed a we-subject) by internalizing the third. A common enemy and a common project enable members of the group to relate to one another, not in a purely dyadic manner, but in terms of the third. Each group member is a third for the other and the group is a third for each dyad. This group does have reality of at least an evanescent sort for Sartre in the *Critique*—which is a difference from *Being and Nothingness*. It rests not only on the recognition of the social-psychological process of shared internalization of the external (a process that would be a relatively superficial phenomenon in the terms of *Being and Nothingness*) but also on the importance of political and social action (hardly discussed in the earlier work). One must, however, recall the dubious nature of the distinctions drawn on related topics in *Being and Nothingness*. And in the *Critique* the conception of the group-in-fusion is not without its difficulties.

The group-in-fusion is the apocalyptic moment in the *Critique*. Sartre's treatment of it has often been seen as a theoretical anticipation of the events of May-June 1968 in France. Existential Marxism in theory seems to have been justified retrospectively by existential Marxism in practice (or even prospectively, since *gauchiste* student leaders such as Daniel Cohn-Bendit had read Sartre). But the status of the group-in-fusion in the *Critique* is problematic. First, in contrast to *Being and Nothingness*, the apocalyptic moment occurs not in a footnote but in the principal text. Yet the footnote status of apocalypse in the earlier work came along with the notion (however empty of content) that a radical transformation of the vicious circles explored in the principal text was possible. In the *Critique*, although the apocalyptic moment takes place in the principal text, by the same token it is presented as a "moment" within the vicious circle of alienation in history and not as a possible way out of it. This view seems more pessimistic about the possibilities of radical change, if more realistic about its context. Indeed, in the principal text of the *Critique*, no way out is presented, even on the level of contentless apocalypse or blind hope. Second, the group-in-fusion is an evanescent though nearly perfect moment. It apparently cannot be stabilized into some ongoing form of community or institution. It gives way to a reign of terror, as a terroristic oath or pledge (*serment*), inspired by fear of disintegration, converts all opponents and critics into traitors. (Here Merleau-Ponty's *Humanism and Terror* as well as the experience of the French Revolution were quite important for Sartre.) And this scapegoating scene is followed by functional differentiation, structure, institutionalization, the rise of a sovereign (who provides the collectivity, through personal identification with him, with a mystified surrogate for the participatory and democratic community of the group-in-fusion), and a fall back into serialization and the practico-inert. Third, there is a difference between the status of the individual and that of the group in the *Critique*. Sartre at all costs wants to avoid the idea of the group as a superorganism and can see no alternative, in combating this idea, to the interpretation he provides. The translucent praxis of the organic individual is the basis of a *constituting* dialectic that is the ultimate origin of all that follows. The intentional praxis of the individual, like that of the for-itself in *Being and Nothingness*, is the generating source of meaning and value in the world. The praxis of the group, while not "unreal" or without ontological status, is nonetheless related to a *constituted* dialectic dependent upon the originating role of individuals. The group-in-fusion in its participatory democracy seems to approximate the "translucency" of the praxis of the individual. But it still depends upon the relation to the third. In terms of *Being and Nothingness*, one might say that the praxis of the individual is initially on the level of immediacy of the prereflective consciousness, while the group depends upon reflection and the role of the other. Or, in Sartre's later preferred terminology, the praxis of the individual is initially on the level of lived experience, while the relation of the group to this level of phenomenological immediacy or spontaneity is in some sense derivative.

These considerations point to further problems in the conceptualization of the *Critique*. The structures (or ideal types) discussed in the *Critique* are explicitly presented as simultaneous. They do not necessarily indicate a historical sequence, and they may merge or blend with one another in complex ways in any real historical context. Yet, at the same time, there is an apparent diachronic dimension to the discussion whose relation to its synchronic side is not altogether clear. In addition, the difference between the constituting dialectic of the organic individual and the constituted dialectic of the group is not congruent with the assertion of the synchronic nature or simultaneity of the structures in question. In comparison with *Being and Nothingness*, the *Critique* seems more militantly individualistic while at the same time it is more concerned about society and politics. And it does not furnish the elements that problematize individualism in the earlier work. In a sense, the *Critique* straightens out the argument of Part Three of *Being and Nothingness* at the expense of omitting most of the self-critical aspects of the earlier work. Furthermore, the entire sweep of the *Critique* does seem to indicate that the sequence it presents constitutes at least a highly possible, perhaps probable, historical sequence. This sequence falls into a larger pattern of relatively hollow repetition, or *corsi* and *ricorsi*. The most rampant historicity seems to merge with the most empty repetitiveness. Besides the obvious reference to Vico (the detailed development of which would lead us too far astray), Max Weber might be considered here. Weber both presented his ideal types as simultaneous structures and tended to believe in the probability—if not inevitability—of the "bureaucratization of charisma" and the rise of large, impersonal, "serialized" institutions in the modern world, headed by more or less "charismatic" leaders or sovereigns. Weber allowed for outbursts of participatory groups, but they would be evanescent and not create lasting changes in institutional structures or viably relate the individual and the community. Their ultimate result would be the intensification of bureaucratic rigidity. Indeed, it might be argued that the *Critique*, in its initial methodological individualism, its neo-Kantian assumptions, its delineation of ideal types, and its apparent notion of probable historical sequence, seems much moré Weberian than Marxist in basic conception. The obvious and significant difference, of course, is that Sartre maintains the commitment to dialectics and Marxist revolution in spite of the structure of his argument, if not because of it.

From a dialectical perspective, the major difficulty with the *Critique* is the very limited notion of mediation it develops. At least at one crucial juncture of the argument, scarcity is hypostatized. Analytic oppositions become regulative. Social revolution and a viable socialist regime seem to be unfounded hopes. As a result, Sartre furnishes a set of concepts and possible processes that enable an analysis of alienation from the inside. The point I would stress is the restricted nature of Sartre's treatment of the problem of institutions. In his major works, Sartre never makes a sustained investigation and immanent critique of existing institutions (for example, those of capitalism) or a set of specific recommendations for major institutional change. Instead, he combines general indictment, apocalyptic tremor, and threats of violence. Specific criticisms and alternatives come, if at all, in interviews where they are not subjected to careful development and theoretical "grounding." What Sartre seems not sufficiently to realize is that the shift from morality to politics raises the institutional problem in an especially forceful form. Even on the most general level of theory, Sartre can conceive of institutions only in terms of rigid structure, the practico-inert, and serialization. The institution is separated by a total divide from the group-in-fusion, which can in no sense be stabilized as an ongoing community. The institution is not perceived as a "third" that may both mediate and supplement human relations in ways that are simultaneously structured and open to contestation and even to forms of excess. Nor is the institution seen in terms that need not identify alterity with alienation, that is, in terms that allow for an interplay between self and other in which difference overlaps similarity. Institutional forms at times more highly developed in other societies—such as ritual, feast, gift-exchange, carnival—are not perceived as possible models for more creative "repetition" in institutional life that limits historical change by playing with and, within limits, playing out excess. To some extent, language itself may be taken as the paradigm of the institution in this sense—a perspective on language that Sartre for the most part resists.[15]

In his understanding of the institution, Sartre retains the one-dimensional phenomenological prejudice that identifies truth with immediacy to the "things themselves," prereflective consciousness, and the lived. Structure, by contrast, is on the side of distortion, if not falsehood. This extreme oversimplification or analytic opposition is apparent in Sartre's comments in an important interview of 1969, "Masses, Spontaneity, Party":

The thought and action of each group necessarily reflect its structure. What occurs is therefore the following: the thought of a group-in-fusion—by virtue of the fact that it is born in the fire of a particular situation and not because of some kind of "spontaneity"—has a stronger, fresher, more critical charge than that of a structured group. As an institution, a party has an institutionalized mode of thought—meaning something that deviates from *reality*—and comes essentially to reflect no more than its own organization, in effect ideological thought. It is upon its own schema that is modeled, and deformed, the experience of the struggle itself; while the group-in-fusion thinks experience as it presents itself, without institutional mediation. This is why the thought of a group may be vague, incapable of being theorized, awkward—as were the ideas of the students in May 1968—but nevertheless represents a *truer* kind of thought because no institution is interposed between experience and the reflection upon existence. . . . While recognizing the necessity of an organization, I admit not to be able to resolve the problems that are posed to any stabilized structure. [*S. IX*, pp. 267, 283]

The impossibility of resolving the problem, I would suggest, is related to its formulation exclusively in terms of extreme, limiting cases that reflect the alienation of fatal splits—the lived immediacy and spontaneity-by-any-other-name of the group-in-fusion and the sclerotic, authoritarian rigidity of the undemocratic, hierarchical institution. To the extent that reality approaches these unmediated extremes, something is very wrong, and it cannot be righted by opposing one extreme to the other as truth and reality to falsehood and unreality. The theoretical and practical problem is to work out relations—among the individual, community, alterity, institutional structure, limits, and excess—that both mediate and supplement these extremes.[16]

# 5

# Autobiography and Biography: Self and Other

Homo. Say "Ecce homo!" on the arrival of any person one is expecting.
Idiot. Those who differ with you.
Idolaters. Are cannibals too.

Flaubert, Dictionary of Received Ideas

A writer is always a man who has more or less chosen the imaginary: he needs a certain dosage of fiction. For my part, I find it in my work on Flaubert, which one can, moreover, consider a novel. I even wish people to say that it is a *true* novel.

Sartre, Interview of 1970, Situations IX

As if there could possibly be true stories...

Sartre, Nausea

All this was like being in a balloon at night, in glacial coldness, carried on an endless voyage toward a bottomless abyss, and with nothing near but the unseizable, the motionless, the eternal. It was too much. They gave it up.

Flaubert, Bouvard and Pécuchet

In this dark night, one has the impression of walking, one tries to remember a road that, in fact, has never existed and should be invented.

Sartre, L'Idiot de la famille

His true Penelope was Flaubert.
He fished by obstinate isles.

Ezra Pound, Hugh Selwyn Mauberly

Sartre's project of comprehending man as a concrete universal culminates in his existential biographies. Moving from the study of Baudelaire (1946) to that of Genet (1952) and finally to that of Flaubert (1971-1972)—passing in the process over a number of briefer studies—one becomes enmeshed in an increasingly elaborate spiral of dialectically totalizing discourse. The attempt to reconcile existential psychoanalysis and Marxism receives increasingly long, if not progressively rich, embodiment in the sustained inquiry into another's life, thought, and times. The biographical "look" at the other is complemented by self-scrutiny in *The Words* (1964). The subject of these portraits of the artist as a young man is, on a certain level, the same. Similar questions are raised in them about the relation of reality to the imagination, of truth to fiction. Again, the basic problem is that of the interplay between similarity and difference in Sartre's thought over time and in his understanding of self and other.

For Sartre, the artist, playing the game of loser wins, negates reality and attempts to transcend it in a turn to imaginary totality in fiction. Sartre tries to provide a critical theory of this process in the light of an open dialectical mode of comprehension geared to praxis in the real world and presumably making use of fiction in the service of truth. In what is perhaps the dominant movement of thought in his existential biographies, Sartre returns to the prose/poetry dichotomy of *What Is Literature?* and the notion of an "original choice of being" of *Being and Nothingness*. But, over time, he becomes increasingly aware of the need for a historical and social specification of the situation of man as concrete universal. The open question is whether Sartre's growing emphasis on history effects a significant change in his interpretive framework or largely fills in the background in a manner that may at times even function to conceal the problematic elements in an interpretive framework. Sartre's dialectical totalization is an appropriative mode of discourse that will not let the other be. It centers comprehension of the other on a notion of life, reality, and truth that furnishes the basis for a straightforward, symptomatic or documentary reading of texts. And it can recognize only *en contrebande* tendencies in the other (including the self as other) that radically place in question the movement of dialectical totalization itself.

The subjects of Sartre's biographies share the status of writers of either poetry (Baudelaire) or what is, from Sartre's dominant perspective, poetic prose (Genet, Flaubert). All three were brought to trial—Baudelaire and Flaubert for what they wrote, and Genet for the criminal acts later celebrated in his works. Sartre does not take the way his subjects were treated in courts of law as an object for extended study. He largely neglects this important instance of the way the works or deeds of his subjects were "read" by the *honnête homme* in a key social institution. Instead, Sartre places his subjects on trial once more for playing variations on the game of loser wins. In the case of Baudelaire and, to a certain extent, Flaubert, Sartre is a harsh and relatively uncompromising judge: their choice resembled the one that Sartre perceives in his own early self. In the case of Genet, whose life differed most from his own, Sartre finds mitigating circumstances and indeed is more than lenient. Yet in all three cases, the trial takes place *en huis clos*. The "subject" is rarely allowed to speak in his own voice. Or rather, the texts are not explicitly analyzed in ways that could raise doubts about the case of the prosecutor. And Sartre's own position as existential analyst who explicitly affirms social revolution has an ambivalent relation to that of the *honnête homme* (or, especially in the case of Flaubert, to that of the father as symbol of authority). The fundamental distinctions with which Sartre conducts his investigation have the self-evident and secure status of common sense. Reality is as unproblematic as is the notion of a flight from it into its opposite (the imaginary). And Sartre does not hesitate to use the categories of psychopathology to describe the plight of his subjects, but not to alleviate their responsibility.

Yet, again, there are elements in Sartre's writing that emerge, at least obliquely, to contest his dominant approach and to impugn the validity of the legalistic metaphor in analyzing it. Such elements are most explicit and forceful in *The Words*, but they exist to some extent in the biographies as well. One may note in a prefatory way the peculiar adventure of the central notion of an original choice of being. This notion is itself the apocalyptic moment of dialectical totalization. In it the lived totalization of the subject's life is repeated and presumably comprehended in the discourse of the existential analyst. But, in the biographies, it is applied in a manner that relates reality to the imaginary in ways that seem to render the project of totalization problematic. Early in *Saint Genet*, for example, Sartre offers a story that is supposed to condense the experience of the young Genet. The dreamy, "absented" child is discovered with his "hand in the bag" and branded from behind by his foster parents with the "vertiginous word"—thief—a primal act that predestines Genet to crime and intimates homosexuality. (There is a sense in which Sartre's own dominant analysis repeats this gesture.) Genet's original choice at this point is to take up this categorization of the "other" and to make it his own, thereby making something of what he is made. It is significant, however, that Sartre describes his own story of this "incident" by using almost the same words he had Roquentin use in *Nausea* to describe the way in which the song was composed by the Jew—the song that functions as a metaphor for the vision of pure art that negates, transcends, and salvages existence: "That was how it happened, in that or some other way" (*G*, p. 26; *N*, p. 245). Given both the words themselves and the object to which they are applied in *Nausea*, this telling repetition would indicate that the concept of original choice has at best the status of a heuristic fiction or even a myth designating a virtual object that is required for a unified or totalizing understanding of a life. In providing an "as if" (or what Freud would term a "just so") story to reconstruct a primal scene, Sartre's discourse itself becomes mythomorphic. In his study of Flaubert, Sartre repeatedly refers to the fantastic or fabulous status of his own reconstruction of the "facts." With reference to his own elaborate and almost entirely unsubstantiated account of the absence of the mother's love in the care of the infant Flaubert—an account that plays an enormous role in his interpretation—Sartre asserts: "I confess that it's a fable. Nothing proves it happened this way" (L'Idiot, I, 139). Sartre of course would like to argue that his use of fiction is justified in that it is guided by the "truth" of dialectical totalization. But his actual use of fiction disorients not only the opposition but even any distinction between truth or reality and fiction. The result is extremely confusing. This largely uncontrolled result of his analysis indicates a problem that Sartre does not explicitly confront. Does the very project of open dialectical totalization itself need to be supplemented by a notion of supplementarity that is not entirely controlled by it and that "situates" it as much as it is situated by it? We shall return to this problem repeatedly in the course of the following discussion.

Sartre's relatively short study of Baudelaire offers in skeletal form the model that will be "fleshed out" in the studies of Genet and Flaubert. As Michel Leiris notes in his introduction, Sartre seeks a comprehension of everything that can be known about Baudelaire: "the choice of himself that he made (to be this, not to be that) as all men make it, originally and from instant to instant" (B, p. 11). Sartre assumes a basic continuity between life and texts that obviates an inquiry into the self-contestatory interplay within each and between them. Interpretation is centered on the totalizing intentional structure of consciousness—the world vision—that informs both life and text. Baudelaire's poetry is an emblematic expression and compensatory activity in relation to his life: again, a game of loser wins.

Baudelaire was only six when his father died. He lived his childhood as a mere extension of his mother. Soon after his father's death, his mother remarried and placed Baudelaire in a boarding school. He experienced his mother's remarriage as a loss and a betrayal. (Interestingly, in The Words, Sartre does not discuss his own mother's remarriage, which was apparently followed by a period of kleptomania in his own life.) This traumatic event expelled Baudelaire from oneness with his mother and imposed upon him a state of isolation and otherness: he was de trop and without justification. In an initial existential compensation, Baudelaire tried to fill the hole in his life and reappropriate his otherness as his own—an enterprise later to be repeated in his poetry. In the child is an initial choice of being through which the exterior is interiorized in freedom:

Here we touch upon the original choice that Baudelaire made of himself, this absolute engagement by which each of us decides in a particular situation what he will be and what he is. Abandoned, rejected, Baudelaire wanted to take up again on his own account this isolation. He laid claim to this solitude so that it might at least come to him from himself and not have to be submitted to. He *felt* that he was *an other* by the sudden unveiling of his individual existence. But at the same time he affirmed and took up again on his own account this alterity in humiliation, spite, and pride. Thenceforth, with a brutal and desolate fury, he *made* himself an other. [*B*, p. 21]

What Baudelaire chose in his freedom, however, was bad faith. He arrested himself at the negative moment of freedom as noninvolvement in the world and then sought escape from it in trying to "statufy" himself in the solidity of the thing. Sartre, in effect, presents him as a "real-life" Antoine Roquentin who saw through bourgeois bad faith but did not recognize his own. He had a will to fail and to scandalize the solid citizens who lived in accordance with conventional criteria of success and respectability. But, like Antoine, he was only a rebel and not a revolutionary. His attitude was parasitic upon the status quo, which he needed for his own poses and role-playing. In Baudelaire, however, the fascination for the artificial and the affirmation of the antinatural led to the posture of the dandy. For Sartre, the role of the dandy has existential significance as the extreme exemplification of a purely negative freedom that refuses to be contaminated by the real world.

Baudelaire lived what would today be called the schizoid state. (One is, of course, retrospectively reminded of the work of R. D. Laing, who drew heavily from Sartre in his own elaboration of an existential psychology, as in *The Divided Self*.) Baudelaire experienced a split between an observing self of pure consciousness and a performing self in the social world. He desired the impossible totality which would make him both observer and observed at the same time. In this futile quest, he fled from temporalization by fixating his look on the intemporal past of repetition and by attempting to set up house with the illustrious dead (Maistre, Poe): "In a sense, what Baudelaire fled from into the Past was the enterprise and the project, perpetual instability. Like schizophrenics and melancholics, he justified his incapacity to act by turning himself toward the *already lived*, the already done, the irremediable" (p. 216). In discussing Baudelaire's antiutilitarian "laziness," Sartre asserts: "That it has a psychopathological aspect, I agree.... But let us not forget that the sick people of Janet, due to their state, often have metaphysical intuitions that the normal man tries to mask" (p. 37).

In addition, if Baudelaire was neurotic, his neurosis was chosen within his original choice of being. And it was related to his poetry. His poems were at one with his life, having identical themes and being encompassed within the identical structure of intentionality. Baudelaire chose to be the *poète maudit* just as he chose to be the isolated child, in an attempt to reappropriate his otherness in freedom. The existential foundation of his poetry was the nihilation of the real, the escape from action, the immobilization of time, and the association of evil, beauty, and death. From the ashes of an ugly reality, he created imaginary flowers of evil. His will to fail enabled a poetic victory at the expense of life. A resoundingly rhetorical conclusion—itself a bizarre tribute to the dead flowers of rhetoric that Baudelaire's poems have been revealed to be—brings Sartre's book to a dramatic close:

Every event was a reflection of that indecomposable totality that he was from the first to the last day of his life. He refused experience. Nothing came from outside to change him and he learned nothing. General Aupick's [his stepfather] death scarcely altered his relations with his mother. For the rest, his story is the story of a slow, very painful decomposition. Such he was at the age of twenty; such we shall find him on the eve of his death. He is simply gloomier, more nervous, less alive, while of his talent and his admirable intelligence nothing remains except memories. And such no doubt was his singularity, that "difference" which he sought until death and which was only visible to others. He was an experiment in a retort, something like the *homunculus* in the Second Part of *Faust*; and the quasi-abstract circumstances of the experience enabled him to bear witness with unequalled *éclat* to this truth—the free choice that a man makes of himself is completely identified with what is called his destiny. [p. 245]

Sartre's *Baudelaire* seems to provide a comprehensive grasp of its material that is related both to its schematism and to its brevity. As the interpretive framework is "enriched" or overburdened in *Saint Genet* and even more so in *L'Idiot de la famille,* the seemingly tight fit of the analysis loosens. It is more difficult, perhaps impossible, to summarize the argument, for the skeleton takes on somewhat unruly masses of flesh. The very simplicity of outline of *Baudelaire* is related to its interpretive bite, as well as to the simplistic quality Sartre himself recognized in retrospect. In an interview of 1970, he referred to the book as "very unsatisfactory, extremely bad, even... " (*S. IX,* p. 113). What is repeated in the later studies is the unthematized, largely blind interplay between the explicit attempt at totalizing interpretation and elements that contest or decenter it. For the latter exist even in the short study of Baudelaire.

Toward the end of the book, Sartre makes a comment that places in doubt the status of his totalization: "It would be enough for us to see Baudelaire live, if only for an instant, for our scattered remarks to organize themselves into a totalitarian knowledge" (p. 235). This remark is paradoxically faithful to the phenomenological project of totalizing comprehension. It stresses the importance of the lived and of empathetic vision. But, by this very gesture, it defers and displaces totalizing comprehension from what the words of Sartre's study convey, to a direct intuition of the living Baudelaire, which is impossible. The virtual presence of Baudelaire, necessary to totalize the totalization, is at best "indirectly communicated" by the existential analysis. Baudelaire himself, in this sense, has a fictive or quasi-mythical status that is necessary for the "truth" of the totalizing attempt at comprehension and for the legibility of Sartre's own text.

What is perhaps more disconcerting for Sartre's dominant interpretive framework is his own indication *en creux* of elements in Baudelaire's texts that place it in question. There is no explicit attempt to relate these elements to the dominant interpretation: their presence is also allowed to communicate itself only indirectly. Sartre discusses Baudelaire's "notions" of the infinite and the spiritual in terms that seem to make them substitutes for each other—substitutes in a chain of supplementary relationships that threatens the self-certainty of the dialectical project and its founding oppositions. Toward the end of the study, the "spiritual" is seen as the central theme of Baudelaire's work. Sartre attempts to interpret it with reference to the desire of pure consciousness to become a freedom-thing. But, earlier in the book, Sartre's own account of the "infinite" does not entirely conform to this interpretation, for it seems to shift imperceptibly the teleological quest for the missing totality in the direction of an elusive center, which "poetic" words supplement but cannot fix: "It [the infinite] is what is without being given, what defines me today and will however not exist before tomorrow; it is the term glimpsed, dreamed, almost touched and yet beyond one's grasp, of a directed movement. We shall see later that Baudelaire, more than any other, insisted upon these suggested existences, present and absent at the same time" (p. 44).

When Sartre later returns to this problem, it is in relation to the spiritual. And the language of absence and presence seems inadequate to grasp it:

The spiritual is a *being* and it manifests itself as such. It has the objectivity, the cohesion, the permanence and identity of being. But this being is enclosed in itself like a sort of reserve; it is not completely; a profound discretion prevents it not from manifesting itself but from affirming itself in the manner of a table or a stone. It is characterized by a manner of absence. It is never entirely there, or entirely visible. It remains in suspense between being and nothingness by a discretion pushed to the extreme. One can enjoy it; it does not steal away. But this contemplative enjoyment [*jouissance*] has a sort of secret lightness. It enjoys not enjoying enough. It goes without saying that this metaphysical lightness of the Baudelairean world figures *existence* itself. [P. 220]

But if this lightness of "that" which is in suspense—and which Sartre associates with Baudelaire's fascination with odors wherein the body becomes spiritual and the spirit, bodily—figures "existence," then the (metaphorically supplemented) categories of Sartre's analysis are simultaneously necessary to "describe" it and inadequate to grasp it. And if the "spiritual" is "le fait poétique baudelairien" (p. 220), then that poetry both invites totalizing interpretation and eludes it. The question without sequel in Sartre's account is whether Baudelaire's poetry itself renders problematic the categorical oppositions with which Sartre seeks to comprehend it.

Sartre, half in jest, compared his *Saint Genet* to a funeral oration. It is in any case one of the most implausible prefaces ever written—a verbal monument of more than five-hundred pages that threatens to bury the collected works it introduces. After its appearance, Genet stopped writing for a number of years. One may suggest two opposed yet perhaps complementary interpretations of why Sartre's study blocked Genet's writing. The book brought Genet to a higher level of self-insight and responsibility, requiring a radical reconstruction of his original project. It unceremoniously stripped Genet naked, betrayed him, and repeated the verbal assault from behind—an assault that Sartre identifies as the occasion for Genet's original choice of being. It is significant that an ambivalence or indecision between these two interpretations characterizes Genet's own reaction to Sartre's study:

It [*Saint Genet*] filled me with a kind of disgust because I saw myself stripped naked—by someone other than myself. I strip myself in all my books, but at the same time I disguise myself with words, with attitudes, with certain choices, by means of a certain magic. I manage not to get too damaged. But I was stripped by Sartre unceremoniously. My first impulse was to burn the book; Sartre had given me the manuscript to read. I let him publish it because my chief concern has always been to be responsible for my acts. It took me some time to get over my reading of his book. I was almost unable to continue writing. I could have continued turning out a certain type of novel mechanically. I could have tried to write pornographic books mechanically. Sartre's book created a void which made for a kind of psychological deterioration.... I remained in that awful state for six years, six years of the imbecility that's the basic stuff of life: opening a door, lighting a cigarette. There are only a few gleams in a man's life. All the rest is grayness. But this period of deterioration made for a meditation that led me to the theater.... Sartre's book made for the exploitation of something that was already familiar.[1]

The last statement in this quotation reveals the inadequacy of both the interpretations between which Genet himself seems to hesitate. Genet had already written plays before the appearance of Sartre's book (*Deathwatch* and *The Maids*). And the story of his life and his writing organized around a radical break—whether it be interpreted in progressive or regressive terms—must be complicated by the problem of repetition. Indeed, it is the exploration of this problem in the writings of Genet that perhaps constitutes the most significant element of dissonance between them and the totalizing interpretation of Sartre.

Sartre's object in writing a book on Genet is stated in the first words of the final chapter, entitled "Prière pour le bon usage de Genet":

I have tried to do the following: to indicate the limit of psychoanalytical interpretation and Marxist explanation and to demonstrate that freedom alone can account for a person in his totality; to show this freedom at grips with destiny, crushed at first by its fatalities, then returning upon them to digest them little by little; to prove that genius is not a gift but the way out that one invents in desperate cases; to find again the choice that a writer makes of himself, of his life, and of the meaning of the universe, including even the formal characterisitcs of his style and composition, even the structure of his images and of the particularity of his tastes; to review in detail the history of his liberation. It is for the reader to say whether I have succeeded. [P. 645]

In this case, Sartre's success—and his book is extremely successful—would reinforce the success of his subject, because Sartre intends to tell an existential success story in speaking of Genet, a story of liberation. But, at least on the level of Genet's writings, the reason why the story is crowned by success in such markedly positive terms is, I think, unclear. Genet plays the game of loser wins. Like Baudelaire and Flaubert, he writes in a poetic mode that dehumanizes words, obstructs communication with the other, and abandons praxis in the real world for passive activity. Genet also stops history in favor of repetition and turns language inside out in the dispossession of the intentional subject of discourse. Indeed, it is in the study of Genet that Sartre develops most extensively the notion of *tourniquets*, or double binds (a translation I find preferable to "whirligigs"). And it is Genet's writing that mires language in these vicious circles and paradoxical dead ends. The fundamental reason for Sartre's *éloge* of Genet seems to concern Genet's life, and it applies to Genet's writings not as texts but in their existential functions for Genet's personal development. Not so much *what* Genet wrote but *that* he wrote, in his *Bildungsreise* from orphan to thief to homosexual to aesthete to writer, is the existentially significant fact. What he wrote is of relevance in so far as it is interpreted as a symptom of his life process—a conception that itself depends upon an initial dichotomy between life and text, which is overcome only in a totalizing interpretation centered on the life. The very power of contestation in Genet's works is seen by Sartre primarily in terms of Genet's wily power to induce the straight *honnête homme* to identify with the homosexual.

But what if these assumptions of Sartre were themselves at issue in the writings of Genet?[2] What if one had, in the confrontation between Sartre and Genet, another variant of the story fit for an "Anthology of Black Humor"?[3] A writer explores the ambiguity of language and sees man as fully at stake in a play of words and world that he does not entirely control. He stages the problem of "originary" *mimesis* and indicates the limitations of oppositions, revealing how seemingly pure opposites are always already implicit in each other. His notion of language expropriates the author of the text and decenters the intentional subject or agent. He sees his own life as a pretext for his writing, which recounts his legend and his legibility: "My life must be a legend, in other words, legible, and the reading of it must give birth to a certain new emotion which I call poetry. I am no longer anything, only a pretext."[4] He tells us that his victory is purely verbal and that he owes it to the sumptuousness of his words. The power of contestation in his words is related to their subversion of secure oppositions and of the consequent effort to bring everything together in a totalizing interpretation. An overlapping and continually displaced network of differences and similarities between his life and his texts is interrogated in the texts themselves. Along comes an existential analyst and presents a totalizing interpretation that paradoxically concludes with a plea to the reader to allow Genet to have his own "voice" and to allow himself to be affected by the challenge of that voice.

This plea climaxes an analysis centered on the intentional structure of consciousness, which privileges life over text and bases
itself on secure oppositions overcome in a dialectical process of
appropriative interpretation. Language from this perspective is
the practical instrument of man, which poetry perverts and inverts in a queer manner related to femininity. And on the basis
of this interpretation, the analyst would like to hand Genet a
bouquet as the existential idol of our time!

The dissonance between Genet and Sartre is epitomized in
the tension between the quotations from Genet that serve as
chapter headings and the text, in which Sartre adapts them to a
totalizing interpretation. But the dissonance may be indicated in
a more evenhanded manner by pointing outside *Saint Genet* to
another set of texts: Sartre's preface to the *Thief's Journal,* followed by the first words of Genet's text itself. Sartre states:

> Not all who would be are Narcissus. Many who lean over the water see
> only a vague human figure. Genet sees himself everywhere.... The
> disturbing theme of the double, the image, the counterpart, the enemy
> brother, is found in all his works. Each of them has the strange property
> of being both itself and the reflection of itself. Genet brings before us a
> dense and teeming throng which intrigues us, transports us and
> changes Genet beneath Genet's gaze.... Genet is never familiar even
> with himself.... He reassures us only to disturb us further. His au-
> tobiography is *not* an autobiography; it merely seems like one: it is
> sacred cosmogony.[5]

Sartre names Genet's power to disturb only to calm it by
familiarizing the strange in a sublating manner. He begins by
reducing "the disturbing theme of the double" to narcissistic
projection, which presumably characterizes Genet's singularly
uncommon identity. Thus we have securely in hand the element
of continuity to be found in all of Genet's works. Genet's autobiography is not an autobiography but—rest assured—it can
be classified: it is a sacred cosmogony (not $x$, then $y$). Contrast
the defamiliarizing and uncanny play of the opening lines of
Genet, which "burn" the prefatory pages of Sartre:

> Convicts' clothes are striped pink and white. Though it was at my
> heart's bidding that I chose the universe wherein I delight, I have at
> least the power of finding in it the many meanings I wish to find: *There*

*is a close relationship between flowers and convicts.* The fragility and delicacy of the former are of the same nature as the brutal insensitivity of the latter. [*Footnote:* My excitement is the oscillation from one to the other.] Should I have to portray a convict—or a criminal—I shall so bedeck him with flowers that, as he disappears beneath them, he will himself become a flower, a gigantic and new one. Toward what is known as evil, I have, for love's sake, pursued an adventure which led me to prison.[6]

In Sartre's analysis, the exciting oscillation of flowers and convicts, fragility, delicacy, and brutal insensitivity is imprisoned in the conception of it in terms of static essentialism and sterile *tourniquets.*

I have of course barely scratched the surface of Sartre's study of Genet; I have tried only to suggest the discrepancy between the "projects" of the two. On the surface, Sartre seems very far from Genet. Sartre himself would find this view objectionably superficial. In an interview of 1971, he claimed affinity with Genet rather than Flaubert in an argument rebutting the idea that, in his book on Flaubert, he had projected himself into his object of study: "No, I do not think it is valid to say that I unveil myself in Flaubert as one said I did for Genet. It was perhaps more true for Genet because he is closer to me on many levels. But I have very few points in common with Flaubert. Indeed I chose him precisely because he is distant from me" (*S. X,* pp. 103–4).

In at least one respect, this characterization of Sartre's relation to Flaubert is misleading. Sartre does not identify with one important element he sees and condemns in Flaubert: the myth of literature and the cult of Art for Art's sake. But one might argue that this element serves as a "negative identity," which Sartre tells us he did believe in at some point in the past. Sartre is distant from Flaubert in the same sense in which he would like to indicate the distance from himself. Thus, the writing of the book on Flaubert has an exorcistic function in relation to a past identity of Sartre that still evokes denunciatory passion indicative of ambivalent fascination and temptation—that is, a certain proximity. And one may ask whether Sartre's "negative identity" leads him to read into Flaubert what may not be there in the form Sartre sees it (notably, a doctrine of Art for Art's sake).

Before discussing Sartre's study of Flaubert, therefore, I shall turn to his self-analysis in *The Words*, where he examines the role of a myth or cult of literature in his own life. *The Words* also serves to decenter my analysis, for in it Sartre encounters many of the questions I have been trying to raise. *The Words* has a more pronounced and, at times, explicit element of self-contestation than Sartre's biographical studies of others. In certain respects, it might even be compared to *Nausea*, despite its brief and somewhat patronizing reference to that novel.

*The Words* might be read as a serio-parodic story of origins. It begins with a series of mock-biblical "begat's" culminating in the appearance of the child Sartre himself. In this reconstruction of the life of the little Poulou by the fifty-year-old Jean-Paul, a vital question is that of the precise role of parody vis-à-vis the serious business of self-analysis, the demystification of ideology, and self-contestation. In this witty, elegant, and often cutting book, parody plays a number of important roles. It has a function in Sartre's half-joking "castration" of his grandfather. It complicates the nature of existential psychoanalysis and Sartre's relation to Freud. And in its role in the critique of ideology, it is related to Sartre's Marxism. Indeed, the importance of parody and self-parody in this text distinguishes it from Sartre's other biographical ventures. Sartre himself distinguished *The Words* from his study of Flaubert by arguing that one could not show empathy in relation to oneself because one adhered too closely to oneself (*S. X*, p. 103). Parody, however, provided a certain self-distance within this proximity.

Parody in *The Words* is not unambivalent. It appears in at least two mutually contestatory forms. The first is a dominant form (or a form of dominance), in which parody serves as an instrument of "totalizing" mastery and control of the situation. This form, in its most positive aspect, provides an avenue of self-enlightenment through the overcoming of one's situated past and the ideology that mystified it. Jean-Paul as a mature adult of fifty lucidly recounts the history of his lost illusions and thus takes his distance from little Poulou, whose life was the quasi-mythical scene where those illusions originated. In this sense, the work is based on a narrative fiction that the reader must contract to accept on faith since he has no means within the terms of the text to test it against reality. Within the text, moreover, the others—both self as "other" (the child Poulou) and members of Sartre's family—very rarely appear as subjects with their own voices to answer back to the story-telling analyst or interrupt his monologue. They are all the children of the adult who fathers the text. The role of parody in this relatively restricted critical process is related to a myth that Sartre does not explore and explode with the explicit scrutiny he applies to other myths, such as the myth of literature. The myth relatively protected here is that of self-genesis, related to a notion of pure and total freedom. In terms of this potent myth, Sartre identifies autonomy with self-creation *ex nihilo* and attempts to become his own genitor. [7]

A second form, or function, of parody overlaps the first, however, and raises doubts about it. In this second form, parody involves the relation of the adult Sartre to himself and is itself "dialogical": it brings Sartre into a playful but serious process of self-questioning that he cannot entirely master. Freedom becomes simultaneously more radical and less total. The child remains enigmatically within the adult, and the projects of the adult are themselves subject to the threat of childish illusion as combinations of intentional praxis and flight. This play in which the self is involved can be stopped only by a willful decision, which in the text is perhaps the function of the final sentences. They are apparently intended in all seriousness and seem to depart abruptly from the playful mood: "If I relegate an impossible Salvation to the prop room, what remains? A whole man, composed of all men and as good as all of them and no better than any" (*M*, p. 213). I shall return to these sentences.

Poulou is the object of serio-parodic treatment by Jean-Paul. (In a sense, this treatment replicates the status of Poulou in the family as the text describes it.) The child finds himself in an equivocal, "can't-win" position that leads him to play the game of loser wins. His status is most markedly that of fetishized object, especially in the eyes of his maternal grandfather, Charles Schweitzer. Objectively, the little boy is happy and loved. His mother tells him so, and she is right. (In an interview,

Sartre distinguished himself as child from the young Flaubert on the basis that Sartre was himself well-loved as a child, especially by his mother. *S. X*, p. 97) Subjectively, Sartre is unhappy and unwanted: he is *de trop* and feels unjustified. He is a traveler without a ticket whose destination is not stamped in advance and who has come to fulfill no higher-order expectation. The desire to fill the hole in existence and to feel justified leads Sartre toward his original choice as writer.

In what sense is the young Sartre a loser in life who must seek compensation in the imaginary? Half-victim and half-accomplice, Poulou joins in what Sartre terms the "familial comedy." As star performer in this living theater, Poulou was the stopgap that filled the holes in the family's life. This half-willing complicity in bourgeois role-playing induced a schizoid state in Sartre, a dissociation: "I led two lives, both of which were deceitful: publicly, I was an impostor: the famous grandson of the celebrated Charles Schweitzer; alone, I slipped into imaginary sulking" (*M*, p. 109). The mirror was a preferred object for games of *bouderie imaginaire*. In the mirror stage of his own existence, the young Sartre—overcome by events he could not control—would flee to the mirror and make faces at himself in an attempt to recapture his fugitive identity. Reading and then writing brought the child to the other side of the looking glass. The loved objects for reading-as-imaginary-identification were of course adventure stories, cliff-hangers with "to be continued" endings. Sartre confesses that, even as an adult, he prefers grade-B detective stories to Wittgenstein. And he refers to committing "the mad blunder, in a grim century, of taking life for an epic" (p. 96).

These escapist games, Sartre intimates, might have lost their fascination for little Poulou had he been accepted into the real games of other children. But Poulou was "l'exclu des jardins publics"—a child *de trop* in the play of others (pp. 111, 184). And the family play was a game in bad faith, whose master of ceremonies was Sartre's maternal grandfather:

The fact is, he slightly overdid the sublime. He was a man of the nineteenth century who took himself for Victor Hugo, as did so many others, including Victor Hugo himself. This handsome man with the flowing beard who was always in between two *coups de théâtre,* like the alcoholic between two drinks, was the victim of two recently discovered techniques: the art of photography and the art of being a grandfather. He had the good and the bad fortune to be photogenic. The house was filled with photos of him. Since snapshots were not practiced, he had acquired a taste for poses and *tableaux vivants.* Everything was a pretext for him to suspend his gestures, to strike an attitude, to turn to stone. He doted upon these brief moments of eternity in which he became his own statue. [Pp. 15–16]

Charles Schweitzer was a highly significant "other" in Sartre's life, who exercised a deeply ambivalent paternal authority. Sartre was an infant when his own father died. Absent as paternal authority, the father played a role similar to that of the missing God. The significance of his absence is highlighted by Sartre's placement of the following sentence as a solitary paragraph: "The death of Jean-Baptiste was the great affair of my life: it sent my mother back to her chains and gave me my freedom" (p. 11). Sartre adds that he "willingly subscribes to the verdict of an eminent psychoanalyst: I have no superego" (p. 11). The death of the father is related to the notion of freedom in its pure and total form. Sartre was a "child of the miracle," born of an absent God and a young virgin: "I was an orphan without a father. The son of no one, I was my own cause" (p. 91). But this total freedom paradoxically condemned him to total responsibility: he was forced to become his own genitor, to be both giver and gift in relation to himself. And the apparent absence of an internalized authority (superego) brought with it uncompromising, total surveillance and masochistic *conscience de soi:* "My commandments were sewn into my skin: if I go a day without writing, the scar burns me; if I write too easily, it also burns me" (p. 136).

Upon the death of her husband Sartre's mother was relegated by her parents to the dependent status of a child. For her son she was more a sister than a mother; she was not the heir to the lost paternal authority. Sartre's childhood relation to his mother was an egalitarian one in which alterity was not identified with alienation. In one sense, he "identified" with her. He recounts a scene in which the desire of a strange male made mother and child one in an instinctive act of fear and flight (p. 182). At the same time, Sartre was the strange male who desired his mother as "other." (Sartre has himself observed that the idea of an incestuous relationship between brother and sister has always fascinated him and that it is an active theme in many of his works.)

In their study of *The Words,* A. J. Arnold and J.-P. Piriou argue that the mother is associated with images that cohere around the in-itself as a risk to the freedom and spontaneity of the pure for-itself.[8] The in-itself is not a danger in itself but insofar as it threatens to mingle with and contaminate the for-itself. In this regard, the mother is like the spider whose white spittle threatens intentional consciousness in one of Sartre's earliest essays on Husserl. She also evokes the "viscous," the discussion of which in *Being and Nothingness* was laced with a relatively manifest network of incestuous images. More generally, one might argue that the incestuous desire for the (m)other is repeated (or vice versa) in the overlapping interplay of same and other, which elicits the ambivalent response of attraction and repulsion, as in relation to transphenomenality, the viscous, or Antoine's encounter with the chestnut tree. In the largest of senses, it is this uncanny threat in the relation of the one with the other that supplementarity dramatizes, analysis represses and makes taboo, and dialectics attempts to sublate, civilize, and convert into an instrument of progress.

In *The Words,* the "other" as dangerous threat to the freedom and integrity of the self is further related to traditionalism and fidelity to the past in general. The terms of the discussion indicate that the myth of total freedom still has a hold on this text. Sartre makes active use of an entire network of more or less invidious distinctions (speech/writing, simple folk/writers, innocent-looking/lucidity, women/men). The scar of conscience as the motivation for writing, which lives on as an exigent vestige of the past, is compared to "the solemn prehistoric crabs that the ocean throws up on the beaches of Long Island" (p. 136)—the crabs that also symbolize the threat of being caught in an unconscious, unfree "other": "Like them it is a survival of a bygone era. For a long time, I envied the concierges of the Rue Lacépède sitting astride their chairs when summer evenings brought them out on the sidewalk. Their innocent eyes saw without being commissioned to see" (p. 136). The past as a traditional given is here associated with the idyll of innocent vision that exerts its fascination on the philosopher of freedom. Yet this happiness is good only for others, who in being born fulfilled an expectation. The writer for Sartre must confront his own superfluity and, in his alienated freedom, struggle with words themselves alienated from speech: "One speaks in one's own language; one writes in a foreign language" (p. 136). The writer is cast out of the maternal womb of innocent seeing and plain unreflective speaking. He is a *fort en thème* who is condemned to translate from his own language into a foreign or alien language—the written word. At this point in the text, Sartre seems to be in dead earnest: his gesture scapegoats writing in a way that simultaneously debases and elevates it. This point is momentary but significant. Later in the text, Sartre returns to the theme of tradition and states: "I love and respect, however, the humble and tenacious fidelity that certain people—women in particular—keep for their tastes, their desires, their old undertakings, their long-gone feasts; I admire their will to remain the same in the midst of change, to save their memory, to carry to the grave a first doll, a milk tooth, a first love" (p. 199). Sartre half-jestingly contrasts this attitude with his own gift for self-criticism and his attachment, despite the recognition of repetition, to "la jeune ivresse de l'alpiniste" (pp. 199, 201).

Sartre's grandmother Louise has a curious role in the text. Unlike the grandfather, who is half a father (or a father by half), she is not seen as half a mother. She is, however, credited with having seen through the family comedy, including the histrionics of little Sartre himself (p. 24). But she is hardly discussed in the text, perhaps because her presence threatens some of its own fictive strategies. Marginally within the text and often projected outside it, she might be compared to the ideal reader who understands and sees through the fictions that hold the text together but who discreetly remains silent so that the comedy may continue.

"There remained the patriarch. He so resembled God the Father that he was often taken for Him" (p. 14). Sartre's maternal grandfather, Charles Schweitzer, is a highly equivocal other in *The Words*. He is the great remainder, the ambivalent supplement to the absent father. And he is written about in a half-serious, half-parodic way:

Charles had two faces: when he played at being grandfather, I considered him a buffoon of my own kind and did not respect him. But when he spoke to M. Simonnot, or to his sons, when he made the women wait on him at table, by pointing without a word, at the oil and vinegar cruets or the bread-basket, I admired his authority. I was particularly impressed by the play of his forefinger [*le coup de l'index*]: he would be careful not to point, but would move it vaguely in the air, half-bent, so that the designation remained imprecise and the two servants had to guess at his orders. [Pp. 130–31]

The grandfather is half buffoon and half Hidden God. The undecidable play of these two statuses is symbolized in Sartre's indecisive use of two first names for him—Karl and Charles. (Freud in this text has a half-serious, half-parodic status analogous to that of the grandfather, and Sartre works out a relationship to his ideas, such as the "superego," that is simultaneously serious and joking.) In his semidivine status, the grandfather replaces the father at a number of junctures in Sartre's life. In one incident, he is the agent of an inverted castration of Poulou as pride of the family: he takes the child for an ill-fated haircut that transforms the darling, long-tressed, slightly feminine angel into an ugly little boy. Most decisively perhaps, he intervenes in a highly equivocal way in Sartre's "original choice of being" a writer, neither clearly opposing nor "positively reinforcing" the choice of the child. Like the Hidden God, he exercises the enigmatic *coup de l'index* and apparently leaves the predestined choice (the child has the "bump of literature") to the individual in his freedom. Sartre half-jokingly recognizes the way in which the grandfather's role generated at least a partial "superego" in him: "In short, he drove me into literature by the care he took to divert me from it, to such an extent that even now I sometimes wonder, when I am in a bad mood, whether I have not consumed so many days and nights, covered so many pages with my ink, thrown on the market so many books that nobody wanted, solely in the mad hope of pleasing my grandfather" (p. 135).

As part-buffoon, the grandfather has a joking relationship with Poulou, which gives the grandfather the jester status traditionally reserved for the maternal uncle. Karl and Poulou are alternatively actor and audience, king and court, for each other. Within the false drama of the bourgeois family comedy, each filled gaps in the other's existence in a way that masked freedom, boredom, and death: "I was a fief of the sun; my grandfather could enjoy me without possessing me. I was his 'wonder' because he wanted to finish his life as a wonder-struck old man" (pp. 14–15).

In the relation to the grandfather, real-life adventures of epic proportions paralleled the imaginary flights available to the child in reading. But the family comedy was both necessary and unsatisfying. In this ontological spoof, the gaps reappeared as quickly as they were filled. The grandfather was disappointed by the products of the child's first plagiaristic attempts at writing; he had expected a rendition of the family comedy and received only scissors-and-paste copies of cheap adventure stories (whose similarity to his own expectations he refused to recognize). The child had only a clownish half-father, a joking divinity, who did not enable him to overcome the feeling of being unjustified.

The choice of writing is presented as the child's way out of the "neurosis" engendered in him as half-victim and half-accomplice in the family comedy. But this exit and the "choice" related to it were themselves highly equivocal. Writing came originally to the little Sartre in the form of a myth or cult of literature, which displaced and repeated the essentials of the family comedy itself. Within the folds of the myth of literature, writing appeared in a transposed religious framework that was the double of the family scene. Writing was a means of salvation from an existence experienced as guilt-ridden; writing was expiation for it. In the act of writing, the comedian became a martyr, who was still a play actor fleeing reality and masking death in the quest for immortality. The grandfather himself was resurrected in the paradoxical Hidden God whose unseen hand had selected Poulou for no good reason to write great things. And the writer, wishing to "appear before the Holy Spirit as a precipitate of language," mystified himself into believing that he was both giver and gift, pure and free cause of himself (p. 161): "I was born of writing.... Writing, I existed. I escaped the adults. But I existed only to write and if I said 'me,' that signified 'me who writes.' No matter: I knew joy. The foundling gave himself private rendez-vous" (p. 127).

This ideology of writing is what Sartre would like to situate, demystify, and outgrow. But he seems to do so only partially. I have already remarked that the myth of self-genesis, closely related to the myth of literature, is not as fully and as critically scrutinized as the latter, and the superabundant attention paid to the latter may even function to obscure the role of the myth of self-genesis. In addition, it is difficult to date precisely the period during which Sartre believed in the myth of literature and to relate it in terms of distinct stages to later developments. (This problem is symptomatic of the more comprehensive difficulty in dating things or establishing a chronology in this highly repetitive text.) Sartre at one point states that he believed in the myth of literature until the age of twenty (p. 148). This would imply that he was already growing out of it by the time he wrote his well-known works (a view that agrees with my analysis of *Nausea*). He also, however, discusses *Nausea* as if, while writing it, he was still prey to the myth in all its force (p. 210). He still apparently took the pen as a sacrament that absolved the writer from the sin of existing. When he refers to his next stage— that of committed literature— he indicates that in a very significant way he displaced the myth of literature in taking the pen as a sword (p. 211). The fully emancipated position would presumably be a demystified one in which the pen would finally be recognized as a pen—the meaningful tautology achieved by cutting through layers of ideological mystification—and its use be supplemented by direct political action in society.

These considerations raise a final issue. In one sense, Sartre seems to affirm a total liberation and achieve a decisive distance between himself at fifty and the mystified Poulou who endured until some shifting point in his life:

The retrospective illusion has been smashed to bits; martyrdom, salvation, and immortality are falling to pieces; the edifice is going to ruin; I collared the Holy Spirit in the cellar and threw him out; atheism is a cruel and long-range affair: I think I've carried it through. I see clearly; I've lost my illusions; I know what my real jobs are; I surely deserve a prize for good citizenship. For the last ten years or so I've been a man who's been waking up, and who can't get over the fact, a man who can't think of his old ways without laughing and who doesn't know what to do with himself. [Pp. 210–11]

If one overlooks momentarily the self-parodic overlay in these lines and reads them "straight," one might say that Sartre in writing *The Words* has performed successful therapy on himself in the interest of enlightenment. He would thus be the master of parody as an instrument in the critique of ideology. But he would simultaneously still indulge the myth of self-genesis and total freedom. The writing of the text would itself be identical with the act of Sartre's becoming his own father and autonomously giving the spoiled brat that he was the verbal spanking he so richly deserved.

At the same time, however, explicit doubts are woven into the affirmations that raise questions about his mastery of the problems he has explored. The progressive time of the dialectical project of self-overcoming is enmeshed in that of repetition, which is "overcome" only through *truquage* (p. 201). As Sartre writes, he is implicated in the text that simultaneously writes him as it repeats the problems that are seemingly under control. Notice the subtle movement of the text up to the last two sentences:

I have become again the traveler without a ticket that I was at the age of seven. . . .

I have given up the office but not the frock: I still write. What else can I do?

*Nulla dies sine linea.*

It's a habit and, besides, it's my profession. For a long time, I took my pen for a sword; I now know we're powerless. No matter. I write and will keep writing books; they're needed; all the same, they do serve some purpose. Culture doesn't save anything or anyone, it doesn't justify. But it's a product of man: he projects himself into it, he recognizes himself in it; that critical mirror alone offers him his image. Moreover, that old, crumbling structure, my imposture, is also my character: one gets rid of a neurosis, one doesn't get cured of one's self. . . . Griselda's not dead. Pardaillan still inhabits me. So does Strogoff. I'm answerable only to them, who are answerable to God, and I don't believe in God. So try to figure it out. As for me, I can't, and I sometimes wonder whether I'm not playing loser wins and not trying hard to stamp out my old-time hopes so that everything will be restored to me a hundredfold. In that case, I would still be Philoctetes; that magnificent and stinking cripple gave everything away unconditionally, including his bow; but we can be sure that he's secretly waiting for his reward.

Let's drop that. Mamie [grandmother] would say:

"Gently, mortals, be discreet."

What I like about my madness is that it has protected me from the very beginning against the charms of the "elite": never have I thought that I was the happy possessor of a "talent"; my sole concern has been to save myself—nothing in my hands, nothing up my sleeve—by work and faith. As a result, my pure choice does not raise me above anyone. Without equipment, without tools, I set all of me to work in order to save all of me. [Pp. 211–12]

These penultimate lines do seem to expose Sartre to a situation of open questioning and playful self-doubt of which he is not entirely the master. The matter of stages along his way itself becomes a problematic question of degree. And it is significant that, in one of the very few direct quotations of another's voice in the book (actually a quote of a quote), a concluding word is given to the insightful and discreet, although petulant, grandmother—the only member of the family who "read" Sartre correctly. These lines would also seem to indicate that the call to order, including the project of dialectical totalization, comes in a decision related to the recognition of a play of forces subjected to control through explicit choice. This, I think, is the significance of the return to seriousness and the disarmingly frank, if not naive, affirmation of egalitarianism in the final words of the book. In a sense, to the extent that Sartre's autobiographical venture has been successfully self-questioning and "self-deconstructive," he has earned the right to these words (a right that is never based on total success): "If I relegate an impossible Salvation to the prop room, what remains? A whole man, composed of all men and as good as all of them and no better than any" (p. 213).

Sartre's monumental *L'Idiot de la famille* (2,801 pages) seems to return to the totalizing world of *Baudelaire* and *Saint Genet*. Flaubert is seen as a simulacrum of the young Sartre in *The*

*Words,* a pure practitioner of the theory of the imagination in *L'Imaginaire,* an extreme incarnation in "real life" of Antoine Roquentin—an imaginary person writing about imaginary things. Sartre's own past seems to return in the person of a rival other. But projection is vociferously denied. In the same breath that he denies projection, Sartre tells us that his long-standing antipathy to Flaubert has become empathy in the course of writing *L'Idiot* and that empathy is necessary for comprehension (*S. X,* p. 102). One may nevertheless ask whether empathy is paradoxically present largely in so far as Sartre's object of study is the precipitate of his own discourse. The dialectical attempt at total comprehension overwhelms its subject as it overwhelms the reader. Indeed, one does not read this philosophical *Bild-ungsroman cum roman fleuve;* one sinks and swims in it by turns, thereby emulating the rhythm of Sartre's writing. It is a work in which the sheer mass of analysis, hypothesis, and speculation far exceeds the critical point of comprehension, to leave the most patient reader with the unsettling feeling that he understands the subject less well after finishing it than before.[9]

The fiction of the bewildered reader (a fiction not entirely divorced from reality, as more than one review of *L'Idiot* will testify) serves to introduce a problem. In *L'Idiot* Sartre's totalizing intention gives birth to an often deviant flow of words that threatens to abort the dialectical project. The labor pains of a new epic, a "true novel," seem to generate an unintentional parody of the epic, which is difficult to situate in terms of genre or form. The true novel seems not to sublate truth and fiction in a higher-order synthesis but to dismember comprehension to the point where one can no longer tell what is true and what is fictive in the account. A disconcertingly simple interpretive schema (Flaubert plays loser wins: he escapes from active life into the imaginary and pure art) is so overburdened with allusion, analysis, context, and guesswork as to be rendered virtually unrecognizable. The "model" of dialectical totalization, integrating existential psychoanalysis and Marxism, is monster enough to kill off prematurely and devour all possible heirs. Awesome ambition spawns awful result. *Hubris* knows no limits, as the book grows like topsy and can be only arbitrarily terminated, not ended. A handful of facts induces hypothesis upon hypothesis, as the "true novel" metamorphoses into the pretext for a speculative mania whose relation to anything named "reality" seems purely coincidental. Positivism seems inverted, as a plethora of significance replaces fact. One looks in vain for the connective tissue of mediation between a paucity of information and an excess of interpretation about its putative meaning. As Sartre wins in his appropriative discourse, he simultaneously seems to lose. The existential shaman risks alienating his public, for there is no basis for a viable exchange between writer and reader in a mutual recognition of freedom. Sartre's Flaubert—the *homunculus* of his own discourse—almost emerges as the parricidal David who kills the generating Goliath. Or—to change the metaphor once again—counter-finality seems to be crowned king. For, in spite of what Sartre would like to say, the text somewhat perversely shows what Flaubert seemed to be saying all the time: You just can't win but you keep trying anyway. The apparent difference is that Flaubert said it (among other things) in an explicit parody of the epic, with considerably more style and mercifully fewer words.

The point reached by these reflections is, however, at best the beginning rather than the end of even the most schematic analysis. Let us start with the short preface to *L'Idiot*. As intimated earlier, the preface in a work of dialectics is the exterior formality or inaugural ceremony that presents what is to come and then effaces itself as it is interiorized and sublated by the principal text. Yet the very existence of the preface is paradoxical, for it is a remnant that in dialectical theory need not be there at all. It is like an intention that should never be articulated to be effective. That it is typically added to the principal text after the fact and is called "preface" only by polite convention makes its existence doubly enigmatic. When the preface explicitly announces themes that are at odds with the principal text and is, moreover, heavily supplemented by further "outside" texts that explicate it, its function is problematic in the extreme. Such is the case with the short preface to *L'Idiot*—an antechamber to which the principal text in one important respect never returns.

Sartre tells us in the preface that *L'Idiot de la famille* is the sequel to *Search for a Method (Question de méthode)*. It tries to answer the question: "What can one know of a man today?" The risk in the undertaking is that one may arrive at only "heterogeneous and irreducible levels of meaning." But, asserts Sartre, "this book attempts to prove that irreducibility is only apparent and that each bit of information put in its place becomes part of a whole that never ceases to make itself and simultaneously reveals its profound homogeneity with all the others" (*L'Idiot*, p. 7). In an interview of 1971, Sartre is even more insistent on this point, and his formulation takes a curiously positivistic turn: "The profound project of this book on Flaubert is to show that everything can be communicated and that— without being God, being a man like any other—one can arrive at a perfect understanding of a man if one has all the necessary elements. I can foresee Flaubert, I know him, and that is my goal, in order to prove that every man is perfectly knowable provided that one uses the appropriate method and has the necessary documents" (*S. X*, p. 106).

The totalizing dialectical method can prove itself and arrive at the whole truth about a life only in relation to a man taken as a concrete universal. Hence the question: "What do we know of Gustave Flaubert, for example?" The example is itself a manifestation of the whole that never ceases to totalize itself. But why does Sartre take Flaubert in particular as the *pars pro toto*? Sartre gives three reasons, enigmatically supplemented by an unnumbered fourth. (This is also the fate of the fourth in dialectics. Totalization does not account for the mediating "third" as a "fourth" that supplements in a way not sublated by the dialectical movement.)

The first reason is the personal feeling Sartre had ever since his rereading of the *Correspondance* in 1943 that he had "an account to settle" with Flaubert. He adds to these fighting words the assertion that his "initial antipathy has changed into empathy, the only attitude required for comprehension." Second, Flaubert "objectivated himself in his books." Sartre continues: "Anybody will tell you: 'Flaubert is the author of *Madame Bovary*.' What is then the relation between a man and his works? I have never accounted for it until now. Nor has anyone else to my knowledge. We shall see that it is double: *Madame Bovary* is defeat and victory; the man who portrays himself in the defeat is not the same as the one required in the victory; we must understand what that means" (*L'Idiot*, p. 8). Third, the thirteen volumes of Flaubert's first works˙and his correspondence appear "as the strangest of confidences, the most easily decodable: you would think you are listening to a neurotic freely associating [*parlant 'au hasard'*] on the psychoanalyst's couch." In this sense, Flaubert is presumably an easy subject for Sartre's difficult method. Finally, the unnumbered fourth reason: "I add that Flaubert, creator of the 'modern novel,' is at the crossroads of all the literary problems of today" (p. 8).

With reference to an interview of 1971, I have already discussed briefly the problem of empathy and projection raised by Sartre's first reason. In an interview of 1972, Sartre complicates the problem by stating that he was interested in Flaubert "because he was the imaginary": "With him, I am at the limits, at the very frontiers of the dream.... Flaubert represents for me the exact opposite of my own conception of literature: a total disengagement and the quest for a formal ideal that is not at all mine.... Flaubert began to fascinate me precisely because I saw in him, from every point of view, the contrary of myself. I asked myself: 'How is such a man possible?'" (*S. IX*, pp. 115–17). This train of thought provides another perspective on the account to be settled with Flaubert. For Flaubert is represented here as the radical "other"—at best the past that Sartre would like to believe he has entirely transcended. And the terms of Sartre's formulation do suggest exorcism, projection, scapegoating, and the denial of internal alterity.

The second reason is highly paradoxical in light of the text that follows. Sartre takes Flaubert's statement "Madame Bovary, c'est moi" literally. Not only does Flaubert "feminize" himself in Emma Bovary as a character. He *is* in some special sense the author of *Madame Bovary*. Yet, except for a few relatively allusive analyses, the study of *Madame Bovary* is to be the orphan of the principal text. It is the inquiry promised as the ending of the whole protracted cliff-hanger of an interpretation that follows. Yet it is the ending that is continually deferred and that finally never appears. One result for Sartre's story is that we see his conception of Flaubert's defeat, but we do not see clearly how he would conceive of Flaubert's victory. In this respect, it is interesting to compare two different statements by Sartre from interviews—the first from 1971, when he still expected to write the fourth volume of *L'Idiot*, and the second from 1975, when he recognized that, like Godot, it would never come.

In the interview of 1971, Sartre develops the theme of the relationship between defeat and victory in the writing of *Madame Bovary*. In a first moment, Flaubert as author "inscribes his defeat in the book," for he has never entirely transcended the problems he had as a child. But the book as victory requires "an author other than the unhappy Flaubert who projected himself into his book—the one I describe in the first volumes." Sartre, however, immediately adds: "In reality, there is only one Flaubert who oscillates constantly between the two poles. If I study the life, I can only find the defeated Flaubert, and if I study *Madame Bovary*, I am obligated to discover what makes Flaubert victorious." These judgmental terms provide little idea of the specific changes in the approach to the problems required by the shift of focus from life to works. On this point, Sartre is equivocal, for he both affirms and denies the importance of the text. Immediately following the last quoted statement, he asserts: "In other words, there is a moment in research when it is the *text* that must be looked into: it is the moment of victory." And stylistic analyses will involve the use of "'structuralist' techniques," which are affirmed by Sartre to be related to "totalizing criticism" (*S. X*, pp. 108–9). Just before these words, however, Sartre declares that he is "completely opposed to the idea of the text" (*S. X*, p. 106). And just after them he associates the "old formalism" of Bakhtin in his study of Dostoevsky with the "new formalism" of semiotics and sends them both packing: "On the whole, what I reproach these studies for is that they lead to nothing: they do not encircle their object; they are forms of knowledge that dissipate themselves" (pp. 109–10). At the very least, the highly problematic notion of combining some form of textual analysis with the encircling discourse of dialectical totalization would make the study of *Madame Bovary* an important part of Sartre's project, if not its teleological culmination.

In an interview of 1975, Sartre decisively changes his views on the significance of the study of *Madame Bovary* for his work. One wonders whether the decisiveness of the change is related to the possibility that, given the nature of his approach in the earlier volumes, it is no longer feasible to assert that the volume on *Madame Bovary* would add a significantly different twist to the "totalizing" movement. In any event, by 1975 Sartre apparently believes that the study of *Madame Bovary* either would be redundant or could be easily extrapolated from the earlier volumes:

> I will not finish my Flaubert. But I am not very unhappy because I think that I said essentially what I had to say in the first three volumes. Someone else could write the fourth on the basis of the three I wrote.
>
> All the same, this book on Flaubert weighs on me like remorse. "Remorse" is perhaps too strong a word. After all, I had to give it up by the force of things. I *wanted* to finish it. And, at the same time, the fourth volume was simultaneously the most difficult for me and the one that interested me the least: the study of the style of *Madame Bovary*. But, I tell you, the essential is done, even if the work remains in suspense. [*S. X*, p. 151]

The tension in the movement of the second paragraph is indicative of that in both Sartre and his project. The study of *Madame Bovary* might have been the most interesting part of the whole work precisely to the extent that it would have posed the greatest challenge to the totalizing dialectic. Indeed, *Madame Bovary* as a text might have deconstructed the very type of discourse with which Sartre apparently would have tried to comprehend it.

Sartre's third reason for his turn to Flaubert is somewhat deceptive: the surfeit of confessional literature. One of Sartre's problems was to be the scarcity of information about Flaubert's earliest years. Sartre would use "imagination" to invent not only hypotheses but also "facts." As he puts it: "In these conditions, one must choose: abandon research or glean indices everywhere, examine documents in another perspective, in another light, and rip from them other information. Of these two alternatives, I choose the second" (*L'Idiot*, I, 56). The intimation that information may be ripped untimely from the womb is borne out. Sartre does not privilege "real" letters over fiction in the interpretation of a life. But this is only because he places both on the same documentary or confessional level as homogeneous objects of a straightforward, symptomatic reading. In relation to the fiction, his task is somewhat (but not altogether) facilitated by the fact that he devotes preponderant attention to the juvenilia. In relation to the correspondence, he rarely perceives that Flaubert's letters are texts at times as intricate and highly staged as Flaubert's fiction. His homogenization of fiction and correspondence as objects of symptomatic reading, moreover, prevents him from raising the "intertextual" question of the sometimes contestatory and sometimes reinforcing interplay between the two. Time and again, in reading the fiction or the letters, Sartre asserts that $x$ "symbolizes" $y$ in the unproblematic sense that $x$ univocally means $y$.

The fourth, unnumbered reason for choosing Flaubert is, I think, related to Sartre's initial belief that the study of *Madame Bovary* would have been the "ending" of his story. Flaubert, after all, was not significant in the history of the novel for his juvenilia. The "totalizing" approach is, by any standard, obliged to confront the great works that make Flaubert historically significant. The study of *Madame Bovary* would have required Sartre to say why he thought Flaubert "creator of the 'modern novel,' is at the crossroads of all the literary problems of today." As it is, his references to this question hardly fulfill the expectation created by the preface. Or, if they do, it is obliquely, for the comments in the principal text on this problem are as marginal as is the status of the fourth reason in the preface. There are perhaps two especially significant passages in which Sartre gives his reasons why Flaubert was crucial in the history of the novel. Here is one: "Flaubert created the modern novel for this precise reason: he never knew how to *tie* his books *together*. It is our good fortune that he was ignorant of the 'rules of composition' and if *Madame Bovary* has the cohesion of a growing plant and the flowing unity of a slow stream, if we find in it, despite the 'constructed scenes' ['*scènes à faire*'], a stammering *natural* harmony, it is because he was perfectly incapable of planning: we will return to this" (*L'Idiot*, II, 2023).

In this passage, Sartre relates Flaubert's innovative role to the childhood problems imputed to him in *L'Idiot*. The "creation" seems rather directly to flow from the "failure" of the child to take an active, assertive relation to language that would enable him to tie things together in an intentional project itself securely tied to praxis in the "real" world. The "passivity" of Flaubert is evoked in the curious reference to "natural harmony" (which recalls Lukàcs's reference in *The Theory of the Novel* to the putative continuity of time as *durée* in *The Sentimental Education*). One might argue in radical contrast to Sartre's approach in this passage that Flaubert was in novelistic practice not ignorant of the "rules of composition" that tied together the traditional novel. These rules were precisely the objects of deconstructive strategy at work and at play in his novels. This deconstruction of the traditional novel (as well as of the epic) is "what" made Flaubert significant for writers that followed, including, for example, the Sartre of *Nausea*. The impression of a "stammering *natural* harmony," to the extent that it exists, is itself the *trompe-l'oeil* effect of a highly constructed and staged technique that Flaubert's writing both papers over and discloses. One may observe this movement in the shifts of narrative perspective in *Madame Bovary*, which are often drastic. Yet they seem to flow naturally and even appear "realistic," given Flaubert's strategy of simultaneously writing on a recognizable level with reference to traditional expectations and critically excavating those expectations on a second level. The shift from a first-person to a third-person narrative at the "beginning" of *Madame Bovary* sets the stage for more subtle shifts in narrative perspective to follow. The "effect" of this strategy, one might argue, is to produce a text in which multiple narrative "positions" create indeterminacy of voice and tend to cross out or erase one another. In this way, the text approaches the limit of language in which the "author" (implied or otherwise) is nonpertinent or decapitated. This shifting role of narrative perspective is one significant way in which Flaubert writes the traditional novel *sous rature*. [10]

Let us turn briefly to a specific case. The fiacre scene in *Madame Bovary* is especially interesting for the problem of shifts in narrative perspective. And it is one scene in *Madame Bovary* to which Sartre devotes a relatively extended analysis in *L'idiot* (II, 1275 ff.). The fiacre scene seems to be written from no one's point of view: it is almost "pure" text, writing itself. Sartre finds in it a dehumanizing failure of dramatic illusion in the narrative because of a "malignant intention" he imputes to the author who manipulates characters as puppets instead of seeing them "from the inside" as human beings. Thus Sartre sees in this scene only the supposed problems of Flaubert as a writer and not the limitations of his own approach to the text. The difficulty in Sartre's approach is that there is no reason to believe that Flaubert was striving for dramatic illusion—which was precisely one element of traditional narrative deconstructed in his works. And the imputation of malignant intention can be made only from a perspective centered on man or author, which Flaubert's text itself places in question. On one level, the fiacre scene might be compared to Sartre's own "defamiliarizing" treatment of the Sunday ritual of bourgeois greeting in *Nausea*. On a more general level, it might be read as an allegory of the problem of language in the modern world—a problem at issue in all of *Madame Bovary*. In this scene, the enclosed fiacre, which resembles a funeral wagon and which houses the copulating couple (Emma and Léon), hurtles aimlessly through the streets of the provincial town. The bewildered coachman who "conducts" it obeys orders that are shouted impatiently from within the coach and that lead nowhere. The scene ends in this way:

> One time, around noon, in the open country, just as the sun beat down most fiercely against the old plated lanterns, a bare hand appeared under the yellow canvas curtain, and threw out some scraps of paper that scattered in the wind, alighting further off like white butterflies on a field of red clover all in bloom.
> Then, at about six o'clock the carriage stopped in a back street of the Beauvoisine Quarter, and a woman got out, walking with her veil down and without looking back.[11]

The scraps of paper are torn fragments of Emma's intended farewell letter to Léon. One might suggest that what Sartre's purely negative analysis fails to evoke is the force of this scene with reference to a history of the novel and even to a Marxist critique of modern bourgeois society. Even if one admits in

Flaubert the thematic intention to dehumanize man and demoralize the reader, this sinister project would depend for its effectiveness upon the techniques that Sartre's analysis refuses to recognize. As Jonathan Culler observes, "The reader would not be demoralized, after all, by a tale told from the point of view of an order which he could identify and adopt as his own."[12]

The second of the passages in *L'Idiot* relating to Flaubert's innovative role in the history of the novel is the following: "The Flaubertian revolution comes from the fact that this writer, distrusting language since childhood, begins—in contrast to the classics—by postulating the principle of the noncommunicability of the lived" (II, 1986). Here Sartre sees Flaubert's revolution in terms that allow it to be appropriated by his own attempt at totalization. Flaubert postulated the principle of the noncommunicability of the lived—the "principle" that Sartre will account for and sublate in the dialectic between comprehension and conceptual knowledge. A specific avenue of appropriation is the identification of lived experience with Flaubert's "l'indisable." The paradox is that in Flaubert *l'indisable*—whose spelling, as Sartre noted, departed from the ordinary *l'indicible*—apparently could not be specified in unambiguous terms and seemed to indicate "unsayable" problems that could not be decided through dialectical totalization. For Sartre, *l'indisable* is Flaubert's lived experience as the neurosis that, through the game of loser wins, led to and was totalized in his original choice to be a writer.

It would be futile to attempt to trace in detail Sartre's labyrinthine effort to totalize the lived experience of Flaubert as family idiot. Sartre makes every effort to show how the child is father to the man while not taking from the man the ultimate responsibility for what he makes of what he is made. For our purposes, a few indications of the more problematic features of Sartre's principal text must suffice.

In the first two volumes of *L'Idiot*, Sartre focuses on Flaubert's interiorization of the exterior in his family. In the third volume, he turns to the exteriorization of the interior in Flaubert's relation to his times. In this third volume, Sartre argues that there was an affinity between Flaubert's neurosis and the collective condition of France under the Second Empire. The regime of Napoleon III was itself an imaginary construct superimposed upon a hollow reality—a superstructure that lacked an adequate infrastructure. As such, it was the fitting context for Flaubert's own imaginary labors. Sartre argues that the reason for Flaubert's decline in productivity and loss of creativity at the time of the fall of the Empire and the coming of the Third Republic was that Flaubert after 1870 experienced himself very much as a fish out of water. With more specific reference to aesthetics, Sartre argues that there was a special relationship between art and neurosis in Flaubert, the poetics of his time (to which he contributed) and the expectation of readers. Art for Art's sake was the neurotic poetics of postromanticism. Its attempt to negate reality and assert the formal purity of art was an ideological conception of art in neurotic terms as a derealization of the real and a realization of the imaginary. To be born to pure Art, the artist had to die to social reality. Readers of the time expected the writer to be neurotic. Flaubert's greatness, for Sartre, was related to the fact that he was a genuine neurotic (at least as a hysteric). Pseudo-neurotics like Leconte de Lisle only play-acted at being mad but lacked the lived experience to make their game genuine. Flaubert corresponded in a privileged way to the "objective spirit" of the time—its culture, which for Sartre was the way in which the time fell into the practico-inert. Yet, while the poetics and the readership of the time associated art and neurosis, this association was ideological. It did not fully apply to the work of art itself—*Madame Bovary*, for example. Flaubert's neurosis was the means of writing *Madame Bovary* (*L'Idiot*, III, 24–25). But the work of art is not itself simply a morbid document: "Horror is never presented; it haunts the book without giving itself to be seen. Ceaselessly aimed at [*visée*], it escapes. Precisely for this reason, *Madame Bovary* does not enter into the categories of pathology. In itself it does not refer one to the subject who wrote it or to his obsessions" (III, 30).

The sweep of the analysis in the third volume is impressive. Yet if there are difficulties in applying the categories of pathology to a work of art, there are also problems in applying them to an aesthetic theory, the expectations of a readership, or the ideology of a society. At least one must account for the institutions and norms that inform society and culture on all of these more or less related levels. There are a number of empirical difficulties in Sartre's approach, aside from the theoretical problems he does not so much confront as hurdle. Sartre offers little if any evidence that the readers of the time expected the writer to be neurotic or that they gave themselves over to a simulated neurotic experience in reading. This notion is plausible only if one identifies neurosis with escapist reading—and this type of reading of Flaubert was possible only on a "naive" level, which his work simultaneously invited and undermined. If one takes the trial of Flaubert as an index of the way he was read in the context of at least one crucial social institution, the expectation was not that of neurosis but that of conformity to moral and religious norms. One might argue that this manifest concern masked a neurotic involvement. But the more pertinent problem, I think, is the way in which a work like *Madame Bovary* was scandalous, not because of the reason stated at the trial— deviance from moral and religious norms—but because of its extreme problematization of the distinctions or oppositions on which those norms—and the trial itself—were founded. *Madame Bovary* neither praises adultery and pollutes marriage nor attacks adultery and defends marriage. (These alternatives are highly significant in the "reading"—or systematic misreading—at the trial for both the prosecution and the defense. For important ideological reasons, the trial had to repress the ways in which the novel undercuts the grounds for trial.) The novel subverts the opposition between adultery and marriage by threatening to show that in certain contexts they amount to the same thing. It is this incestuous complicity of dominant and presumably opposed categories that produces the shock effect of the novel, in its own time and in ours. One might perhaps suggest that its scandalous power operates in an analogous way for the organizing oppositions of Sartre's own analysis—including those of normality and pathology, activity and passivity. The novel discloses their tenuousness in its world

and, by implication, in our world. And it suggests that a radically different way of approaching problems may be necessary.

A further difficulty in Sartre's analysis is that after the fall of
the Second Empire Flaubert wrote what are for many commentators his most forcefully "Flaubertian" works—the *Trois Contes*
and *Bouvard et Pécuchet*, for example. Sartre rarely refers to these
works, and when he does discuss a post-1870 work (*Saint Julien
l'Hospitalier*), it is simply to show its uncreative redundancy. But
these later works are no less (or no more) "Flaubert" than
*Madame Bovary* and, while they certainly involve and explicitly
treat the problem of repetition, they are susceptible to an
analysis rather different from Sartre's.

One especially problematic feature of Sartre's approach generally in volume three is that he implicitly takes Marx's analysis
in *The Eighteenth Brumaire*, which Marx applied to events leading
up to the foundation of the Second Empire, and applies it to that
regime once established and operating. The problem is that the
analysis, as the reference to Marx itself shows, can be applied to
other periods or phenomena, including the Third Republic. The
historical analysis related by Sartre to crucial differentiations (for
example, in Flaubert's work) threatens to be nondifferential.
One might almost infer from Sartre's account that the Third
Republic was the possessor of some original purity denied to the
Second Empire.[13] From a Marxist perspective, the similarities
between the two periods (especially beginning with the so-
called "liberalization" of the Second Empire in the 1860s) would
be more striking than their differences. And it is dubious
whether the differences can be explicated in accordance with
Sartre's criteria. For, if the Second Empire was a sham empire,
the Third Republic was somewhat a sham democracy—even
from non-Marxist perspectives.[14]

The first two volumes of *L'Idiot* attempt to show how
Flaubert's life within his family generated the tangle of double
binds that led from the neurotic child to the neurotic writer. The
absence of a mother's love was especially significant for Sartre in
creating Flaubert's "bad insertion into language"—his feeling of
being a passive object or "signified" of words rather than an

active, speaking subject. His father rejected him when he was still unable to read at the age of seven. The father was an extremely successful doctor—a self-made man who dominated the family and expressed an ideology of secular rationalism. All the father's hopes were placed in Flaubert's elder brother, who succeeded brilliantly everywhere that Flaubert had an almost intentional will to fail. The elder brother was designated legitimate heir to the father's profession and Flaubert was destined to inferiority. The mother was from an aristocratic family and had religious inclinations. She was a stark contrast to the husband who dominated her and whose reaction to Gustave she shared. Gustave was (presumably) handled with meticulous care as an infant but was denied the warmth and genuine affection of the mother. She attempted to relive more happily her own somber early years in the person of Gustave's younger sister Caroline, who was also the ambivalent object of Gustave's love and lasting devotion.

Within this complex family structure, Flaubert developed into a passive being with a strong sense of fatality and an inability to relate actively to the "real" world. He became, for Sartre, a genuine hysteric who imitated schizophrenia. Art via neurosis played out the game of loser wins through which Flaubert both repeated his childhood scene (in ways that Sartre attempts to detail extensively) and somehow came to terms with it (in ways Sartre only suggests). The passage from even remote association with "active life" in the preparation for a hated legal career to a sequestered life as writer came most dramatically, in Sartre's view, at the time of Flaubert's famous fainting fit at Pont l'Evêque—a "peak" experience that is the object of some 350 pages of analysis toward the end of the second volume of *L'Idiot*.

In what is perhaps the interpretive dénouement of his text, Sartre inquires into the relationship of Flaubert's fit at Pont l'Evêque to *The First Sentimental Education*: "One night in January '44, Achille and Gustave are returning from Deauville, where they had gone to look over the châlet. It is dark out, as black as the inside of a furnace; Gustave himself is driving the cabriolet. Suddenly, somewhere near Pont l'Evêque, as a wagon overtakes them on the right, Gustave drops the reins and falls thunderstruck at his brother's feet" (II, 1771). Chapters 26 and 27 of *The First Sentimental Education* were added after this fiacre scene in Flaubert's own life. For Sartre, the experience at the bridge was the locus of Flaubert's original choice of being—"a moment in which a life totalizes itself and realizes the destiny it has been bearing within itself" (p. 1799). The fit at the bridge divides Flaubert's existence into a "before" of activity and an "after" of sequestered escape from reality and dedication to pure art. It simultaneously "bridges"—through a beautiful correspondence—the gap between the lived experience of Flaubert and Sartre's own totalizing comprehension of that experience, in this sense shoring up the intuitive validity of Sartre's interpretation. Dialectical understanding corresponds (dialectically?) to the dialectic of the lived. Sartre will deemphasize the importance of recurrent breakdowns in Flaubert's life: they simply confirm the original totalization in the fit at the bridge and are, in a sense, mere commentaries on it. It is the crisis at the bridge that is the epitome of Flaubert's neurosis as it is the epitome of Sartre's interpretation. Through this hysterical conversion, Flaubert dramatically somatized the psychic by fainting away from a seemingly predestined "real-life" career in law and into an "imaginary" life as a writer. The cumulative binds of the "can't-win" situation of his life were passively acted out and in some sense actively passed over. Similarly, the difficulties of Sartre's interpretation are overcome inasmuch as it receives its crucial experimental test in the comprehension of Flaubert's apocalyptic moment of truth—his radical conversion experience, his identity crisis, his rite of passage. For this experience was of quasi-religious proportions: "What the convert of Pont l'Evêque is trying to recover is that identification of the Father with God which once guaranteed his personal identity" (II, 2083). What Sartre himself is trying to recover is the confirmation that the dialectical totalization of existential Marxism represents the use of fiction in the service of truth—that it is the real thing.

For Sartre, the last two chapters of *The First Sentimental Education* "symbolize" the fit at the bridge and the passage from active life to pure art. Sartre devotes his most extended analysis of any single work of Flaubert to chapters 26 and 27 of this early novel—some 185 pages of sustained inquiry. These two chapters seem to tell it all. In them, Flaubert "recuperates his neurosis" (p. 1923). And, through these chapters, Flaubert's experience at the bridge further "symbolizes" the convulsive death rattle of romanticism and the birth pangs of the new poetic order of Art for Art's sake: "These ultimate pages . . . contain an *Art poétique* that could serve as a manifesto for postromantic writers and that in any case define brilliantly the future work of Flaubert" (p. 1924). This analysis by Sartre is perhaps the one that renders superfluous the projected study of *Madame Bovary*. For, from the time of the fit at the bridge, Flaubert's works as well as his life mark time within the original existential choice of being. The discussion of chapters 26 and 27 of *The First Sentimental Education* (1845) is immediately followed in *L'Idiot* by a discussion of *La Légende de Saint Julien l'Hospitalier* (1875). The earlier framework of Flaubert is seen to be repeated almost mechanically in the later work. And repetition is not interpreted by Sartre as a challenge to his totalizing comprehension but as its simple confirmation.

Sartre's analysis of the last chapters of *The First Sentimental Education* moves predominantly on the level of a straightforward symptomatic reading. Jules in the novel is a projection of Flaubert. The fit at the bridge is "symbolized" by Jules's encounter with the dog at the bridge in chapter 26. After his fit, Flaubert believes what Jules presumably comes to believe in chapter 27: salvation is to be found in turning away from active life toward pure art. Let us inquire into Sartre's pivotal analysis in terms of the intimately related questions of the "symbolic" expression of the fit at Pont l'Evêque and the status of pure art: "There is nothing in *The Education* that is the *realistic* equivalent of the accident of Pont l'Evêque. If one reads well, however, there is an entire chapter which describes *symbolically* the rupture of Jules with his past, that is, the instant when the convert in fear and trembling sees his life totalized, in all its ugliness, and is tempted to fall back upon it, then takes flight and escapes by sequestration. It is the episode of the dog" (II, 1927).

Before chapter 26, the novel seemed to be largely about

Henry, the seemingly successful man of the world, and only marginally about Jules, his more aesthetic childhood friend and correspondent. In chapter 26, Jules is propelled to the center of the text, and he seems to undergo a transformative experience. Jules, "already well along the path to conversion[,] encounters one evening" a mangy dog (p. 1927). Sartre quotes Flaubert in observing that "Jules saw in it 'only one of those dogs that have lost their master, that one chases off with shouts, that wander aimlessly in the countryside, that one finds dead on a roadside'" (p. 1927). Yet this seemingly ordinary dog is also epiphanic: it evokes in Jules the ambivalent feelings of horror and fascination. For Sartre, "this dog, so repulsive, so unkempt, represents the very life of Flaubert" (p. 1928), and Sartre compares it to a surreality that is close to the sacred (p. 1929). The dog in this sense is *l'indisable* as the lived, neurotic experience of Flaubert. Sartre summarizes the story of this strange beast's sinister tracking of Jules to the point where Jules, exasperated by the confrontation, resorts to violence and beats the dog off. Jules returns home and "'reflects on what has just happened to him.'" Sartre quotes Flaubert further and adds his own italics: "'In all that had happened between him and the monster, in everything related to this adventure, there was something so intimate, so profound, and at the same time so precise [*net*] that one had to recognize a reality of another sort and as real as vulgar reality although it seemed to contradict the latter. *What existence offered of the tangible, of the sensible, disappeared in his thought as secondary and useless, as an illusion which is only the surface*'" (p. 1928). Sartre then refers to Jules's strange desire to see the dog again. Jules goes down the stairs of his house and opens the door: "'The dog was curled up on the threshold.'" These are the last words of chapter 26. The following chapter begins in this way: 'This was his last day of pathos [*pathétique*]; after that he got over his superstitious fears'" (p. 1928).

Sartre immediately begins his next paragraph, not by noting the blank that separates the two chapters, but by attempting to fill or recuperate it by interpreting the meaning of the dog. He presents the meaning of *l'indisable*: "The dog is the temptation of pathos; at the same time, it is his past life, his loves, his excesses, Lucinde, the desperate hours when he thought of suicide, a few instants of illusory happiness" (pp. 1928–29). After continuing in this vein for a few more sentences, Sartre returns obliquely to the blank between chapters 26 and 27 only toward the middle of the paragraph:

Curiously we do not assist at the definitive rupture: Jules goes down, opens the door, the dog is there; what happens? It is very significant that Flaubert says not a word and that he declares in the following chapter: 'This was his last day of pathos.' As if, between the last lines of chapter 26 and the first of chapter 27, there was situated the true crisis. . . . One can imagine anything except that, upon seeing the beast, he calmly closed the door and went back to bed. For he was still *pathétique* at this instant. What brought it about that the next day he ceased to be it forever? In any case, the encounter with dog is the *cover-event* [*l'évènement-couverture*] which simultaneously reveals and masks the true event of Pont l'Evêque. [II, 1929]

From a different perspective, related to a different interpretation of *The First Sentimental Education*, the true crisis indicated by the blank between chapters is that of Sartre's own analysis—the critical point at which the dialectical totalization itself meets the beast that both tempts it to engage in the hunt and eludes it. In this sense, the dog would "be" the "symbol" that is both too full and too empty for totalizing interpretation—the uncanny "presence" in the text of the unconscious, the absent center, the supplement to totalization. It would also be the *piège à cons* that both invites a recuperating or appropriating interpretation and frustrates it. In the blank between the two chapters, the reader's expectation of some meaningful interpretation of the final, mock-melodramatic encounter with the dog is aborted. The cupboard is bare, and the reader (or the existential analyst) is in the same position as Jules: he is not given the satisfying bone of meaning for which the text has made him pant. He can only—as in some sense he must—set up a totalizing howl to "compensate" for his loss.

One might further argue that what is explored in Jules's encounter with the dog is not simply the experience of Flaubert at the bridge but the relation of that experience to its fictional "representation." One has in this enigmatic encounter an allegory in the text of the very problem of the text—that of writing autobiographical fiction with its disconcerting, "mimetic" play between the real and the imaginary. Sartre's totalizing interpretation is an attempt to tie down and domesticate the dog by stopping the play of the text and fixating it in a univocal manner. For Sartre, the encounter with the dog symbolizes the "real" experience at the bridge, and the imaginary can be ultimately reduced to the real. Before the encounter, Jules (or Flaubert) is one thing, *pathétique* for example; after it, he is dramatically another—although he was paradoxically well on his way to conversion before it. Yet the dog seems almost literally to lie on the threshold of ambiguity between Jules and itself—between Jules and Flaubert, between the text and the reader, between Flaubert and Sartre, between the real and the imaginary, and so on. This endless series of possible substitutions is itself "related" to the problem of the dog as "symbol." The dog "as" supplement to totalization both elicits the attempt at domestication and contests it. One has here another side of the relation of Sartre to Flaubert, which Sartre himself saw in terms of the relation to the imaginary. Flaubert is the beast of the imaginary for Sartre and, rather than explore the enigmatic interplay suggested by that status, Sartre would prefer to master it.

Neil Hertz observes in an excellent article that the question of totalization is itself at issue in *The First Sentimental Education*. While recognizing the richness and energy in Sartre's interpretation, Hertz raises doubts about its accuracy (some of which we have already mentioned). Chapter 26 contains a complex textual development which Sartre does not fully trace. As the chapter opens, Jules experiences a "serenity" that soon dissolves into feelings of wonder and anxiety: "Turning inwards he finds nothing but a painful 'confusion, a whole world whose secret, whose unity, he could not understand.' . . . In Sartre's terms, we might say that Jules is confronted by all that is apparently 'heterogeneous and irreducible' in his life."[15]

At this point Jules imagines that, through "art, pure art," the scattered fragments of his life might be arranged into a meaningful whole that is teleologically oriented. Jules has a vision of totality that seems to recuperate the blanks and ambiguities of his life. But it is precisely this apocalyptic vision of totality that is disrupted by the barking of the dog. The dog first appears in the text not to fulfill the totalizing vision that encapsulates a life but to displace it: "Jules tried to discover some difference in the monotony of these furious, plaintive and frenetic sounds; he forced himself to guess at and seize the thought, the prognostic, the tale or the complaint that they were trying to express; but his ear could hear nothing but the same vibrations, almost continuous, strident, always alike."[16] Jules tries to appropriate the meaning of this disconcerting experience by running through the same possible interpretations that Sartre himself mentions with reference to the meaning of the dog! But, in the text, they do not succeed in taking hold.

The supplementary "position" of the dog in the text is further suggested by the relationship between Jules's encounter with it and the problem of pure art. Is the status of pure art in this text unproblematic as a saving belief or credo of Jules, which by extension "symbolizes" the ideology of Flaubert? Or is there something suspicious in the association of pure art with what is, at least on one level, a mangy dog story?

Hertz observes that pure art is discussed in chapter 26 before the encounter with the dog at the bridge as well as in chapter 27 after that encounter. Before the dog appears, Jules already looks to pure art as a way out of his difficulties—and one might add that only at this point does the text explicitly refer to "art, pure art":

Jules' state of mind here is, it would seem, indistinguishable from what it will become after his encounter with the dog; if anything the language of these pages is more convincing, because considerably less inflated, than that of Chapter 27. And indeed Sartre, in the course of a discussion of how Jules is represented *after* his conversion, draws repeatedly on these earlier pages . . . as though there were no compelling reason to differentiate the two moments in Jules' progress (cf. in particular p. 1932, where Sartre constructs a long question out of a medley of fragments from both sections of the novel; also pp. 1926–37, 1966–67). But if no such differentiation is necessary, what becomes of the notion of conversion, of that "definitive rupture" that Sartre would locate in the lives of both Jules and his creator?[17]

One might intensify the force of this question by adding that art, when it does re-emerge in chapter 27, is open to question precisely because the language with which Jules and Flaubert surround it is so inflated and *pathétique*. Not only was the day of his encounter with the dog decidedly not the last day of pathos in Jules's life, but the highly staged onslaught of pathos-ridden clichés and bloated sentiments that introduces Jules's "commitment" to art also functions as an almost Pavlovian signal of what the text itself has led the wary reader to suspect. Indeed, chapter 27, until the discussion of art—especially the catalogue of distinctions between Jules the artist and his opposite number in "active life," Henry, who reappears in this chapter after being left out of the picture in chapter 26—resembles the bathetic parody of the epic and encyclopedic quest in *Bouvard et Pécuchet*. This is quite significant to the extent that salvation through art is the object of Jules's quest. There are excessively numerous and somewhat fragile, if not confusing, distinctions to oppose Jules and Henry in chapter 27 and serve as the textual support for Jules's affirmation of art. One obvious question—of a sort that also arises time and again in *Bouvard et Pécuchet*—is whether these distinctions have sufficient thematic force to bolster a real difference between the two men. Does not a surfeit or excess of distinctions lose organizing power and threaten to collapse the different into the same—Jules into Henry, both of whom are fictive (if not incestuous) "projections" of the same writer, Flaubert? (And is there not a similar problem in *L'Idiot* itself in regard to the relationship between Flaubert and Sartre?)

The point is whether Art for Art's sake is not a doctrine or credo but a highly self-conscious fiction whose problematic status is recognized in *The First Sentimental Education*. One might perhaps speak of the Golgotha of pure art in Flaubert's works—but in which the cult object is necessarily threatened with desecration and demystification. It is, moreover, interesting that *The First Sentimental Education* is the last novel in which Flaubert directly treated pure art and created a fictional alter ego in the person of a writer. And, in a sense, the treatment of pure art as the road to salvation resembles its treatment in Sartre's *Nausea*. (Through a somewhat burlesque "elective affinity," the status of the dog in the text is itself comparable to that of the chestnut tree in *Nausea*.) In both novels, salvation through art is subject to ironization. In Flaubert's later novels and stories where art is treated analogically or allegorically, its agonistic contest with irony and parody remains. But it is fought or played out in more indirect and subtle ways.

Significantly, Flaubert not only tested the totalizing interpretation in his fiction but also subscribed to it himself in his *Correspondance* with reference to the experience at Pont l'Evêque. In a now famous letter (which Sartre discusses) written two years after the crisis, Flaubert referred to the event at the bridge as dividing his life into "two distinct existences" with an irreversible directedness leading from "active life" to "something else." Flaubert thus underwrites Sartre's view and reveals his own desire to make full and satisfying sense of things. Yet the question one may ask is whether the relation of the totalizing interpretation and elements that contest it is more compelling and even more "realistic" in the fiction. Should one "read" the life in this case not in the terms of the letters but in those of the fiction?

In contrast with its treatment of the crisis at the bridge, the *Correspondance* does not reinforce Sartre's view with reference to the closely related problem of the status of pure art. The *Correspondance* does not present Art for Art's sake or a formalistic aesthetics as the simple object of an ideology or credo. On this issue, one may juxtapose two famous selections from the *Correspondance*—both of which were written apropos of *Madame Bovary*. First is part of the letter (January 16, 1852) on the notorious "livre sur rien":

> What seems beautiful to me, what I should like to write, is a book about nothing, a book dependent on nothing external, which would be held together by the strength of its style, just as the earth, suspended in the void, depends on nothing external for its support; a book which would have almost no subject, or at least in which the subject would be almost invisible, if such a thing is possible... from the standpoint of pure Art one might almost establish the axiom that there is no such thing as subject, style in itself being an absolute manner of seeing things. [Vol. II, p. 345]

This passage seems relatively straightforward in its affirmation of formalistic, self-referential art. But one must note the difficulty in the analogy with the earth, which brings up the problem of gravity. And one must further note the triple "almost"—"almost no subject," "almost invisible," and "almost establish the axiom"—as well as the qualification in the clause "if such a thing is possible." A second famous passage about *Madame Bovary* (in a letter of July 12, 1853) seems to convert the conditional possibility of pure Art into an unconditional impossibility: "What drives one to despair is thinking that, even if it is successful in attaining perfection, this [scene in *Madame Bovary*] can only be acceptable [*passable*] and will never be beautiful because of its very subject [or content—*à cause du fond même*]. I do the work of a clown; but what does a *tour de force* prove, after all? No matter: 'God helps those who help themselves.' The cart is, however, at times quite heavy to be extricated from the mud" (vol. III, pp. 276–77). Here the subject or content contaminates the purest of styles and makes the writer himself subject to the very dangers, for example, those of stupidity or *bêtise*, from which he would like to distance himself. In the *Correspondance*, I would suggest, is evidence of what is fully exemplified in the novels and stories: Art for Art's sake is not a simple doctrine or ideology in Flaubert. It is at best a self-conscious fiction with a tenuous, problematic status that is poignantly recognized by a writer who at times would like to believe differently.

I would not, however, conclude with the impression that one can reduce *L'Idiot de la famille* to its thematic *Bovarysme* (the quest for the "true novel") or reverse roles by presenting Sartre as the naive *con* whom Flaubert might have invented if he did not exist to provide the analyses that Flaubert both invited and radically placed in question. The project of demoralizing the reader, the hatred of the human race, a negative critical outlook verging on nihilism, a deadly desire to transcend an ugly reality—these tendencies do exist in Flaubert's texts, although not in the unproblematic, unqualified form asserted in Sartre's totalizing interpretation. And the enigma of *L'Idiot* itself is that, in his confrontation with the imaginary, Sartre writes beyond his intentional project. The explicit goal of providing a totalizing dialectical interpretation of the other—who is himself a surrogate for the imaginary—gives way to a discourse that is not entirely controlled by this finality. The totalizing project generates its own

Flaubert (who is at times supported by the "real" Flaubert) and accounts for him. But it is continually exceeded by questions that suggest both another Flaubert and another Sartre whose dialogue about the real and the imaginary might be a different story. In the face of this other Flaubert (so close to the other Sartre), the author of *L'Idiot* protests too loudly and anxiously generates a monumental stream of appropriative interpretation. The stream reaches floodlike proportions, I think, because the totalizing Sartre does not explicitly investigate the conditions that allow the floodgates to open: the relationship between the totalizing project itself and the problems Flaubert referred to in terms of *l'indisable*. The other Sartre might have been more cognizant of Flaubert's deconstructive approach to traditional paradigms. But this other Sartre rarely makes an appearance in the major theoretical works, including the existential biographies.

The question is whether this other Sartre could still make the Marxist commitment to basic change in society. Indeed, it is perhaps Flaubert's own subversion of faith in dialectics more than his explicit, antiproletarian political views that have made him such a *bête noire* among Marxist theorists. Are a deconstructive strategy and Marxism compatible? Does Marxism require an unproblematic faith in dialectics or might its antiauthoritarian incentive require different theoretical bases? Can one reject the explicit political views of a Flaubert yet take up his critical strategies in more affirmative terms?

# 6

# In Lieu of a Conclusion

Teems of times and happy returns. The Same anew. . . . The Vico road goes round and round to meet where terms begin.

James Joyce, *Finnegans Wake*

Essential thinkers always say the Same. But that does not mean the identical. Of course they say it only to him who undertakes to think back on them.

Heidegger, *Letter on Humanism*

The prefix "un" is the token of repression.

Freud, "The 'Uncanny'"

That which stands behind negation is by no means nothingness but the "other side" of that which is denied, the carnivalesque upside down. Negation reconstructs the image of the object. . . . Negation and destruction of the object are therefore its displacement and reconstruction. . . . The nonbeing of an object is its "other face," its inside out. . . . Carnival celebrates the destruction of the old and the birth of the new world—the new year, the new spring, the new kingdom. . . . Positive and negative elements are, of course, inherent in every word of a living speech. There are no indifferent, neutral words; there can only be artificially neutralized words. In the most ancient forms of speech the merging of praise and abuse, that is, a duality of tone, is characteristic. . . . Time itself abuses and praises, beats and decorates, kills and gives birth; this time is simultaneously ironic and gay, it is the "playing boy" of Heraclitus, who wields supreme power in the universe.

Mikhail Bakhtin, *Rabelais and His World*

The questions that end the preceding chapter mark a beginning point of current French thought and of related thought elsewhere. I shall not pretend to answer these questions. Rather, I shall briefly address them in terms that suggest both the limits of this book and the way it broaches certain larger issues.

The popular reputation of Sartre has been that of a scandalous thinker and an extreme revolutionary in every respect. He has been seen as the prototypical modern French thinker, perhaps the modern intellectual *tout court,* partially because of the widespread acceptance of his appropriating interpretations of the past. But in the light of the interests of Baudelaire, Flaubert, Mallarmé, Breton, Genet, Foucault, and Derrida—to limit oneself to this series of figures—Sartre seems both more eccentric in relation to modern if not revolutionary tendencies and more wed to traditional assumptions than is ordinarily believed. (Indeed, Sartre's very popularity may in part stem from the frequency with which he does more to confirm prevalent assumptions than to contest them radically.) The ultimate paradox of Sartre lies in his attempt to take a firm stand on the tail end of traditions of thought that he himself places in question. In what is perhaps his dominant tendency, Sartre explicitly rejects traditions and yet more covertly repeats nearly exhausted traditional assumptions in his own approach to problems. In this sense, the limitation of his critique of tradition is related to the limited nature of his attempt to think through traditional assumptions to the point of disclosing their nature, his own necessary indebtedness to them, and the difficulties involved in the theoretical and practical effort to transcend them.

A notion of supplementarity helps to articulate often submerged tendencies in Sartre's thought and (if one may continue to speak in terms of such hazardous concepts) in the tradition that threatens to reappropriate it. Supplementarity and related notions reveal how freedom is "always already" situated and why the dialectical project of totalization must remain open and give rise to continually displaced "centers," or final terms and referents. These notions may also suggest the manner in which thought and action are to be referred to a "carnivalesque" process of interplay between excess and limits. The denial of supplementarity short-circuits this interplay and its possibly regenerative functions. The result is the endless, empty repetition of disabling dissociations, vicious circles, and the blind quest for "totalization." A recognition of this interplay may provide a basis for a more balanced mode of thought and action— especially with reference to institutions—which situates irony and other disconcertingly oblique forms of contestation in a more comprehensive social and cultural process. In terms of this process, comprehension and mastery are never complete; but "deconstruction" may be related to reconstruction, which attempts to affirm and to institute a more viable interchange between excess and limits, freedom and structure, openness and mastery, "ambiguity" and definition. It is the possibility of this process that Sartre fails to explore as the horizon of modern thought and action. Instead, in Sartre, knowledge tends to be identified with power or cognitive control of the object. The denial or de-emphasis of ambiguity, repetition, play, and supplementarity fosters equivocation, empty repetition, and unthematized inconsistency. It also inhibits the emergence of notions of regenerative "ambivalence" and critically constructive "repetition" through which active remembrance of the past is related to the "overcoming" of its alienating features and the affirmative "re-petitioning" for a radically transformed way of life—a way of life more open to the play of difference and sameness as nonidentity (which cannot be identified with alienation). In this sense, remembering is neither the mechanical marking of the hollowed-out time of double binds nor the "interiorizing" repossession of a lost totality (*Erinnerung*); it is the same as the affirmative attempt to begin again and to make old things new in a world where absolute beginnings and endings are recognized as (necessary) utopian dreams.

But what do these "abstract" considerations have to do with politics, which has increasingly been Sartre's primary concern? The present study has not rejected the importance Sartre attributes to politics, nor has it denigrated the value of certain of his specific political stands. But it has attempted to raise doubts about the theoretical foundations for politics in Sartre and to suggest that a significantly different perspective may be necessary to defend the demand for basic change in modern societies. Indeed, one of the more promising features of the anticapitalistic and antibureaucratic protest during the May–June 1968 events in France was the attempt to assert the need for more "supplementary" and even "carnivalesque" forms of relationship in modern institutional life. To this extent, these events may have been more "advanced" than the analysis in Sartre's *Critique* that is often seen as their theoretical analogue.

To furnish a critical perspective on Sartre, I have made relatively discriminating use of the thought of Derrida and have often "supplemented" it through an explicit or implicit reference to the work of other theorists. At the risk of oversimplifying it, I have attempted to render the challenge of Derrida's thought more accessible, especially for the intellectual historian. If the result has been a "socialization" of his approach to problems that retains some measure of its critical force, the inevitable losses may be counterbalanced by a few gains. But I have not attempted, for example, to emulate (or parody) Derrida's style, nor have I entered wholeheartedly into the *errance joyeuse* of his methodically mad, disseminating play on words or his energetically diasporic *mise en abyme* of the text. In general, I have kept a certain distance from the more extravagant (and at times more critical) overtures of his approach to the problem of textuality. On the level of what I shall call his "minimal" program, Derrida has affirmed the importance of the contest and the contestation between structure and play and has suggested that the problem with the dominant philosophical tradition is the sacrifice of open contestation in favor of either the alienation between identity and difference (and analogous contrasts) or the related utopian hope of a total reconciliation of opposites.

Derrida's approach does not sterilize utopian hope, but it does situate the object of this hope as a critical fiction that at times approaches the status of a functional "reality." In addition, Derrida has developed a notion of limits that does not disqualify even the daring attempt at dialectical totalization, but that does go beyond ontological fiat and the "common sense" appeal to human fallibility in showing why the dialectic must remain open. A limit in Derrida's sense is not an absolute or fixed barrier beyond which thought may never go. It is "something" necessary for structured thought (or life) that must periodically be transgressed or exceeded, for it traverses the field of knowledge in continually displaced forms that recurrently render founding concepts and oppositions problematic—but not useless or meaningless. Among the problematic oppositions are those between life and text (or practice and theory) as well as those between the political and the apolitical. Derrida has generalized the problem of the text and of political power (as did Nietzsche). Life and text supplement each other in a number of different ways that the clear, distinct, and unproblematic opposition between them—whether in favor of "life" or of "text"— serves to repress or all too easily negotiate. Life repeats text in another place and vice versa. The text is always a power structure that questions itself in more or less explicit and forceful ways. "Thought" itself is based on institutions that are not the less constraining for passing unobserved. And these "intellectual" institutions are heavily indebted to metaphysics and its "common sense" analogues even (and perhaps most defenselessly) when traditional metaphysics is simply rejected or bracketed without being "deconstructed." One implication of this view for research is that the intellectual historian cannot accept "ready-made" the precritical conception of "the context" or "the times" provided by some other area of history. This notion of context may function as a detour around the texts and the issues they raise, thereby reinforcing the most conventional traits of the dominant culture. The problem of the intellectual historian is to work out a notion of context that informs a reading of texts and to explore its possibilities and limits.

At the very least, Derrida's work serves to raise questions about the attempt to found revolutionary politics on an unproblematic notion of dialectical totalization related to a relatively conservative understanding of the text. It may even function to raise doubts about ordinary conceptions of politics and what is politically relevant. It clearly brings up the question of the relationship of one's own discourse to the political "ends" one seeks. More broadly, it raises the issue of the relationship between forms of language and forms of life. But Derrida himself has addressed relatively little explicit attention to these questions. It would perhaps be both too facile and too tempting to extend his thought in a certain direction and to argue that, in significant ways, it provides the cogent "theoretical foundation" for certain of Sartre's own explicit political goals. Derrida's approach does not simply reject analysis and dialectical totalization, but it does situate them in a critical framework that is not exhausted by the alternatives they pose. And it conveys—at times in too overwhelmingly unbounded a "form"—an affirmative sense of play, which even the most seemingly open dialectical perspectives may interpret in a truncated, subjectivist manner or leave theoretically unsituated. Its sustained critique of power structures and of all "arches" might be related to a notion of decentered or decentralized democracy that cannot simply be identified with traditional forms of anarchism. And it would seem to relate the "overcoming" of alienation to the affirmation of (internal) alterity and (external) sameness—more precisely, to the open play between the same and the other that is repressed and dominated by "clear and distinct" oppositional splits, which themselves rely on a scapegoating mechanism. Even its seeming excesses take on a somewhat different color when they are seen as uncanny "carnivalizations" of traditional assumptions. In any event, Derrida's approach does render problematic Sartre's combination of radical politics, dialectical totalization, unproblematic notion of "reality" or "life," dismissal or reduction of the "text," and relatively blind apocalyptic hope.

Among recent thinkers critical of Sartre, Foucault has been

preoccupied with the problem of politics. For some, the relationship between text and politics might almost be formulated in terms of the relationship between Derrida and Foucault. I do not intend to invoke Foucault at this point as a *deus ex machina*. Only the topic of the present study and its very selective use of Derrida and (to a much lesser extent) Foucault has enabled me to avoid both a sustained confrontation between these two recent *monstres sacrés* and an attempt to disentangle their problematic relationship. In an appendix to his *Histoire de la folie*, Foucault has violently reacted to Derrida's critique of the earlier edition of this work in "Cogito et histoire de la folie" (included in *L'Ecriture et la différence*). Aside from the discussion of specific points of interpretation concerning Descartes's treatment of madness, Foucault issued a general indictment against Derrida as the purveyor of a decadent textual problematic that reduces "discursive practices" to "textual traces," escapes from the world of political events, and provides professors with an alibi to go on explicating texts in traditional detachment from social issues. I find these charges—which are remarkably reminiscent of the charges Sartre has leveled against others—defensive, excessive, and in good part misguided. The "textual" strategies of Derrida may of course function in an escapist way. But this function depends upon an abusive mishandling of them. Taken in a certain way, Derrida's strategies not only "deconstruct" the oppositions that are essential both to escapist or apolitical uses of them and to Foucault's critique of them. They may also provide theoretical insight of a more penetrating sort into the very political project of Foucault (whose own theoretical formulations often suffer from obscurity, if not confusion).[1]

Foucault is most important precisely in the area that the present book has explored only in limited ways: the interaction between discourse and institutions, in the ordinary sense of the term. Foucault, moreover, has been politically active. It is somewhat curious that Sartre, even in some of his most recent comments, still seems to be doing battle against a relatively hidebound "structuralism," which he perceives as a methodology of the "practico-inert" that denies the role of agents in history. Whatever their differences, neither Derrida nor Foucault holds to this conception of structuralism, and it is dubious to what extent other figures labeled "structuralist" may be seen in its light. The more interesting challenge of Derrida and Foucault for Sartre lies in their critique of traditional philosophical assumptions, including those at the basis of "humanism" and dialectics. This is the critique employed in the present study, in a relatively selective and reserved way, to inform its discussion of Sartre.

In one important respect, this critique of Sartre has been faithful to one of Sartre's own cardinal principles: the importance of contestation and self-contestation. And, even with respect to the limited problem of interpreting Sartre, this book might serve as a preface to another that would take it into account, contest it, and formulate problems in a different way. One might, for example, attempt a reading of *Situations* as a "single" text that internally places itself in question by revealing heterogeneous tendencies. Indeed, *Situations* might even be seen as Sartre's exemplary text—the one closest to his understanding of freedom in a situation. And in certain respects, it may be misleading to follow existing commentaries in taking the *Critique* as the quintessential expression of Sartre's existential Marxism. Perhaps a better work for the understanding of Sartre's recent thought and action is *On a raison de se révolter* ("One Is Right to Revolt"). In the text of this new kind of book—the revised transcript of Sartre's conversations from 1972 to 1974 with two younger men, Pierre Victor and Philippe Gavi—it is often difficult to locate unambiguously Sartre's own authorial voice; and the most interesting dynamic is the shifting, contentious, but friendly interchange among highly militant yet open people. More generally, all of the elements in Sartre's writings, which I have designated as marginal vis-à-vis his dominant framework, might become central in another interpretation. In relation to this approach, which I have tried to render more possible, the present critical "preface" has itself often been too "traditional" and too insistently "parricidal," but perhaps this was necessary to bring out Sartre's own largely unexplored relation to traditional assumptions in his most famous and influential writings.

Finally, it must be recalled that this book has contested only a dogmatically "totalizing" and progressivist notion of dialectics and that it is compatible with a "supplemented" dialectical model, which might well prove to be what the most forceful and critical form of dialectics has always been, for example, in Marx. Only the limited nature of this book has permitted the elision of a more direct and sustained inquiry into the difficult problem of the relationship between "supplementarity" and an "open" or "unfinished" dialectic. In the present context, it may suffice to note again that an "open" dialectic may require, for its own intelligibility, a theoretical appeal to supplementarity and related notions such as repetition. Dialectics itself may be seen as displaced agonistic ritual or "re-creative" carnivalization, and the most elementary dialectical progress may lie in overcoming a society dominated by notions of progress, toward a society whose traditions and institutions are healthy enough to allow for genuine contestation in all its forms, including powerful laughter. But it would be the height of self-deception to believe that one has understood something when one declares that it must be approached "dialectically." This notoriously protean term may readily function as a magic word or *épithète élogieuse*, which conceals all that we do not know about something, including the meaning of "dialectics." When a term threatens to lose all meaning, the time has come to render it problematic in order to restore what is of value in it—that which recurrently calls for contestation, self-criticism, and the regenerative "overcoming" of exhausted traditions.

# Notes

## Introduction

1. In limited ways, the critical approach to Sartre attempted here has implications for important tendencies in contemporary historiography. Especially to be noted is the proximity of Sartre's assumptions to those of two significant schools of historical research. First, Sartre's quest for a dialectical, total history bears comparison with the approach of the *Annales* school of social history. In however seemingly alien a language, Sartre to some extent provides the theoretical basis for assumptions that the social historian either accepts on faith or refuses to pursue on a philosophical level. In this respect, one might profitably compare Sartre with Fernand Braudel in his more theoretical moments, as in the seminal essay, "Time, History, and the Social Sciences," included in *The Varieties of History*, edited by Fritz Stern (New York: Random House, 1972), pp. 403–430. Second, much that is "Sartrean" appears in Quentin Skinner's influential notion of an intellectual history that privileges the intentions of authors in response to contexts (or situations) and seeks to elicit the network of communication formed by the interaction of intentional projects. As Skinner puts it, "There *is* no history of the idea to be written, but only a history necessarily focused on the various agents who used the idea, and on their varying situations and intentions in using it" ("Meaning and Understanding in the History of Ideas," *History and Theory* VIII, no. 1 (1969), 38). Skinner's critique of purely internal and external approaches to intellectual history is impressive, as is his integration of the methods of analytic philosophy with tendencies that culminate in Sartre. But he does not fully perceive the problematic nature of an approach that centers intellectual history on intentions, or what authors meant to say. It may further be suggested that Sartre's thought readily opens itself to appropriation by analytic philosophy, although the attempt to see Sartre predominantly through the prism provided by the concerns and categories of analytic philosophy involves significant reduction and distortion of his approach. Two especially successful ventures in the analytic interpreta-

tion of Sartre are those of Arthur Danto, *Jean-Paul Sartre* (New York: Viking Press, 1975), and Anthony Manser, *Sartre* (London: Athlone Press, 1966).

2. For a suggestive approach to Camus, see Geoffrey Hartman, "Camus and Malraux: The Common Ground," in *Beyond Formalism* (New Haven: Yale University Press, 1970), pp. 85–93. The best general study of Camus is that of Donald Lazere, *The Unique Creation of Albert Camus* (New Haven: Yale University Press, 1973). On Merleau-Ponty, see Albert Rabil, Jr., *Merleau-Ponty: Existentialist of the Social World* (New York: Columbia University Press, 1967). Probably the best single work on Lévi-Strauss is that of Yvan Simonis, *Claude Lévi-Strauss ou la "Passion de l'inceste"* (Paris: Aubier, 1968). For Lévi-Strauss's later works, see Eugenio Donato, "Lévi-Strauss and the Protocols of Distance," in *Diacritics* V (Fall 1975), 2–12. For a creative interpretation of Foucault, see Edward W. Saïd, *Beginnings: Intention and Method* (New York: Basic Books, 1975). See also the excellent article by Hayden V. White, "Foucault Decoded: Notes From Underground" in *History and Theory* XII, no. 1 (1973), 23–54. For the general problem of structuralism, see Fredric Jameson, *The Prison-House of Language* (Princeton: Princeton University Press, 1972), and Jonathan Culler, *Structuralist Poetics* (Ithaca, N.Y.: Cornell University Press, 1975). For analyses of Derrida, see Gayatri Chakravorty Spivak, translator's preface, *Of Grammatology* (Baltimore: The Johns Hopkins Press, 1976), pp. ix–lxxxvii; Geoffrey Hartman, "Monsieur Texte: On Jacques Derrida, His *Glas*," *Georgia Review* XXIX, no. 4 (1975), 759–797 and "Monsieur Texte II: Epiphony in Echoland," *Georgia Review* XXX, no. 1 (1976), 169–97; and Sarah Kofman, *"Un Philosophe* 'unheimlich'" in *Ecarts,* edited by Lucette Finas (Paris: Fayard, 1973), pp. 109–204. For approaches to Nietzsche inspired by Derrida, see Bernard Pautrat, *Versions du soleil: Figures et système de Nietzsche* (Paris: Editions du Seuil, 1971), and Sarah Kofman, *Nietzsche et la métaphore* (Paris: Payot, 1972). See also Jacques Derrida, "La Question du style," in *Nietzsche Aujourd'hui?* (Paris: 10/18, 1973), pp. 235–87, and Paul de Man, "Genesis and Genealogy in Nietzsche's *Birth of Tragedy,*" in *Diacritics* II (Winter 1972), 44–53.

3. Parts of the preceding discussion appear in substantially the same form on pp. 241–43 of my essay "Habermas and the Grounding of Critical Theory," in *History and Theory* XVI, no. 3 (1977), 237–64, which forms a companion piece to this book.

4. For the former view, see Mark Poster, *Existential Marxism in Postwar France: From Sartre to Althusser* (Princeton: Princeton University Press, 1976). Poster's interpretation is in good part inspired by that of Fredric Jameson in *Marxism and Form* (Princeton: Princeton University Press, 1971), pp. 206–305. See also the convergent analysis of István Mészáros in "Phases of Sartre's Development," *Telos,* no. 25 (Fall 1975), 112–32. All of these interpretations are both leftist in perspective and

sympathetic to Sartre. For the latter view, from a leftist perspective not sympathetic to Sartre, see Ronald Aronson, "Sartre's Individualist Social Theory," *Telos*, no. 16 (Summer 1973), 68–91.

## 1. Early Theoretical Studies: Art Is an Unreality

1. Quoted in Michel Contat and Michel Rybalka, *Les Ecrits de Sartre* (Paris: Gallimard, 1970), p. 108.

2. Sartre in *L'Imaginaire* would also like to maintain a total divide between the dream—which is on the side of the imaginary—and reality. To counter Descartes's argument (in the *First Meditation*) in favor of a possible confusion between the two, Sartre relates the dream to fiction: "A dream does not offer itself—contrary to what Descartes thought—as the apprehension of reality. On the contrary, it would lose all meaning, all its own nature [*toute sa nature propre*] if it could for an instant posit itself as real. It is above all a story [*une histoire*] and we take the same kind of passionate interest in it that a naive reader takes in the reading of a novel. The dream is lived as fiction and it is only in consid- ering it as a fiction that it is given such that we can understand the kind of reaction it produces in the dreamer" (*L'Imaginaire*, pp. 225–26). Sartre here argues not that the dream is recognized as fiction from the "awak- ened" perspective of a "realizing" consciousness but that it is lived as fiction. In the latter case, two eventualities arise and both are damaging for his argument. First, if the dream posits itself as fiction, it involves a contrast between fiction and reality and a confusion between the two becomes at least theoretically possible. Moreover, the dream is then beyond itself just as a naive reading of a story that sees itself as naive would for that very reason no longer be simply naive. Second, the dream is lived as fiction in a sense that does not involve a contrast between fiction and reality. But, in this event, the distinction between dream and reality would break down—and it was precisely this eventu- ality that Sartre's argument was intended to prevent. In more general terms, Sartre's desire or intention in this argument is to generate a clear and distinct opposition or separation between dream and reality. Yet his argument, in displacing the problem of the relation of the real to the imaginary onto the problem of the relationship among the real, the dream, and fiction, itself repeats the dream process (displacement) in trying to account for it. It is interesting to note further that, according to Foucault, the "Classical Age" presented the dream (in contrast to the "waking" or blind "dream" of madness) as a phenomenon involving no judgment or affirmation about the truth or reality of its object. Foucault interprets this view of the dream in terms of a more encom- passing reduction, in the "Classical Age," of both the dream and mad- ness to nonbeing or empty negativity, and he finds in Descartes the philosophical exponent of this reduction (see *L'Histoire de la folie* [Paris:

Plon, 1961], chapter 4). Sartre's analysis indicates that this reductive approach did not find a simple exponent in Descartes. But Sartre himself goes further than Descartes in conforming to the characterization of the presumably dominant "classical" view of the dream as it is presented by Foucault. I would also observe that the problem of the relationship between reality and the imagination is explored by Sartre in an early short story, "The Room," in a manner not entirely accounted for by his theoretical formulations.

3. Joseph Fell, *Emotion in the Thought of Sartre* (New York: Columbia University Press, 1965),pp. 133–34.

4. Ibid., p. 106.

5. Translated by Bernard Frechtman (New York: Washington Square Press, 1966). It may be noted that in an interview of 1971 Sartre asserted: "I have reconsidered certain notions set forth in *L'Imaginaire*, but I must say that, in spite of the criticisms I have been able to read, I still hold this work to be true: if one takes only the point of view of the imagination (outside of the social point of view, for example) I have not changed my opinion: evidently it is necessary to take it up again from a more materialist point of view" (*S. X*, p. 102).

6. Sartre presents the case of the impersonator Franconay imitating Maurice Chevalier as a problem in a double inscription or double reading, which he explicitly attempts to analyze in terms of two distinct, heterogeneous readings. But his "description" threatens to escape his analysis. And it is unclear what is simultaneous and what is successive in the process he discusses: "The object that Franconay produces by means of her body is a feeble form that can constantly be interpreted on two distinct levels: I am constantly free to see Maurice Chevalier in image or a little woman who makes faces. Thus one has the essential role of signs: they must clarify, guide consciousness.... The artist appears. She wears a straw hat; she sticks out her lower lip; she inclines her head. I cease to perceive, I *read*, that is, I undertake a signifying synthesis. The straw hat is at first a simple sign, just as the cap and scarf of the realistic singer are the sign that he is going to sing an apache song. That is, at the very first, I do not perceive the hat of Chevalier through [à *travers*] the straw hat, but the hat of the *fantaisiste* refers to [*renvoie à*] Chevalier, just as the cap refers to the 'apache milieu.' To decipher the signs is to produce the concept 'Chevalier.' At the same time I judge: 'She imitates Chevalier.' With this judgment, the structure of consciousness is transformed. The theme at present is Chevalier. By its central intention, consciousness is imagining; it is a question of realizing my knowledge [*savoir*] in the intuitive matter furnished to me" (*L'Imaginaire*, p. 42). The slippage in Sartre's terminology is significant. In terms of his theory, the concept has no place in the imagining consciousness. And the relationship among the imagination, reading, and the interpretation of signs brings up unexplored problems that might mitigate the opposition between the imagination and perception.

7. For a critical attempt to show how Sartre's thought—especially *Being and Nothingness*—unintentionally recapitulates both traditional metaphysical assumptions and the ideology of free competition, individual transcendence, and self-realization, see Herbert Marcuse, "Existentialism: Remarks on Jean-Paul Sartre's *L'Etre et le néant*," *Journal of Philosophy and Phenomenological Research* VIII (March 1948), 309–36. See also Ronald Aronson, "Interpreting Husserl and Heidegger: The Root of Sartre's Thought," *Telos*, no. 13 (Fall 1972), 47–67, and "Sartre's Individualist Social Theory," *Telos*, no. 16 (Summer 1973), 68–91. Aside from their partially misleading emphasis on Sartre's early individualism, the often cogent essays of Marcuse and Aronson rely overmuch on the argument that Sartre "ontologizes" (or "reifies") the historical and fails to develop a truly dialectical approach to problems. They fail to observe that the concepts of "history" and "dialectics" are already heavily "ontologized" and that they cannot be deconstructed and recast through the simple and uncritical opposition between "ontology" and "history" or "dialectics." It is the very understanding of "history" and "dialectics" that is at issue. Despite its own unexamined leanings toward "identity-theory" and the total reconciliation of opposites, Marcuse's *Eros and Civilization* provides important bases for an alternative approach to Sartre's. Especially significant is its notion of the imagination as both mediation and supplement vis-à-vis the senses and reason.

## 2. Literature, Language, and Politics: Ellipses of What?

1. Michel Contat and Michel Rybalka, *Les Ecrits de Sartre* (Paris: Gallimard, 1970), p. 161.

2. One may of course raise the question of the social conditions underlying the role of structuralism in French thought from the late 1950s to the late 1960s. One's response depends upon an initial characterization of structuralism that furnishes the terms to be explained or accounted for. Although he has not offered an extensive social explanation (other than in the relatively indirect form of the general argument concerning the "practico-inert" in the *Critique* or the study of Flaubert), Sartre sees structuralism as an analytic, neopositivist methodology that denies the importance of human praxis in history. "Structure" is for him an acceptable notion only as it designates the moment of the practico-inert in a more comprehensive dialectical process. (See especially "Jean-Paul Sartre répond" in *L'Arc* 30, 1966, 87–96.) For an attempt to explain the rise of structuralism, which is highly critical of Sartre yet characterizes structuralism in terms comparable to Sartre's own, see Michel Crozier, "The Cultural Revolution: Notes on the Changes in the Intellectual Climate of France," in *A New Europe*, edited by S. R. Graubard (Boston: Houghton Mifflin, 1964). Crozier places the change from the post-Liberation period to the 1960s in a traditional

cyclical pattern that moves from a "romantic period of crisis, when the irresponsible and creative individual partially succeeds in exploding the social structures, to a period of routine and retreat where the structures again become dominant" (p. 623). France of the 1960s represents "the dead part of the cycle" when the weight of social constraint is felt and the more charismatic intellectual (such as Sartre himself in the 1940s) is out of place. Thus, the 1960s are marked both by social and economic optimism and by intellectual disillusionment and soul-searching that foster a "climate of formalism and detachment" (p. 622). Structuralism is a symptomatic expression of this intellectual climate. Crozier's alternative to the vicious cycle that includes detachment as one of its moments is the formation of responsible, informed intellectuals and agents who know how institutions work and how they must operate within them to effect "realistic" change: "The necessity for revolution has disappeared or has at least changed direction. The fashion today is for reform by concrete commitment, for contacts through participation, for responsibility" (p. 624). Although the conclusions of Crozier's analysis—which are in practice relatively moderate and which provide little intimation of what would occur in France in 1968—depart significantly from those of Sartre, his analysis shares with Sartre's an over-simplified characterization of the phenomenon to be explained: "structuralism." Whether such accounts are taken to be superficial or probing in their characterization and explanation of phenomena, they do not in any case address the specific problem of the use by Sartre in "A Plea for Intellectuals" of certain notions often associated with "structuralism."

3. Roland Barthes, *Writing Degree Zero and Elements of Semiology*, translated by Annette Lavers and Colin Smith, with a preface by Susan Sontag (Boston: Beacon Press, 1970). All references to *Writing Degree Zero*—abbreviated as *WDZ*—are to this edition. In terms of a more immediate context for "A Plea for Intellectuals," another "discursive" event was possibly significant in helping to bring about Sartre's shift in perspective. "A Plea" (delivered as lectures in September and October of 1965) was preceded in December 1964 by a public debate among six intellectuals (Simone de Beauvoir, Yves Berger, Jean-Pierre Faye, Jean Ricardou, Sartre, and Jorge Semprun). The most interesting feature of this debate was the opposition between Sartre and young members of the *Tel Quel* group (Ricardou and Faye). In the "Plea for Intellectuals," Sartre might be seen as attempting to assimilate certain features of the *Tel Quel* conception of textual or scriptural praxis that he had resisted rather ineffectively during the debate. On this issue, see the transcript of the debate in *Que peut la littérature?* Présentation par Yves Buin (Paris: Union générale d'éditions, coll. "L'Inédit" 10/18, 1965). See also Jean Ricardou, "Fonction critique," in *Tel Quel: Théorie d'ensemble* (Paris: Editions du Seuil, 1968), pp. 234–67, and *Problèmes du nouveau roman* (Paris: Editions du Seuil, 1967). Barthes, of course, was an important reference

point for the *Tel Quel* group, and Ricardou had made use of Barthes's distinction between the *écrivain* and the *écrivant*. In any larger study of recent French thought, one would have to examine the importance of Philippe Sollers and other members of the *Tel Quel* group in attempting to work out a relationship between a theory of the text and Marxist politics. And the *telquelistes* immediately recognized the key role of Derrida's "deconstructive" criticism in this attempt.

4. Northrop Frye, *The Anatomy of Criticism* (New York: Atheneum, 1970; 1st ed., 1957), p. 81.

5. For analyses of Mallarmé and Valéry that bring out the limitations of the account of "symbolism" reproduced above, see Jacques Derrida, "La Double Séance," in *La Dissémination* (Paris: Editions du Seuil, 1972), pp. 198–317; and "Qual Quelle," in *Marges de la philosophie* (Paris: Editions de Minuit, 1972), pp. 325–63. For a study of the mutually deconstructive interplay of "prose" and "poetry" (or "representational" and "nonrepresentational" language) in the writings of Mallarmé, see Paul de Man, "Lyric and Modernity," in *Blindness and Insight* (New York: Oxford University Press, 1971), pp. 166–85.

6. Quoted in Contat and Rybalka, *Les Ecrits de Sartre*, p. 261. The authors observe: "The radicalism of the literary project of Mallarmé— what Sartre calls his 'terrorism of politeness'—confers upon his work, however 'uncommitted' it may seem, a revolutionary status [*une portée révolutionnaire*]" (p. 261). Sartre, however, does not provide a detailed analysis of the "negative work" at play in Mallarmé's writings.

7. This line of argument is developed by Jacques Derrida in a commentary on Lévi-Strauss's distinction between *bricolage* and engineering—a distinction similar in certain ways to that between the literary and the literal. See "Structure, Sign and Play in the Discourse of the Human Sciences," in *The Structuralist Controversy*, edited by Richard Macksey and Eugenio Donato (Baltimore: The Johns Hopkins Press, 1970), pp. 255–66.

8. Joseph Halpern's *Critical Fictions: The Literary Criticism of Jean-Paul Sartre* (New Haven: Yale University Press, 1976) came to my attention too late to be taken into account in the present study.

## 3. *Nausea:* "Une Autre Espèce de Livre"

1. Quoted in Michel Contat and Michel Rybalka, *Les Ecrits de Sartre* (Paris: Gallimard, 1970), p. 64.

2. Ibid., p. 399.

3. Frank Kermode, *The Sense of an Ending* (New York: Oxford University Press, 1966). Kermode is himself traditionalist in that he presents the departure from the apocalyptic narrative structure in terms of nostalgia and loss and insists that this structure must exist at least on the level of the reader's expectations. He fails to account for elements that

exist in counterpoint to his view. The work (or play) of deconstruction and double inscription of traditional forms may become an explicit and self-conscious strategy in the writing as well as the reading of the text. This process applies to *Nausea* in a sense unrecognized by Kermode. And the deconstruction and reinscription of traditional forms may be related to a sense of affirmation and joy "beyond" nostalgia, as they are in the writings of Nietzsche. The formality of this entire problem is explored in Jacques Derrida, "Structure, Sign and Play in the Discourse of the Human Sciences," in *The Structuralist Controversy,* edited by Richard Macksey and Eugenio Donato (Baltimore: The Johns Hopkins Press, 1970), pp. 247–65.

4. *Hegel: Texts and Commentary,* translated and edited by Walter Kaufmann (Garden City, N.Y.: Doubleday & Co. 1965), p. 30. For an excellent discussion of related problems, see J. Hillis Miller, "Tradition and Difference," *Diacritics* II (Winter 1972), 6–14.

5. Quoted in Contat and Rybalka, *Les Ecrits de Sartre,* p. 61.

6. See Jonathan Culler, *Flaubert: The Uses of Uncertainty* (Ithaca, N.Y.: Cornell University Press, 1974), in which Flaubert's deconstruction of the traditional novel is one important theme of the analysis.

7. To be precise, Sartre both inverts and overdramatizes the "truth" in his fictive account of the origin of "Some of these Days." It was written by a black and recorded by Sophie Tucker, who was of eastern European Jewish immigrant background. In her autobiography Ms. Tucker recalls how she came upon the song that was to be virtually identified with her:

"One day Mollie [Tucker's black maid and confidant] came and stood in front of me, hands on hips, and a look in her eye that I knew meant she had her mad up.

"'See here, young lady,' said she, 'since when are you so important you can't hear a song by a colored writer? Here's this boy Shelton Brooks hanging around, waiting, like a dog with his tongue hanging out, for you to hear his song. And you running around, flapping your wings like a chicken with its head chopped off. That's no way for you to be going on, giving a nice boy like that the run-around.'

"'All right. I'll hear his song,' I promised. 'You tell him.'

"'You can tell him yourself,' said Mollie. And she brought him in.

"The minute I heard 'Some of These Days' I could have kicked myself for almost losing it. A song like that. It had everything. Hasn't it proved it? I've been singing it for thirty years, made it my theme song. I've turned it inside out, singing it every way imaginable, as a dramatic song, as a novelty number, as a sentimental ballad, and always audiences have loved it and asked for it. 'Some of These Days' is one of the great songs that will be remembered for years and years to come, like some of Stephen Foster's.

"Later Shelton Brooks wrote 'Darktown Strutters' Ball,' which I sang too. But nothing else he ever did touched 'Some of These Days.' " [*Some of These Days* (Garden City, N.Y.: Doubleday, Doran and Co., 1945), p. 114]

8. One may compare my discussion of *Nausea* with the partially convergent analysis of Georges Raillard in *La Nausée de J.-P. Sartre* (Paris: Hachette, 1972). One may also profitably consult the study of Gerald Joseph Prince, *Métaphysique et technique dans l'oeuvre romanesque de Sartre* (Geneva: Librairie Droz, 1968).

## 4. From *Being and Nothingness* to the *Critique:* Breaking Bones in One's Head

1. Michel Contat and Michel Rybalka, *Les Ecrits de Sartre* (Paris: Gallimard, 1970), pp. 87, 339.

2. Ibid., p. 339.

3. Fredric Jameson, *Marxism and Form* (Princeton: Princeton University Press, 1971), pp. 208–9.

4. It is significant that Sartre, who is so concerned with a totalizing intentionality in his interpretations of others, has shown relatively little interest in relating his earlier works to his later ones. The self-image in terms of which he would like to see the *Critique* is faithfully reflected in the analysis of Mark Poster: "In the *Critique de la raison dialectique*, Sartre wrote 'against himself,' becoming ill and driving himself almost to a heart attack. It was a dramatic moment in his life. Over fifty years old, he compelled himself to alter his most cherished positions in order to account for his own experience. Although the *Critique* conserved much of *Being and Nothingness*, it was also a change in which he called his own past into question. In Sartre's own terms, the *Critique* was a conversion, a reconstituting of his original project by which he threw himself into the anxiety of nothingness, enacting his own concept of freedom. In 1960 he formulated his second existential Marxism, which was, as the dialectic prescribes, a richer and more concrete synthesis" (*Existential Marxism in Postwar France: From Sartre to Althusser* [Princeton: Princeton University Press, 1976], pp. 264–65). I would suggest that the notion of a totalizing conversion experience or an original choice of being functions in good part as an ideological cover for a repetitive process of a more complex, though less melodramatic, nature—one more proscribed than prescribed by the dialectic.

5. Jacques Derrida, "La Différance," in *Marges de la philosophie* (Paris: Editions de Minuit, 1972), pp. 21–22. The essay is translated by David B. Allison and included in *Speech and Phenomena and Other Essays on Husserl's Theory of Signs* (Evanston, Ill.: Northwestern University Press, 1973), pp. 129–60 (quote on p. 152).

6. Compare the statement by Simone de Beauvoir: "If Marxism and psychoanalysis had so little effect on us, although a great number of

young people went over to them, it was not only because we had only a rudimentary understanding of them; we did not want to look at ourselves from afar with the eyes of strangers. It was first important for us to coincide with ourselves" (*La Force de l'âge* [Paris: Gallimard, 1970], p. 26).

7. This model is a crucial foundation of the analysis of the passage from *Being and Nothingness* to the *Critique* in Mark Poster's *Existential Marxism in Postwar France* (see especially p. 278). It is derived from Fredric Jameson's discussion of the "third" in *Marxism and Form* (pp. 242 ff.).

8. This notion would be comparable to Merleau-Ponty's "intermonde." It is noteworthy that Merleau-Ponty found that *Being and Nothingness* "remained too exclusively antithetical" ("La Querelle de l'existentialisme," in *Sens et non-sens* [Paris: Editions Nagel, 1966], p. 125). The problems of ambiguity, supplementarity, play, among others, might provide the basis for a reinterpretation of the relationship between Merleau-Ponty and Sartre in terms not entirely exhausted by the more restricted political issues that divided them. Mark Poster's discussion of Merleau-Ponty in *Existential Marxism in Postwar France* heads in this direction; but it is not made to challenge the dominant interpretive framework of the book, which seeks a dialectical reconciliation of all recent tendencies in French thought in terms that privilege Sartre's thought as the center of the *Aufhebung*. It is perhaps no accident that Poster pays almost no attention to the work of Jacques Derrida, which offers one of the most radical critiques of the framework upon which Poster relies, both in general terms and in reference to the interpretation of recent French thought.

9. One may note that Mikhail Bakhtin's studies of Dostoevsky [*Problems of Dostoevsky's Poetics*, Ann Arbor, Michigan: Ardis, 1973] and of Rabelais [*Rabelais and His World*, Cambridge, Mass.: The M.I.T. Press, 1968] provide notions of play and "carnivalization," which are often resisted in Sartre's theoretical works.

10. Fredric Jameson's attempt to offer a more dialectical formulation of the relationship between the two works is misleading: "The *Critique* and the brief *Search for a Method* that precedes it attack the same problem from opposite directions: the former as a theory about the collectives in and through which our individual lives are pursued, the latter as a method of interpreting those individual existences from within, working back from the individual life to the objectivity of history. This pamphlet therefore completes the task Sartre had set for himself at the end of *Being and Nothingness*, that of laying the groundwork for a theory of existential psychoanalysis" (*Marxism and Form*, pp. 209–10). To the extent that this type of formulation is at all accurate, the opposite of Jameson's conception could be maintained, for, while the *Critique* does not inquire into the "lived" quality of individual experience, it does "begin" with the individual in a sense in

which *Search for a Method* does not. The more basic question is of course that of the extent to which the two works supplement and displace rather than dialectically complement each other. On the problem of the relationship between the two works and, more generally, on the question of the interpretation of the *Critique,* the reader is also referred to: Raymond Aron, *Histoire et dialectique de la violence* (Paris: Gallimard, 1973); André Gorz, "Sartre and Marx," *New Left Review,* no. 37 (1966), 33–52; George Lichtheim, "Sartre, Marxism and History," *History and Theory* III, no. 2 (1963–1964), 222–46; and Leonard Krieger, "History and Existentialism in Sartre," in *The Critical Spirit: Essays in Honor of Herbert Marcuse,* edited by Kurt H. Wolff and Barrington Moore, Jr. (Boston: Beacon Press, 1967), pp. 239–66.

11. On the problem of the preface, see Jacques Derrida, "Hors livre," in *La Dissemination* (Paris: Editions du Seuil, 1972), pp. 9–67. This problem is discussed in an especially insightful way by Gayatri Chakravorty Spivak in her preface to her translation of *Of Grammatology* (Baltimore: The Johns Hopkins Press, 1976).

12. Poster, *Existential Marxism in Postwar France,* p. 278.

13. Here are selections from Simone de Beauvoir's well-known description of the psychological conditions under which Sartre wrote the *Critique:* "Sartre managed [in the midst of extreme emotional tension due in part to events during the Algerian war] by writing furiously his *Critique of Dialectical Reason.* He did not work as he usually did, with pauses, erasings, tearing up pages, beginning them again. For hours at a stretch, he sped from page to page without rereading them, as if waylaid [*happé*] by ideas that his pen, even at full tilt, could not keep up with. To keep up this pace, I could hear him crunching corydrame capsules, of which he swallowed a tube a day. By the end of the afternoon, his gestures would become uncertain, and often he would get his words all mixed up. We spent our evenings at my apartment. As soon as he drank a glass of whisky, the alcohol would go straight to his head. 'That's enough,' I'd say to him; but for him it was not enough; against my will I would hand him a second glass; then he'd ask for a third; two years before he'd have needed a great deal more; now he lost control of his movements and his speech very quickly, and I would say again: 'That's enough.' Two or three times I became violently angry and sent a glass crashing against the tiled floor of the kitchen. But it exhausted me to quarrel with him. And I knew that he needed to let himself go, that is to say, to destroy himself a little .... What had happened during these horrible days is that Sartre had barely escaped an attack .... To think against oneself is fine, but in the long run it takes its toll. By breaking bones in his head he had damaged his nerves" (*La Force des choses* [Paris: Gallimard, 1963], pp. 407, 474).

14. A similar point is made by Pietro Chiodi in what is probably the best study of Sartre's Marxism, *Sartre e il Marxismo* (Milan: Feltrinelli, 1965). Fredric Jameson, in *Marxism and Form* (pp. 238–39), provides a

useful summary of Chiodi's argument, but inserts it in his text without using it in any significant way in his own dominant interpretation of Sartre.

15. Sartre's treatment of gift-exchange in the *Critique* (pp. 187 ff.) is perhaps paradigmatic of his understanding of institutions in general. The discussion comes in a peculiar place in the text: after a brief discussion of language along the lines of *Being and Nothingness* and an analysis of the way in which two "serialized" workers separated by a wall are objectified and unified by the look of a "third" in the person of a vacationing petty-bourgeois intellectual (Sartre himself). And the treatment of gift-exchange is intended as an illustration of the problem of the "third." Sartre refers to both Lévi-Strauss and Marcel Mauss on this problem and observes: "Mauss strongly marked the ambiguous character of potlatch, which is simultaneously an act of friendship and of aggression" (p. 187). But, in Sartre's own analysis, the role of ambiguity in gift-exchange is not strongly marked. It is significant that Sartre discusses, not the more balanced forms of gift-exchange, but the extreme form of the potlatch, which Mauss saw as the limiting "monster child" of the gift system. For Sartre, the potlatch becomes in its turn a manifestation of alienated relations. What Sartre fails to discuss is everything that was vital in gift-exchange for Mauss: the cycle of reciprocity and ambiguous interplay that is, in a sense, broken by the gesture of unilateral domination or sovereignty in potlatch. But who or what is the "third" in the potlatch for Sartre? The third is "the only one who can by his mediation make appear the *equivalence* of the exchanged goods and, consequently, of successive acts. For him, who is exterior, the use value of the exchanged goods evidently transforms itself into exchange value. Thus, to the very extent that he does not figure as an *agent* in the operation, he negatively determines the potlatch; he brings to light, for those who live it, reciprocal recognition. And the third here, whatever may be the society under consideration, is each one and everybody. Thus reciprocity is lived by each one as an *objective and diffuse* possibility" (p. 188). Without discussing extensively all the problems raised by Sartre's treatment of gift-exchange, one may note that what is diffuse in this analysis is his conception of the "third" itself. Sartre is unable to recognize the institutional norm as the mediating "third," which, within limits, may allow for what exceeds it. In addition, he misleadingly uses Marx's conception of market relations under capitalism to account for the gift system, although gift-exchange as a form of ostentatious expenditure or display is generally distinct from market exchanges. In consequence, Sartre repeats one of the earliest forms of ethnocentric distortion in the perception of gift-exchange. By way of contrast, one may refer to the discussion of Jacques Derrida in "Structure, Sign and Play in the Discourse of the Human Sciences," in *The Structuralist Controversy*, edited by Richard Macksey and Eugenio

Donato (Baltimore: The Johns Hopkins Press, 1972), pp. 261–62. In Derrida, a reference to Lévi-Strauss's discussion of Mauss leads, through the "mediation" of notions like *hau* and *mana*, to a discussion of language and supplementarity rather than away from them as in Sartre.

16. A biographical note is perhaps pertinent here. In her memoirs, Simone de Beauvoir refers repeatedly to Sartre's fear of growing up and assuming the "institutional" responsibilities of adulthood. He has lived in barren hotel rooms or small, easily abandoned apartments. His preferred work place is the café. "What attracts me to the café? It is a milieu of indifference where others exist without caring about me and without my bothering about them. Anonymous consumers who argue noisily at a neighboring table inconvenience me less than a wife and children who would walk on tiptoe in order not to disturb me. The weight of a family would be insupportable for me. In a café, the others are there, that's all. The door opens, a pretty woman crosses the room and sits down: I follow her with my eyes and return without effort to my blank sheet of paper: she has passed like a movement in my consciousness, nothing more" (comment of Sartre in 1946, quoted in Contat and Rybalka, *Les Ecrits de Sartre*, p. 145). Sartre turned down the Nobel Prize with the assertion that he did not want to become an institution. His recent affiliation is with revolutionary groups that hold institutionalization in horror. The point is not that Sartre has had "problems" with institutions in his life or that one can moralize about his attitudes from the secure position of "realistic" institutional affiliation. It is rather that Sartre, on any level, seems unable to conceive of institutions other than in highly restricted, one-sided terms as hellish. This is a problem for a social theorist.

## 5. Autobiography and Biography: Self and Other

1. Interview in *Playboy* XI (April 1974), 51–52.

2. In *Glas* (Paris: Editions Galilée, 1974), Jacques Derrida provides an extremely intricate discussion of Genet. *Glas* is printed two columns to a page juxtaposed to each other, with marginal insertions. One main column is devoted to Hegel and the other to Genet. This intercolumnar dialogue, or confrontation, between the philosopher of Absolute Knowledge and the criminal who writes scandalous texts is made with constant contrapuntal awareness of Sartre's study of Genet. Aside from specific references to Sartre, one might argue that Sartre, as a theorist who paradoxically attempted to interpret Genet through the dialectical approach developed most forcefully by Hegel, exists in the silent gap that separates their columns. It is interesting to contrast briefly Derrida's strategy with that of Sartre. Derrida is wary lest his own text assimilate and perhaps immobilize that of Genet: "To try to stop once

more, as in 1952, when, upon your release from prison, the on-tophenomenologist of liberation . . . insisted that he give you back, in your own hand [or, in a clean hand—*en main propre*], in a sure place, the 'keys' of the man-and-complete-works, their ultimate, psychoanalytical-existential signification" (*Glas*, pp. 36–37). (My ellipsis marks a place where Derrida interrupts his own discourse to insert words of Genet.) "Not to arrest the course of a Genet. It is the first time that I am afraid in writing, as they say, 'on' someone to be read by him. Not to arrest him, to lead him backward, to bridle him" (pp. 45–46). The concern that his own discourse not arrest Genet is related to Derrida's belief that nothing he can say will better articulate "what" has already been written in Genet's texts. His reading of Genet is, therefore, discreet and participatory. Its strangeness emulates the uncanniness of Genet's text: "What he would tolerate with greatest difficulty is the assurance I might give myself or others that I have mastered his text. In procuring—they say—the rule of production or the generative grammar of all his utterances [*énoncés*]. No danger. We are far from that and this, I repeat, is preliminary and will remain so. No more names. It is necessary to return to his text, which watches over this one during its play" (p. 229). There is no possibility of summarizing Derrida's "analysis." One may at best suggest the intertextual play of his text. One final quotation may give some notion of its movement: "The rare force of the text is that you cannot catch it in the act of [*surprendre*] (and thus limit it to) saying: *this or that*, or, what comes to the same thing, this has a relation of apophantic or apocalyptic unveiling, a determinable semiotic or rhetorical relation with that; this is the subject, this is not the subject, this is the same, this is other, this text here, this corpus here. It is always a question of still something else. At the limit, nothing [*nulle*]. One should say power of the text. As one speaks of the musculature of a tongue [or, language—*langue*]. . . . What I should like to write is Gallows [*Potence*, with the figurative suggestion of Potency] of the text. I expose myself to it; I tend toward it very much. In any case, the scene will finish badly. He will bear a grudge against me to the point of death" (pp. 223–24). "Glas" may be translated as "death knell." And, in this text, some of Derrida's most extreme and most controversial tendencies are in evidence.

3. Here is Sartre's version of the story: "And now here is a story fit for an Anthology of Black Humor: 'An abandoned child from his earliest years manifests evil instincts. He robs the poor peasants who adopted him. Though reprimanded, he persists. He escapes from the reformatory into which he had to be put, steals and plunders more than ever, and, in addition, prostitutes himself. He lives in squalor, begs, commits petty thefts, sleeps with everybody and betrays everybody: this is the moment he chooses for devoting himself deliberately to evil; he decides that he will do the worst in every circumstance and, as he

has come to realize that the greatest crime was not the doing of evil but the manifesting of evil, he writes, in prison, abominable books that stand up for crime and run afoul of the law. Precisely for that reason, he will leave abjection, squalor, and prison. His books are printed and read. A stage director who has been decorated with the Legion of Honor stages one of his plays which incites to murder. The President of the Republic nullifies the sentence he was supposed to serve for his latest offenses, precisely because he boasted in his books of having committed them. And when he is introduced to one of his former victims, she says to him: "Delighted to meet you, sir. Please continue"''' (G, pp. 628-29).

4. Genet, *Thief's Journal* (Paris: Olympia Press, 1954; 1st ed., 1949), pp. 130-31.

5. Ibid., pp. 7-8.

6. Ibid., p. 9.

7. This theme is important in the analysis by Jeffrey Mehlman, *A Structural Study of Autobiography: Proust, Leiris, Sartre, Lévi-Strauss* (Ithaca, N.Y.: Cornell University Press, 1974), pp. 151-86.

8. A. J. Arnold and J.-P. Piriou, *Genèse et critique d'une autobiographie: Les Mots de Jean-Paul Sartre* (Paris: Minard, 1973), pp. 18-19.

9. Ronald Aronson, in one of the more interesting reviews of *L'Idiot de la famille*, argues that other reviews have not criticized *L'Idiot* enough, but neither have they praised it enough. While Aronson asserts genuine respect for the awesome nature of Sartre's undertaking, the general tenor of his review indicates frustration and becomes largely negative almost in spite of his intention, and he is even led to defend more traditional approaches to biography: "No discrimination or pruning in *L'Idiot*: each and every detail, each moment of Gustave's shaping process, calls out to us with equal urgency. And so we scarcely ever know if we are in the main stream or in the backwaters. This is bad scholarship. No distinction here between investigation and its intelligible, communicable results; no sense of proportion about what is and isn't important; no sense of what constitutes adequate proof. Thus he drones on, hammers home the same points again and again, rebuilds his basic analysis over and over. The subject seems always about to get out of hand, and Sartre seems always to be grasping after it, to be laboring frantically to reproduce it. And so in addition to its sheer length the book takes on a slipshod, chaotic, overstuffed quality. Whatever became of the mutual respect between readers and writer, to the pact between freedoms? Instead of meeting us as equals in the social world of scholarly communication, Sartre imposes on us his more private and subjective world and forces us to accompany *his* journey through each and every turning. The book's every aspect only strengthens our sense of its involuted, inward, unreal quality" ("*L'Idiot de la famille:* The Ultimate Sartre?" in *Telos,* no. 20 [Summer 1974], 102).

In the light of this response, Sartre seems to produce in the reader the effect of bewilderment and disorientation which he radically criticizes as an intentional project of Flaubert. Flaubert, of course, wanted to write a preface to *The Dictionary of Received Ideas* (itself perhaps intended as an appendix to *Bouvard and Pécuchet*) "where one would explain how the work was intended to re-establish the public's links with tradition, order, and social norms, and written in such a way that the reader couldn't tell whether or not one was putting him on [*si on se fout de lui*]" (*Correspondance* [Paris: Conard, 1926-33], vol. II, pp. 237-38, letter of September 4, 1850). For a response to *L'Idiot* similar to that of Aronson, see Robert Champigny, "Trying to Understand *L'Idiot*," in *Diacritics* II (Summer 1972), 2-6. See also Joseph Halpern's critical rejoinder to Champigny in *Diacritics* II (Winter 1972), 60-63.

10. For a somewhat similar discussion, see Jonathan Culler, *Flaubert: The Uses of Uncertainty* (Ithaca, N.Y.: Cornell University Press, 1974). The unexplored paradox of Culler's excellent study is that he freely appropriates from Sartre's *L'Idiot* (at times almost seeming to write its missing fourth volume) and simultaneously employs critical approaches to the problem of the text that contest Sartre's interpretive strategy—apparently without being aware of the tensions between the two movements in his own text or the problems involved in cogently relating them on a theoretical level.

11. *Madame Bovary*, edited, with a substantially new translation, by Paul de Man (New York: Norton, 1965), p. 177.

12. Culler, *Flaubert*, p. 122.

13. This was of course the ideological belief of defenders of the Republic. As late as 1945, Léon Blum, for example, asserted: "The Empire had been guilty, but the Republic was only unfortunate [*malheureuse*]" (*A l'Echelle Humaine* [Paris: Gallimard, 1945], p. 41). Sartre would probably reject this sort of invidious distinction, but the question is whether his text provides the theoretical basis on which to do so.

14. See, for example, the analysis of Stanley Hoffmann, "Paradoxes of the French Political Community," in *In Search of France* (Cambridge: Harvard University Press, 1963), pp. 1-117.

15. Neil Hertz, "Flaubert's Conversion," in *Diacritics* II (Summer 1972), 10.

16. Quoted by Hertz, p. 11.

17. Ibid., p. 10.

## 6. In Lieu of a Conclusion

1. This point might be briefly illustrated by the treatment of continuity and discontinuity in Foucault's "archaeology of knowledge." Foucault asserts the radical discontinuity, or epistemological break, between periods of history defined in terms of synchronic structures. He

is in no theoretical position to pose explicitly the question of the synchronic and diachronic interaction between structures in terms that render problematic asserted relations of dominance or submission. Yet in practice he will at times discuss history in a manner that departs from, if it does not contradict, his theoretical assumptions by presenting a more complex picture of the relationship among structures both at a given time and over time. His actual practice is occasionally closer to the model of repetition that I tried to articulate earlier in this study. Thus, for example, in L'Histoire de la folie, the explicit framework is one of discontinuity among synchronic structures. A synchronic structure defines a period that is separated by a radical divide from another period. But the discussion itself refers to the interaction of structures at a given time (especially in terms of relative dominance or submission) and to the changing position and displacement of structures over time. The "dialogue" between reason and unreason in the preclassical period is, for Foucault, forceful if not dominant. With the "classical age," this dialogue does not simply disappear—indeed, Foucault at one juncture somewhat misleadingly presents it as a "constant verticality" that functions as the counterpoint to "history" in the Western tradition. In the modern period the dialogue goes underground in figures like Nietzsche, and it is clear that Foucault would like to see this underground become a groundswell. Whatever may be the other difficulties in this work, there is a more or less systematic tension between "theory" and "practice" in treating the problem of continuity and discontinuity in history. In Les Mots et les choses, similar problems arise, but the theoretical insistence on discontinuity between synchronic structures is, if anything, more adamant. The epistemè of the "preclassical" sixteenth century is discussed in terms at least as opaque as those of the most obscurantist figures to whom Foucault briefly (and at times misleadingly) alludes. It is interesting to compare Foucault's allusive discussion of "the prose of the world" with the more accessible treatment of analogous problems to be found, for example, in Frances Yates's Giordano Bruno and the Hermetic Tradition (Chicago: University of Chicago Press, 1964). Yates investigates in terms of the Hermetic tradition the problems and phenomena in the Renaissance that Foucault evokes in terms of similitude. She also asserts that this view was dominant at the time, and she supports her assertion with analyses of major figures such as Pico and Bruno, to whom Foucault somewhat perversely does not even refer. But, unlike Foucault, she also notes strong opposition to Hermetic views during the Renaissance, both among theologians and among humanists such as Erasmus. (It is curious that Foucault does not try to relate his own discussion in Les Mots et les choses to that in L'Histoire de la folie. In the latter work, painting in the Renaissance is closer to his delineation of the sixteenth-century epistemè than is prose, but in the former work prose is treated as unproblematically grounded in the presumably dominant *epistemè*.) In the context of Yates's analysis, one might plausibly argue that the Hermetic view was "dominant" in the sixteenth century (especially toward the end) but it was hotly contested during that period itself. In the seventeenth century, Hermetism is explicitly rejected by Mersenne and Descartes. But it does not entirely disappear as a significant force after 1600. Certain problematic elements in the thought of Descartes himself, for example, with reference to the imagination, the fiction of the Evil Demon, the relationship between mind and body, and the question of the foundation of rationalism itself, might be related to concerns of the Hermetics. On a more explicit level, the works of Robert Fludd and Athanasius Kircher, as well as the secret societies of the Rosicrucians and conceivably of the Freemasons, attest, in the seventeenth century, to the fate of once dominant or at least prevalent Hermetic tendencies when they were forced to go "underground." Indeed, the resurgence of displaced, modified, and at times distorted Hermetic tendencies throughout the "modern" period is a many-sided story, which is yet to be told in a sufficiently cogent way. One obvious but crucial point in the story is that the failure to recognize more submerged tendencies in a manner that sets up a viable interplay between them and their "opposite" may well induce their expression in blind or unbalanced forms. The difficulty which Foucault does not adequately negotiate is that of relating critical rationality and active interpretation in a manner that avoids the complementary extremes of "grammarian pedantry" (in Bruno's magnificent phrase) and undisciplined, if not obscurantist, word-magic.

# Index